D1697799

HOT ASSISTANTS

Digital Photography, Lighting and Artistic Input: **Chester Ong**

Graphic Synergy, Design and Art Direction: **Kenneth Wong**

Recipe Research and Support: **Jerome Billot, Taran Chadha, Kwan Chung Man**

Professional Support: **Christopher Lenz**

Words and Text: **R. Christopher Christie**

Tomato Synergy: **Chefs Garden, Ohio, U.S.A.**

Recipe Design Page 20: **Phyllis Lam**

Life Mentors: **Patrick Mc Donnell** and **Hans Göbel**, men of wisdom who departed this earth far too soon

First printing by KHL Printing in Singapore, 2006
Printed and bound in Singapore

ISBN 978-988-99387-1-0
988-99387-1-5

Elite Champ Limited
© All rights reserved. No part of this publication may be reproduced, stored in a retrieval system or transmitted in any form or by any means, electronic, mechanical, photocopying, recording or otherwise without the prior written permission of Elite Champ Limited

Published by
Elite Champ Limited, D,12 F, Block 9
Park Island Ma Wan,
New Territories, Hong Kong
(852) 2340-3422

HOT TOMATOES

by Angelo Mc Donnell

This book is dedicated to my beautiful wife, Blanca and our daughter Kiara
for their never ending love, support and encouragement.

HOT TOMATO FURY

It's an age-old debate waged for centuries. For brevity and the sake of argument, in this book let's consider the tomato a fruit and not a vegetable. Our parents squabbled about it, as did their parents, and so on. But the simple truth of the matter is, botanically, the tomato is a fruit. A tomato begins as the flower of the plant in the same way apples, berries, peaches and virtually all fruit which ends up on our tables, and all of these fruits contain seeds. Herein lies the central point of the debate, as vegetables are generally roots, stems or buds and not the species entrusted seed bearer's of future generations.

I'm certain we can all agree the simple tomato truly is one of nature's gifts. When allowed to fully ripen during long hot summers, its meaty flesh oozes sweet nectar with just the right balance of acidity and explodes with a flavor like no other. For most of us, our memories are filled with wonderful summers of vine ripened tomatoes, although back then we had only a few varieties to choose from.

Unfortunately the tomatoes we buy in the grocery store today are a far cry from the ones we grew up with in our mother's garden. The majority of the commercially grown garden variety red tomatoes on the market are picked immaturely to resist bruising and decay during transportation. Once they reach their destination, they're sprayed with ethylene to persuade the fruit to change from green to red. A true shame for one of nature's original masterpieces.

The tomato makes for a great addition to almost any dish as evident by its global popularity in cuisine, even though this has not always been the case. There are conflicting accounts of where the tomato actually originated. A similar fruit was grown in the Andean mountains of South America and consumed in small quantities by the Indigenous people with recorded evidence of use in cooking as early as the mid 1500's. The early tomato plant, named pomodoro because of its golden-yellow color, began to make its way to Europe in the mid 1500's with returning Spanish and Italian explorers. Mediterranean countries began to cultivate the tomato and introduced it into a wide variety of dishes by the 17th century. It wasn't until the mid 19th century that the tomato appeared in northern France. In 18th Century England, the tomato, or wolf peach, (as it was known) was misclassified a 'poisonous plant' as the leaves of the plant closely resembled those of another toxic foliage. By the mid 1800's, tomatoes appeared in British and American recipes after reclassifying the plant and the flavorful orb soon became a major part of the New World cuisine.

Nowadays, the name list of tomatoes is as extensive and varied as that of a dining room's wine list. There's the brilliant black krim, the momotaro, banana leg, or green zebra, Cherokee purple, plum lemon, black brandywine, ox heart and pineapple heirloom just to name a few. Some of us have been fortunate enough to experience the tastes of these wonderful gifts of nature, distinguishing the different varietals that exist among the species. They vary in size, color, shape, texture and taste as much as the names they are given. In fact, there are four-thousand classified varieties grown throughout the world yet most of us have not seen more than a handful.

Tomatoes are high in vitamins A and C, as well as potassium- all of which can be easily absorbed into the body from the tomato's raw state. Scientific studies suggest eating cooked tomatoes reduces one's likelihood of suffering from cholesterol-related heart problems and digestive tract cancers. When tomatoes are cooked, they release lycopene, a strong antioxidant that gives tomatoes their red color. Lycopene helps to release free radicals from the body which have been linked to cancer in various studies. Lycopene may also help prevent the oxidation of low-density lipoproteins, a suggested form of cholesterol carrier in the blood that is thought to be a cause of heart disease.

Having worked in many different parts of the world, I've had the opportunity to cook with a vast amount of tomato varieties. I love tomatoes not only for their appearance and taste, but for their versatility in cooking. The ideas are endless of what can be done with tomatoes and I'm always on the lookout for something new. As a chef, I find the tomato one of the most interesting foods there's something just a little bit different every time. Perhaps it's the acid, or the amount of juice, or maybe the meatiness, to me each one seems to have a slight nuance different from the other. I like that; I enjoy the newness and excitement. That's what I love about food.

Happy cooking,

Angelo

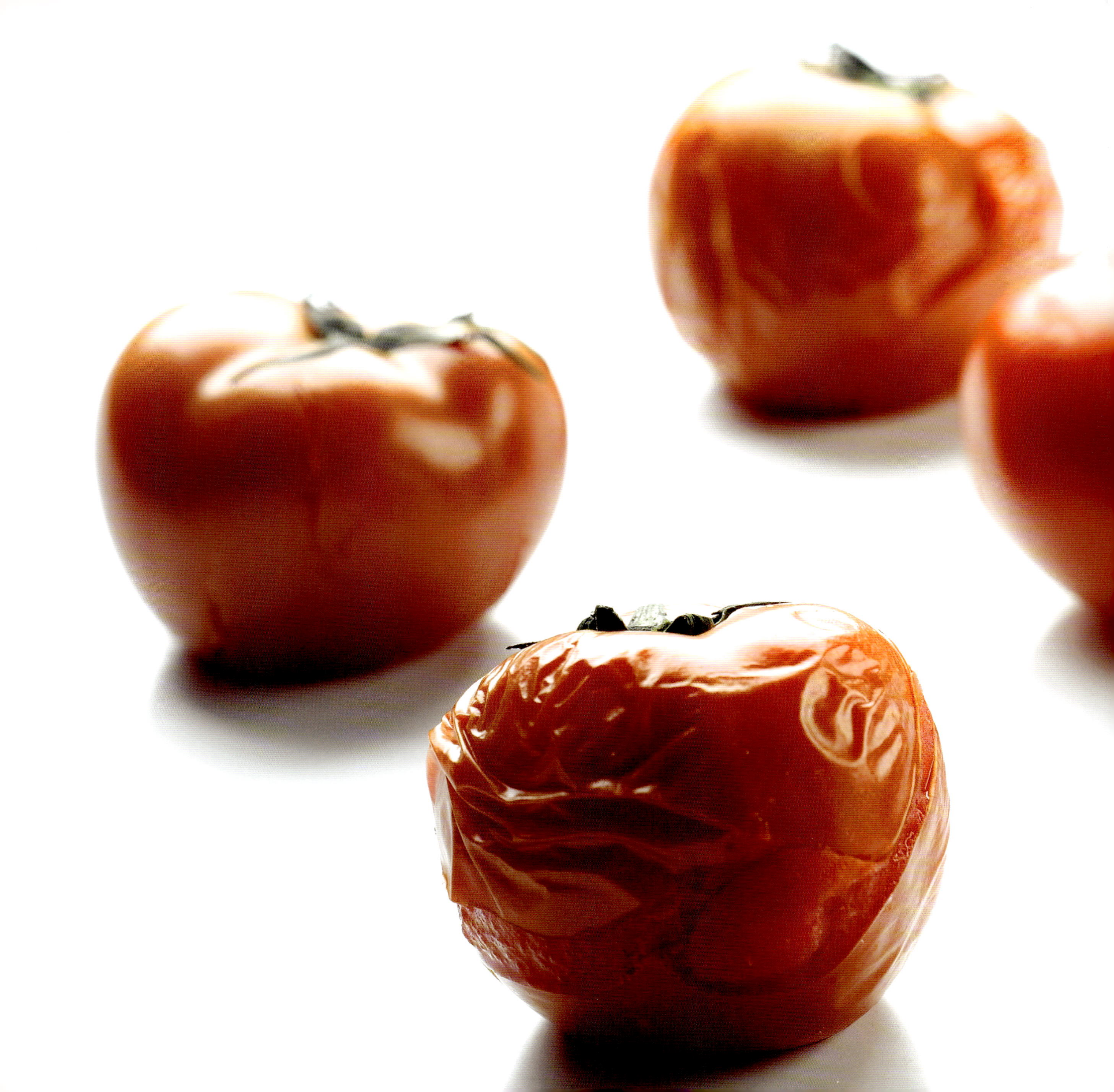

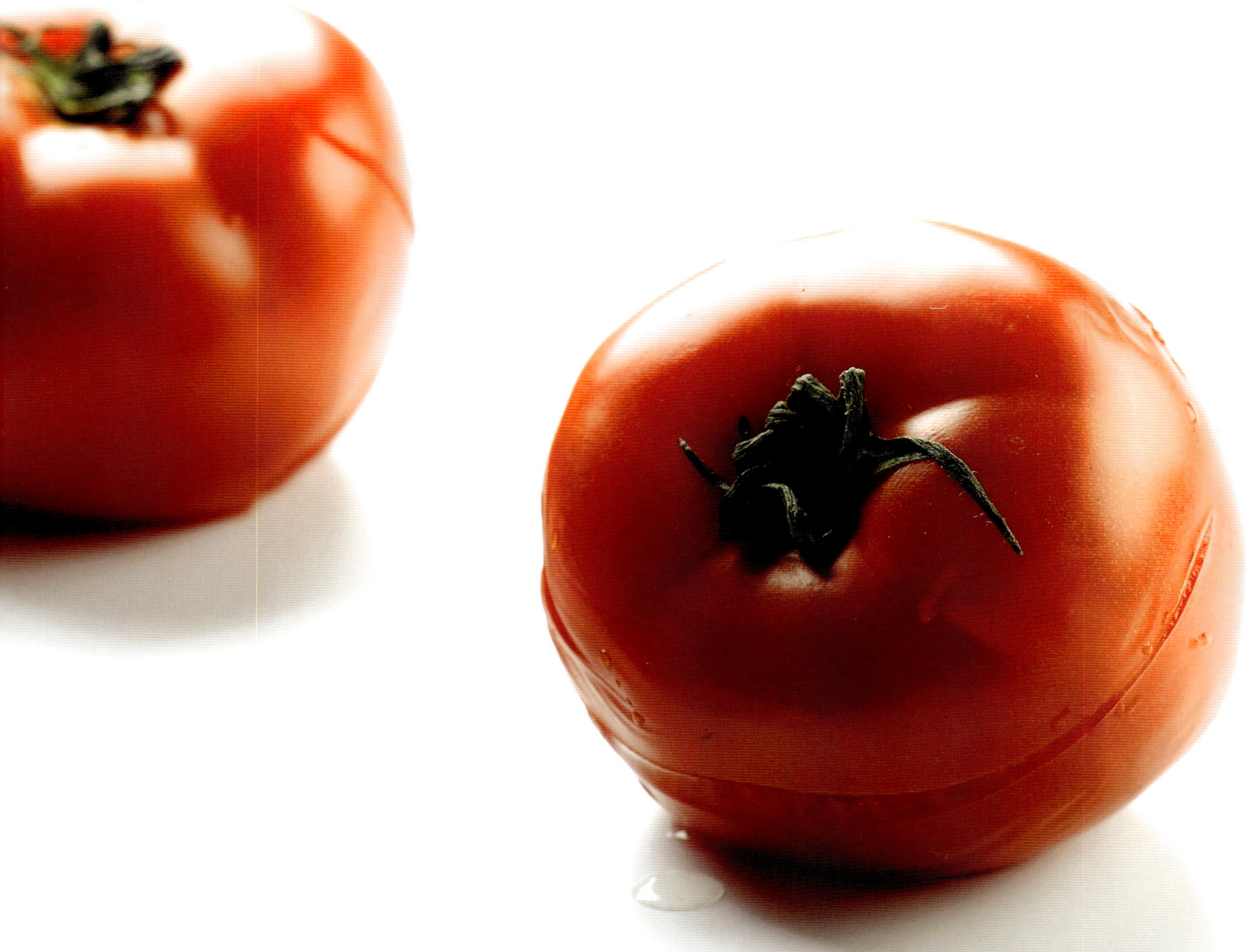

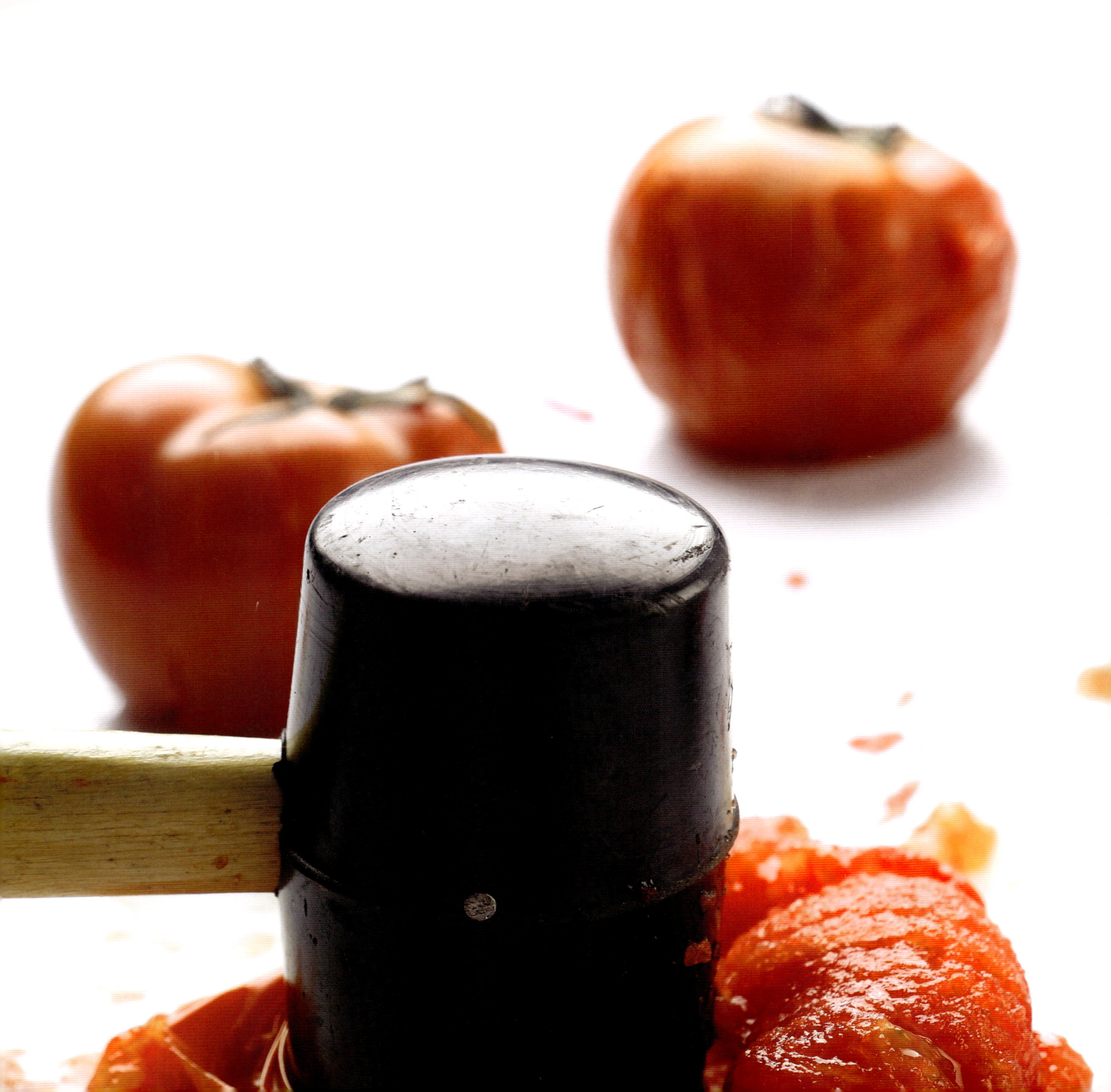

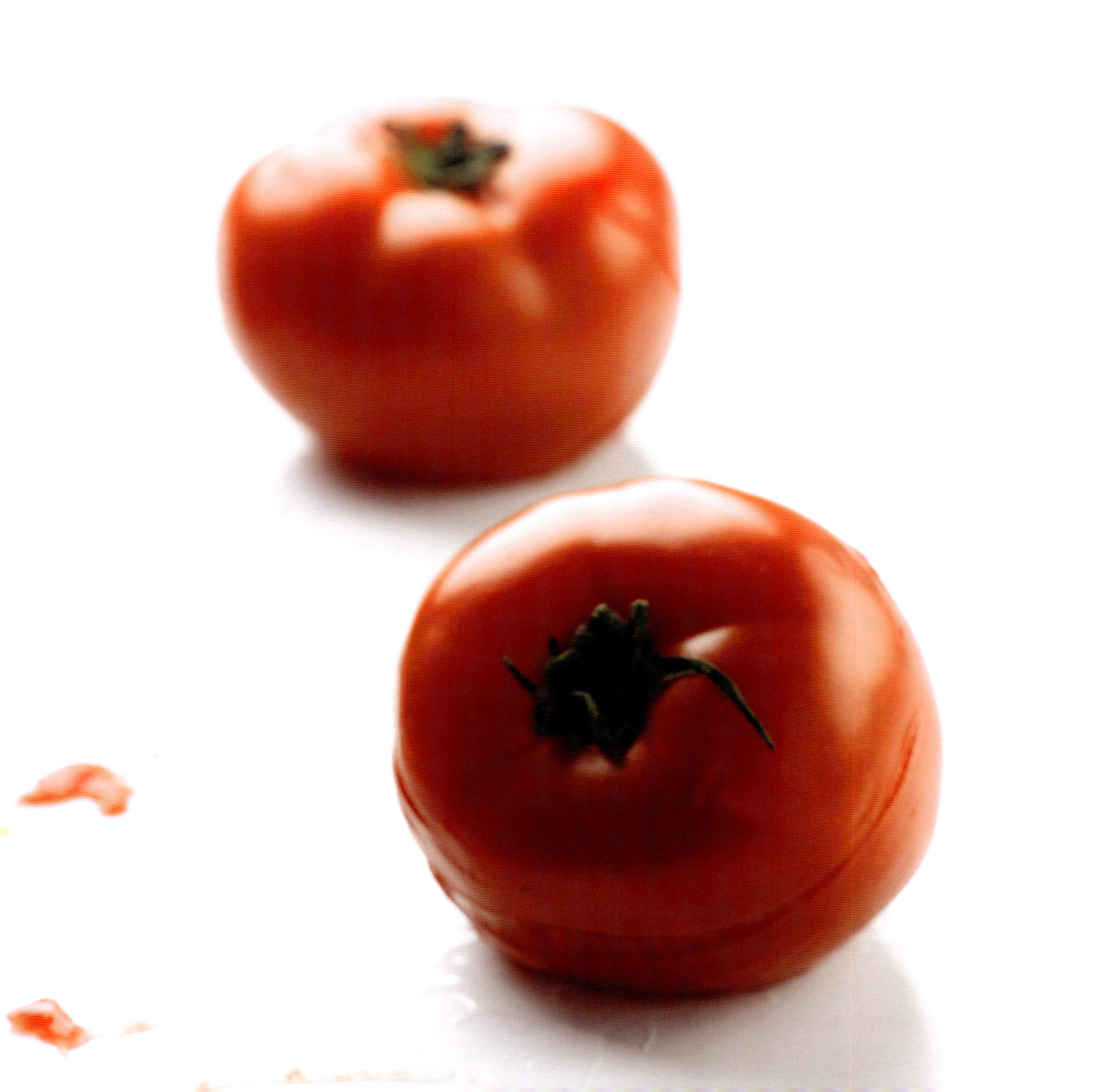

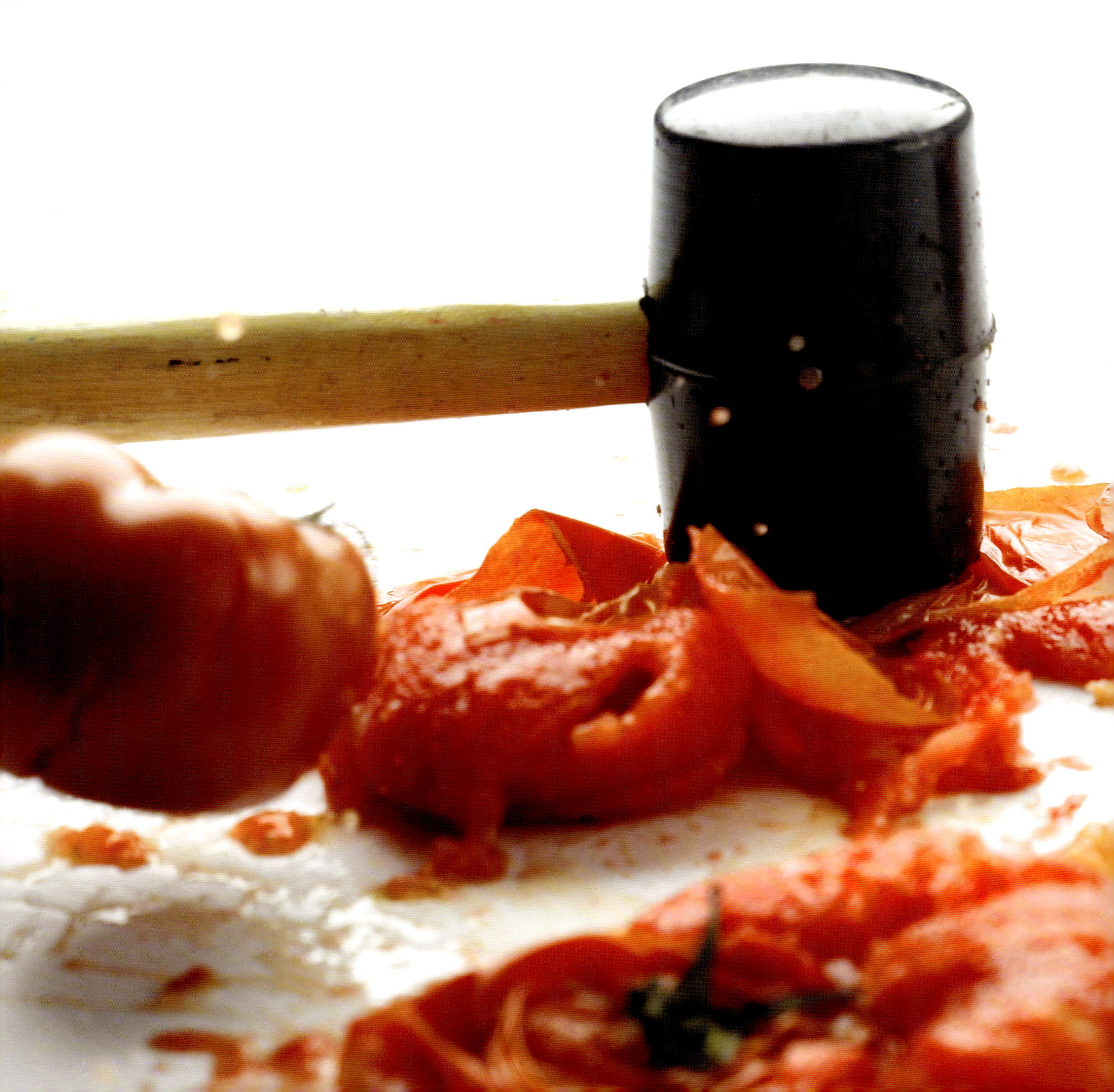

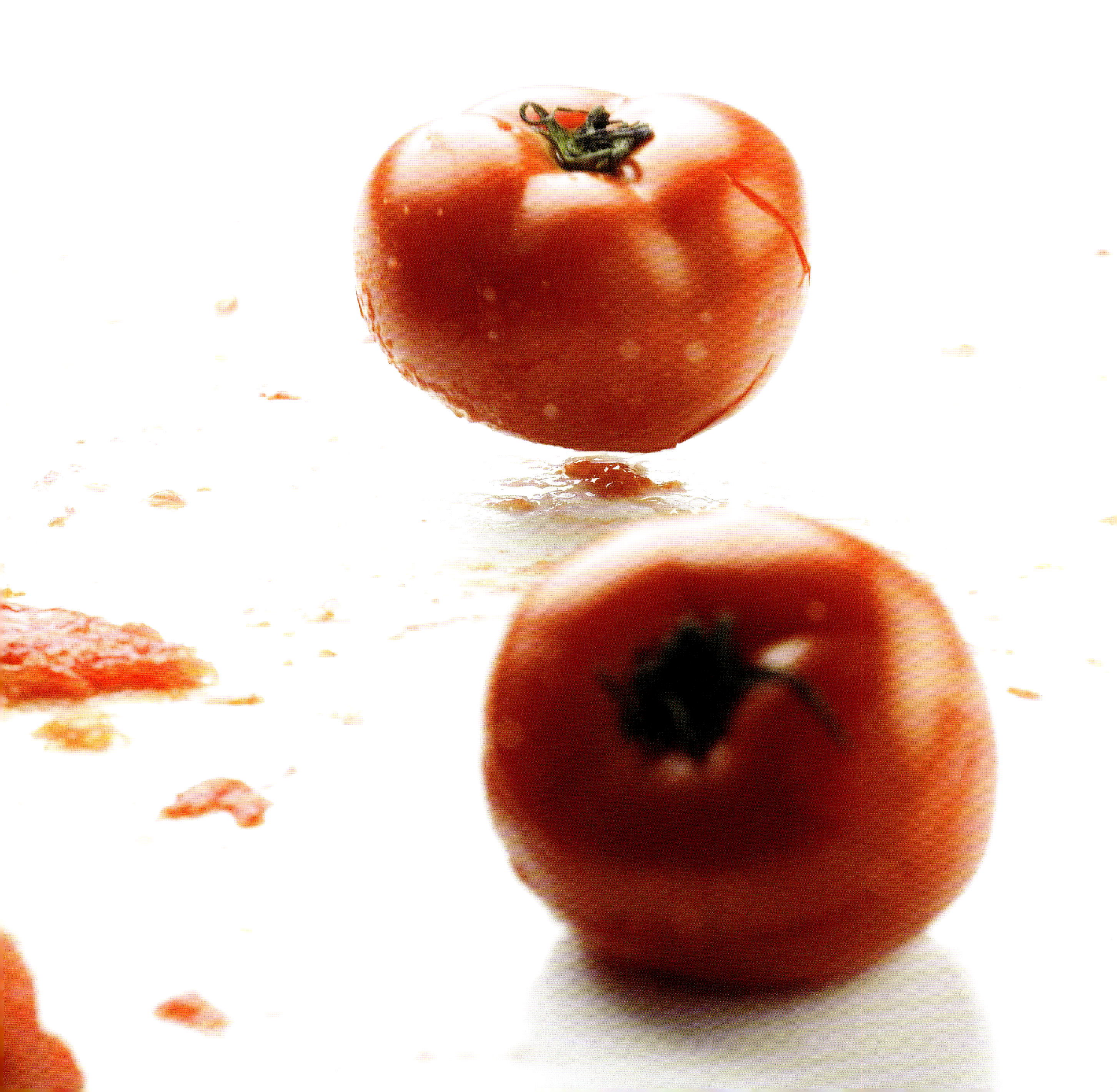

COPIA TOMATO WITH CRISPY BILTONG AND PARMESAN

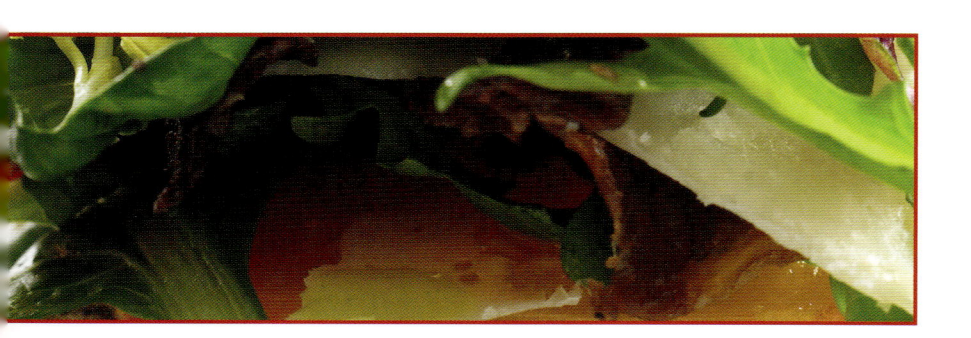

FOR THE BILTONG
- 1 kg   beef sirloin
- 100 ml   achiote paste (see recipe index)
- 20 gr   cumin powder
- 40 gr   coriander powder
- 5 gr   salt
- 5 gr   pepper

Rub the beef with the achiote paste. Blend remaining spices and rub into the beef.
Hang the meat on a hook and air dry in a refrigerator using a fan to circulate the air. The meat should remain in the refrigerator for seven days.

Slice the biltong very thin and oven dry at 80° Celsius for 2 hours.

FOR THE SHERRY VINAIGRETTE
- 300 ml   sherry vinegar
- 600 ml   olive oil
- 15 ml   dijon mustard
- 1 pc   garlic clove chopped
-             salt, pepper

Merge all components.

FOR THE COPIA TOMATOES
- 100 gr   copia tomatoes
- 50 gr   parmesan cheese
- 50 gr   lettuce
- 50 gr   parmesan cheese, shaved
- 30 ml   sherry vinaigrette
-             rock salt and
-             fresh ground pepper

Slice the tomatoes and season with rock salt and pepper. Toss lettuce in sherry vinaigrette and arrange parmesan shavings and biltong with tomatoes. Drizzle with sherry vinaigrette.

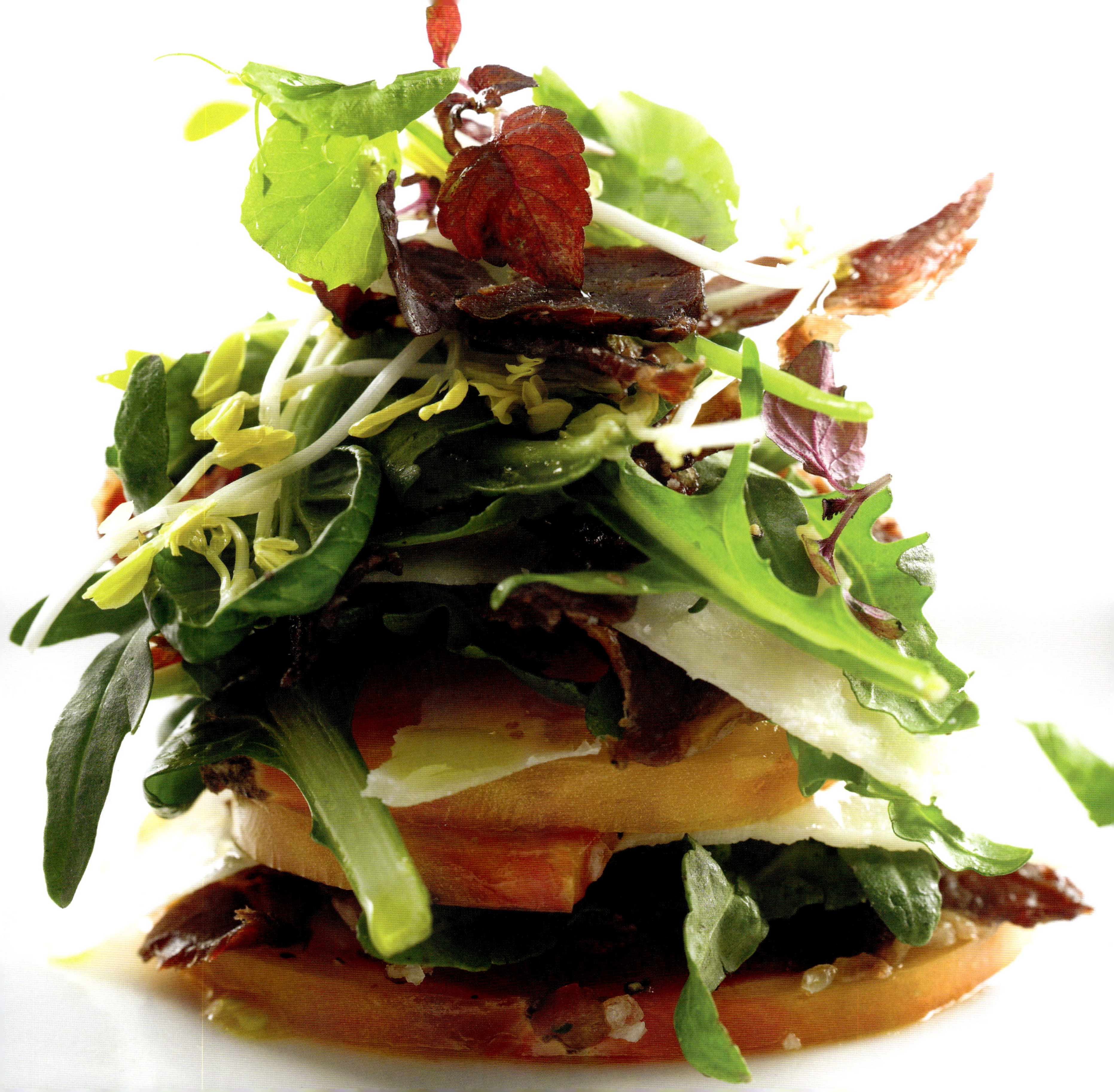

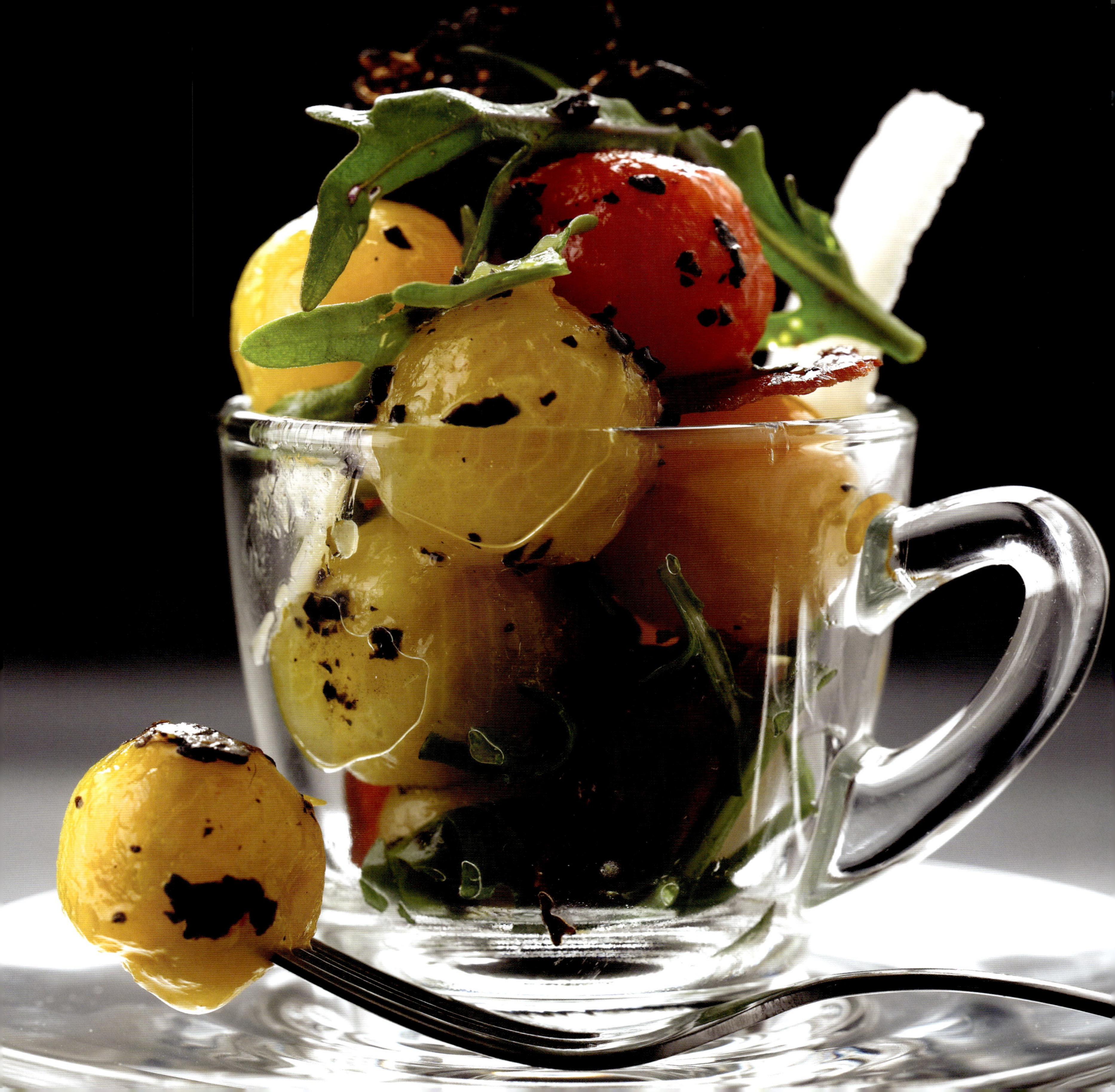

CHERRY TOMATOES WITH TRUFFLES, PARMESAN AND CRISPY SERRANO

FOR THE SALAD
500 gr	red cherry tomatoes
500 gr	yellow cherry tomatoes
100 gr	parmesan cheese, sliced
50 gr	lettuce
30 gr	mache lettuce
20 gr	truffles, sliced
150 ml	truffle dressing
	crispy serrano ham
	salt and pepper

Blanch the tomatoes in boiling salted water for 5 seconds and plunge into ice water. Remove skins.
Merge with all remaining components.

FOR THE TRUFFLE DRESSING
30 ml	truffle oil
200 ml	olive oil
80 ml	white balsamic
10 gr	truffles, diced
	salt and pepper

Blend all components and add diced truffle at the end.

FOR THE CRISPY SERRANO
200 gr	sliced serrano

Lay the sliced Serrano ham on a baking tray lined with grease paper.
Bake in the oven at 100° Celsius for 30 minutes.

BLOODY MARY SORBET WITH TOMATO HONEYCOMB

FOR THE SORBET
- 60 gr vodka
- 5 ml tabasco
- 150 gr tomato juice
- 15 ml lemon juice
- 100 ml sugar syrup
- 10 ml worcestershire sauce
- salt and pepper

Merge all components and place in an ice cream machine. Mix until frozen and remove. Place in the freezer for 3 hours before serving.

FOR THE HONEYCOMB
- 500 gr sugar
- 70 ml water
- 170 gr glucose
- 40 gr tomato juice
- 20 gr baking soda

Make a light caramel with sugar, water, tomato juice and glucose. While still hot, add the soda, stir and quickly pour onto an oiled deep sided tray. Do not shake the tray or the airy mixture will collapse. When cool, break into pieces and freeze for storage.

Garnish with celery leaves.

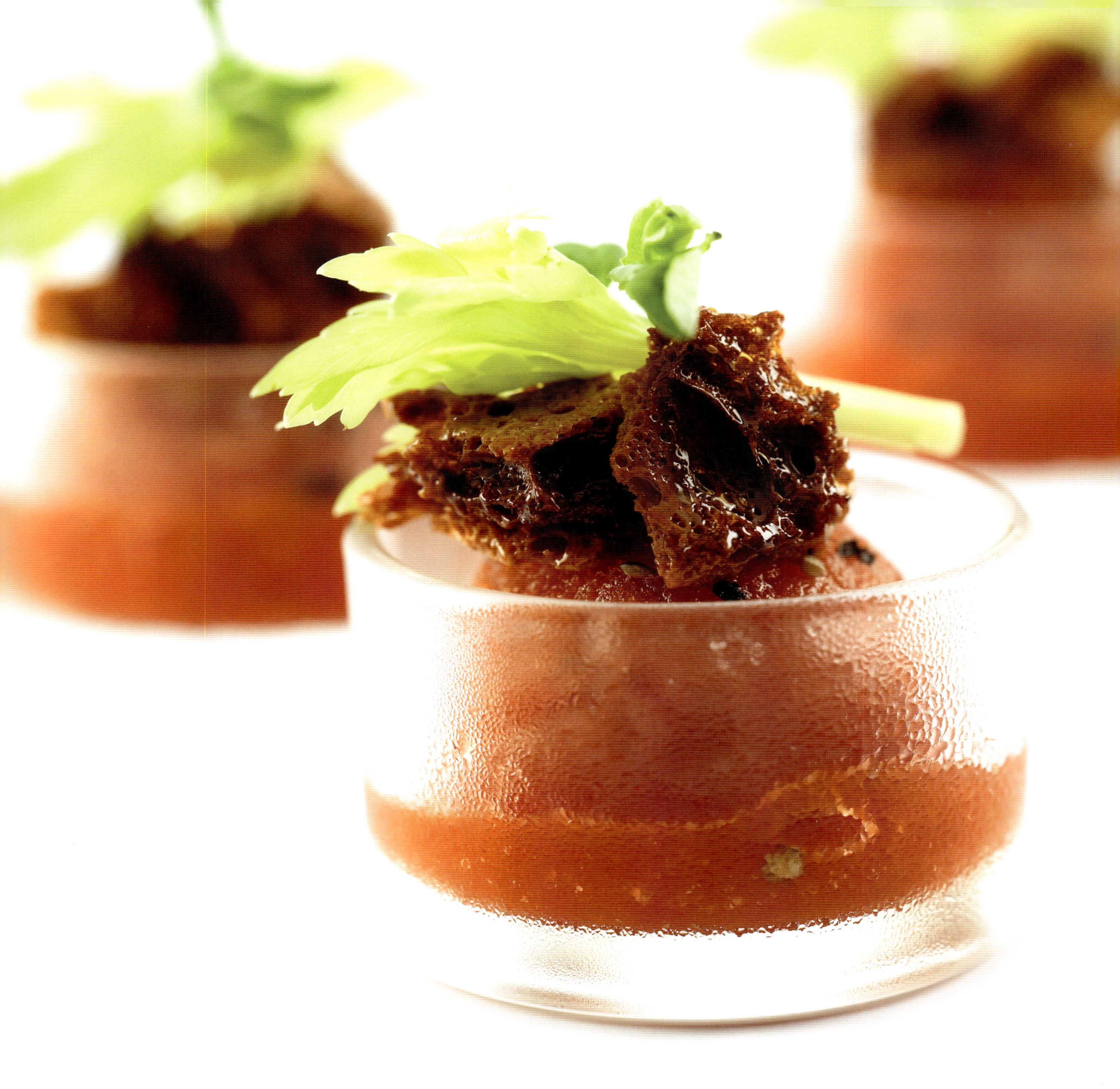

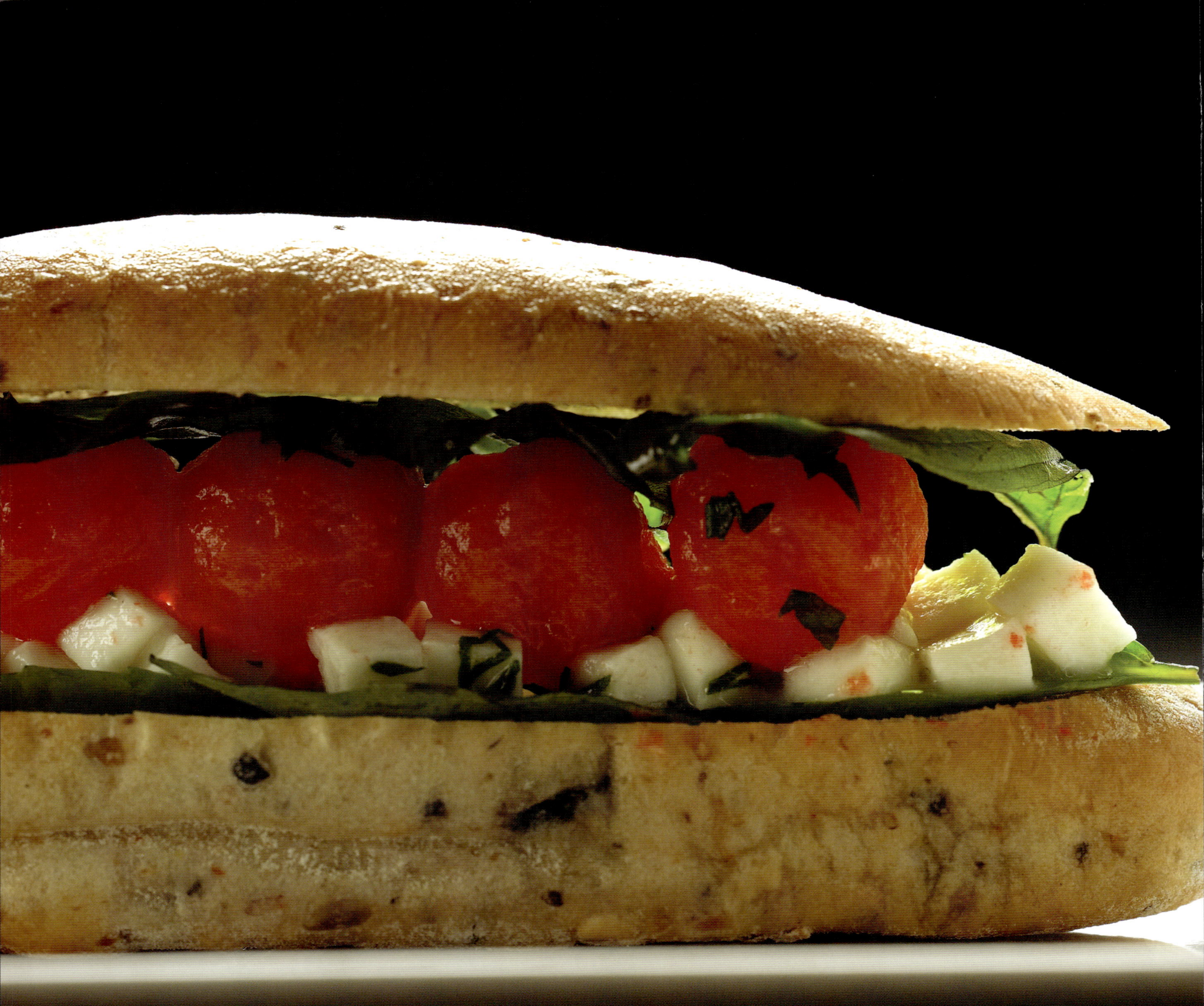

BRUSCHETTA WITH TOMATO, MOZZARELLA AND AFRICAN BLUE BASIL

FOR THE BREAD
- 1 pc crusty black olive baguette toasted
- 1 pc garlic to rub the bread

Rub the toasted bread with the garlic.

FOR THE FILLING
- 50 gr buffalo mozzarella, diced
- 10 pc fresh african blue basil leaves
- 5 pc cherry tomatoes, blanched and skinless
- 5 gr rock salt
- 15 ml white truffle oil

Season the tomatoes and cheese with salt, pepper and truffle oil. Lay half of the basil leaves on the bread. Place the mozzarella cheese on the basil leaves and top with the tomatoes. Julienne remaining basil leaves and place on top of the tomatoes. Sprinkle with rock salt and truffle oil.

CHOCOLATE FONDANT, BALSAMIC AND TOMATO

FOR THE MARSHMALLOW
230 gr	castor sugar
35 gr	glucose
75 gr	water
12 gr	gelatin
50 gr	egg whites
70 gr	vanilla sauce
3 ml	canola oil

Boil water, oil, sugar with glucose at 130° Celsius. Reduce heat to 50° Celsius and add gelatin.
Beat egg whites to stiff peaks.
Mix the sugar syrup and vanilla sauce into the egg whites.

FOR THE CONSOMMÉ
1 pc	lemongrass
100 ml	water
70 gr	castor sugar
1 pc	slice of lemon
15 gr	ginger, sliced
10 ml	lemon juice
15 ml	grand marnier liqueur

Bring all components to a boil for 5 minutes and strain.

FOR THE TOMATO JELLY
200 gr	water
80 gr	castor sugar
15 gr	gelatin
65 gr	white wine
20 gr	strawberry juice
10 pc	candied sliced cherry tomatoes

Merge all components (except candied cheery tomatoes) and boil for 5 minutes. Strain.

FOR THE FONDANT
150 gr	water
100 gr	glucose
400 gr	whipping cream
300 gr	40 % milk chocolate
100 gr	61 % dark chocolate
56 gr	balsamic vinegar

Boil water and glucose at 130° Celsius. Reduce heat to 50° Celsius. Melt both chocolates with the cream.
Merge all ingredients together.

FOR THE CANDIED CHERRY TOMATO
Slice the cherry tomato thinly with skin. Dip in sugar syrup and lay on a greased tray. Place in a preheated oven at 70° Celsius for 3 hours.

In a serving glass pour in tomato jelly and add candied tomato slice in each glass. Let it set for 5 minutes and top with marshmallow.
Add the chocolate fondant and finish with candied tomato.

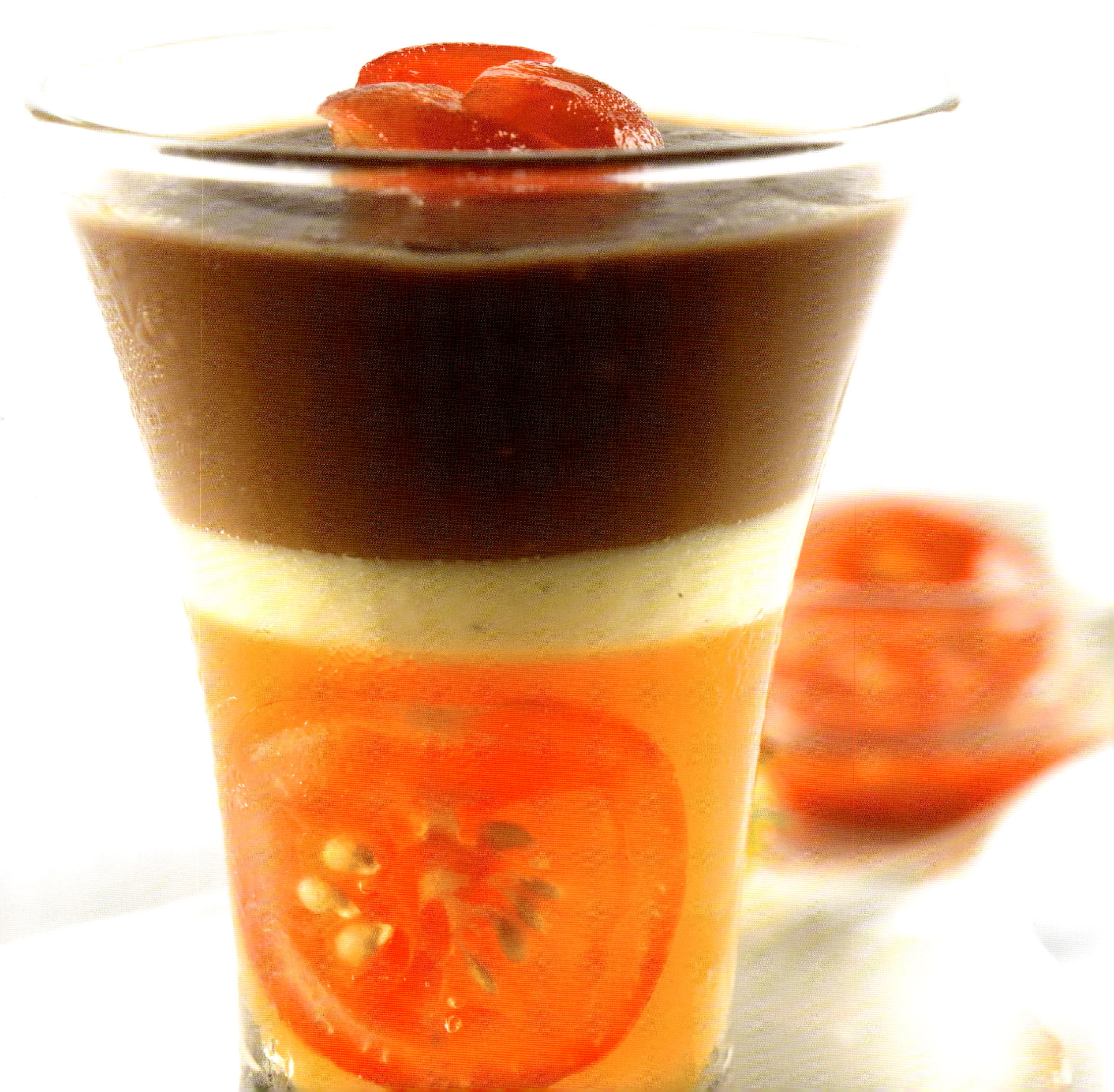

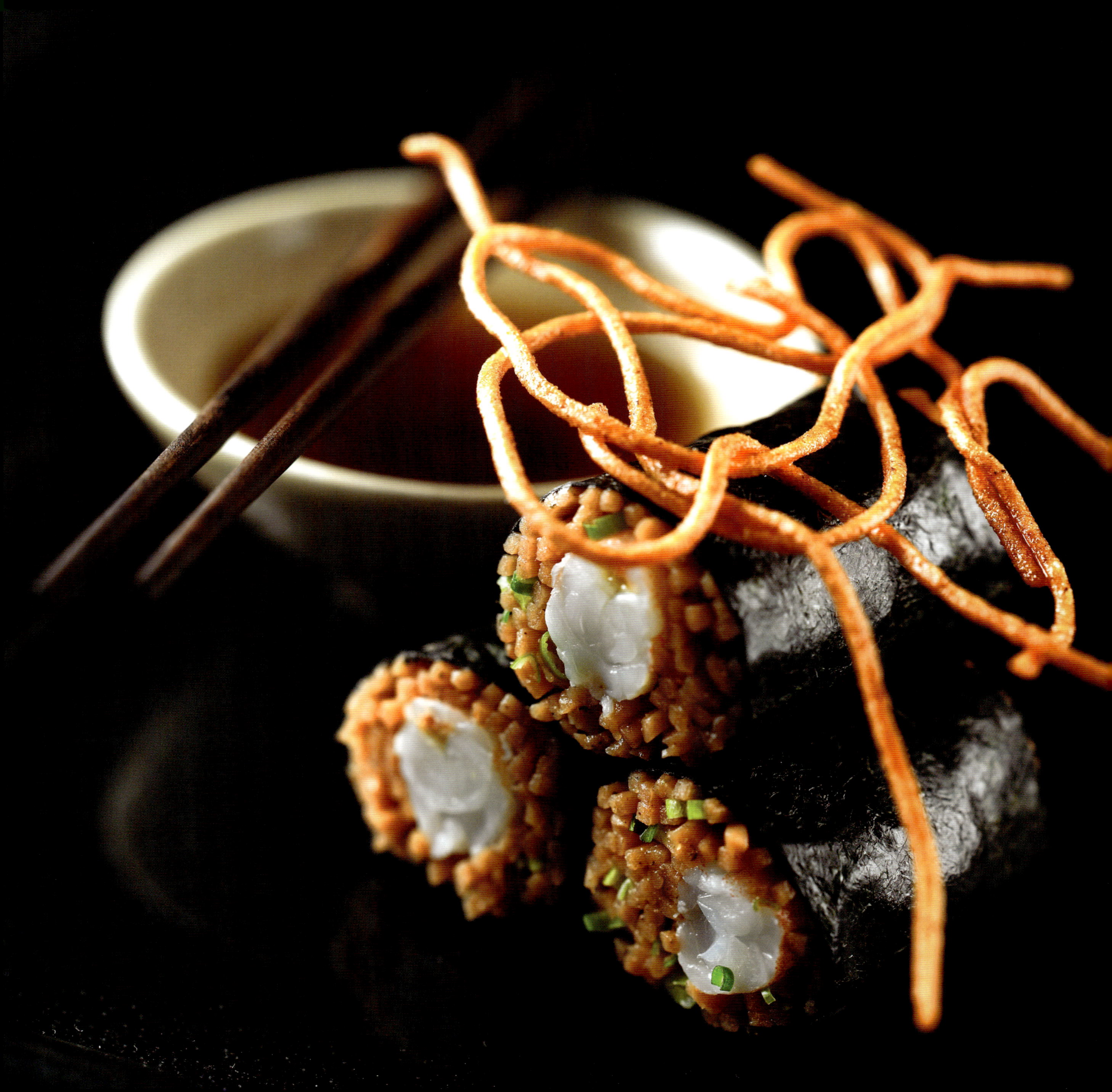

ORDORIKO TOMATO SOBA WITH SPICED SHRIMP

TOMATO SOBA

350 g	buckwheat flour
150 g	wheat flour
250 ml	water
60 ml	ordoriko tomato paste (see recipe index)

Sift flours and mix together. Merge the ordoriko tomato paste and water into flour and knead for 10 minutes. Divide dough into 4 units, cover and rest for 10 minutes. Roll the individual dough units to 2 mm thickness. Using a pasta rolling machine, attach the squared spaghetti cutter and roll dough sheets through machine.

Cook in boiling salted water for 5 minutes. Remove and plunge into ice water.

FOR THE DIPPING SAUCE

10 ml	miso paste
125 ml	soy sauce
1 pc	red chili, chopped
500 ml	dashi (see recipe index)

Merge all components and simmer for 10 minutes. Strain.

FOR THE SHRIMP

Poach fresh live shrimps in boiling salted water until just cooked. Plunge into ice water.
Peel shrimp and discard shells. Season with salt, pepper and shisimi powder.

Lay out nori seaweed sheets and place tomato soba noodles in the center running the length of the sheets. Place the poached shrimp in the center and cover with a layer of tomato soba noodles. Roll up tightly with bamboo roller and slice.

Garnish with crispy fried tomato soba noodles.

TOMATO CRUMPET WITH FOIE GRAS & TOMATO SOFRITO

FOR THE TOMATO CRUMPET

100 ml	tomato juice
450 ml	warm water
20 ml	dried yeast
500 gr	flour
30 ml	tomato paste
15 gr	salt
4 pc	fresh basil leaves
	fresh ground black pepper

Mix the yeast with water and tomato juice. Merge remaining components and mix for 3 minutes to make a light and airy mixture. Cover and allow to rest in a warm area for 20 minutes.
Spoon crumpet mixture into greased ring molds placed on a 160° Celsius flat top grill.

Remove mold after 5 minutes, (the bottom should be slightly brown) and turn crumpet onto the other side. Continue to cook until slightly brown.

FOR THE FOIE GRAS

200 gr	foie gras
	flour
	salt and pepper

Slice foie gras into 50 gram pieces and season with salt and pepper. Dredge in flour and pan-fry until crisp on the outside and soft on the inside.

FOR THE TOMATO SOFRITO

100 gr	tomatoes, chopped
50 gr	sugar
2 pc	basil leaves
15 ml	onion, chopped
1 pc	garlic clove, roasted
30 ml	olive oil
30 ml	cider vinegar

Place all components in a sauté pan and cook over low heat slowly for thirty minutes. Puree and pass through a strainer.

Place toasted crumpet on the serving plate Pour the excess oil from the foie gras pan onto the crumpet. Top with the seared foie gras and spoon sofrito on top. Garnish with sliced dried crumpet wafer and red leaf spinach.

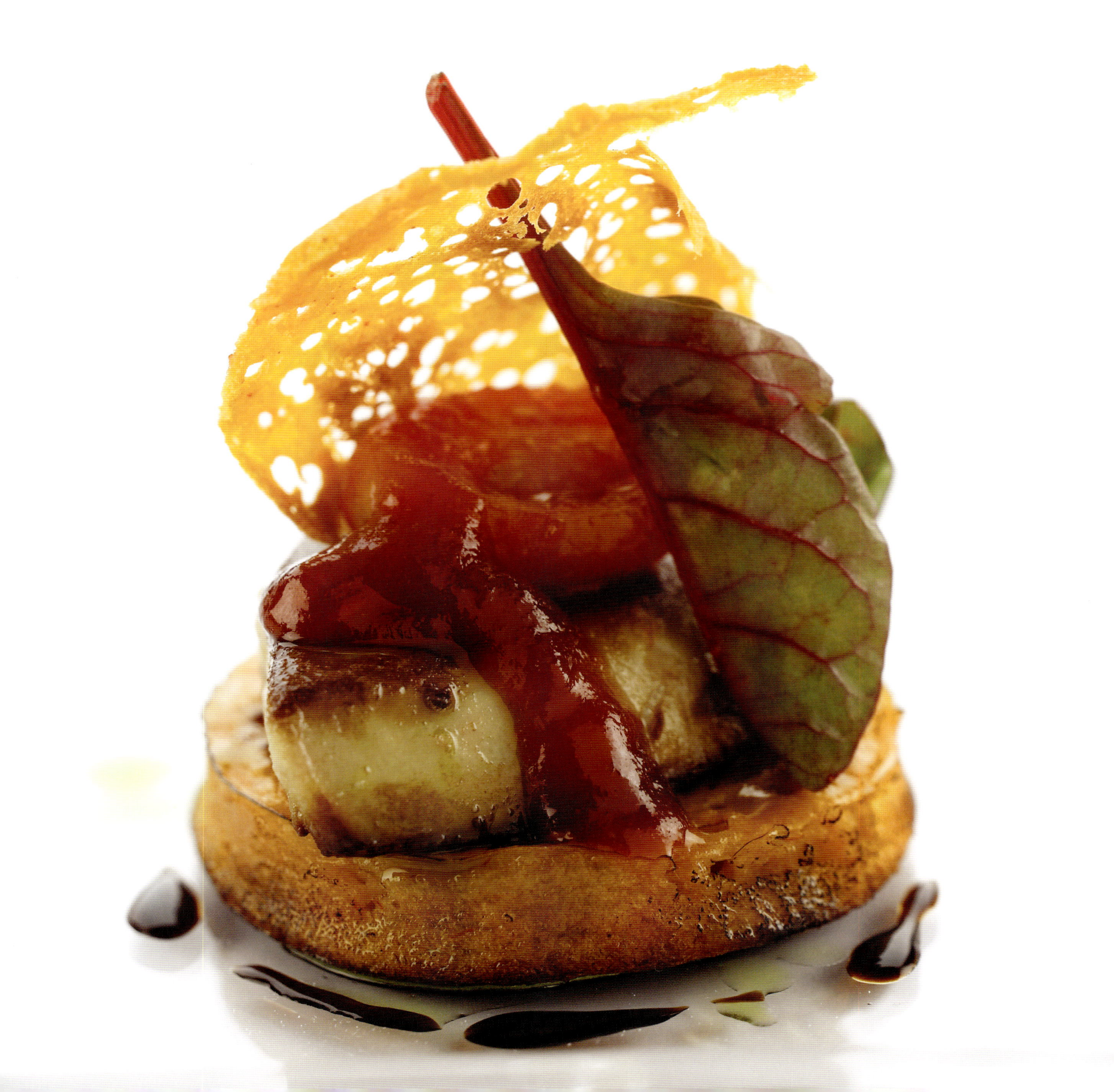

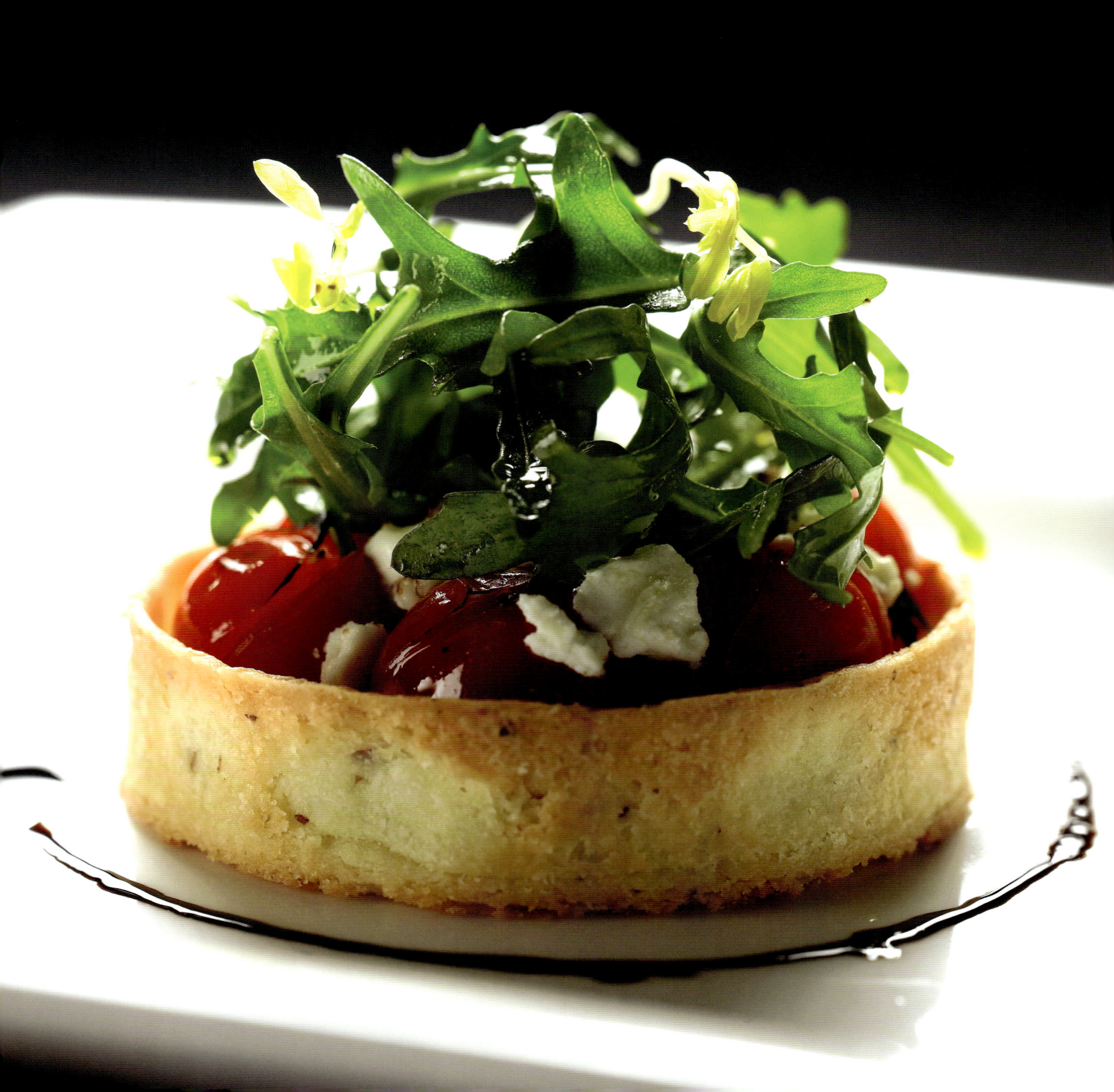

TOMATO CONFIT TART WITH GOAT CHEESE

FOR THE EGGPLANT RELISH
5 pc	elongated eggplants, small dice
50 ml	olive oil
15 gr	garlic
20 gr	capers
	juice of 2 lemons
10 ml	icing sugar
	salt and pepper

Sauté diced eggplant in olive oil for 3 minutes until soft. Drain. Using oil from the sautéed eggplants, sweat the garlic and capers over medium heat. Add lemon juice and sugar.
Mash only half the eggplant into a paste and mix with remaining diced eggplant. Merge with all other components.

FOR THE SAVORY DOUGH
550 gr	butter
10 gr	salt
2 pc	eggs
5 ml	fresh thyme
500 gr	cake flour
500 gr	bread flour
50 gr	water

Merge all components and refrigerate for 1 hour. Roll dough to 2mm thickness and line pie shell molds. Bake.

FOR THE CONFIT OF TOMATOES
250 gr	cherry tomatoes
250 gr	goose fat
1	sprig fresh thyme
1	sprig fresh rosemary
2 pc	garlic cloves, sliced

Make a cross on the top of the cherry tomatoes with a knife. Merge all components and bake at 80° Celsius for 10 minutes.
Remove tomatoes.

ASSEMBLY
1 pc	pre-baked savory tart shell
50 gr	tomato confit
30 ml	eggplant relish
30 gr	goat cheese
2 pc	shredded fresh basil leaves
	salt and pepper

Spoon eggplant relish into tart shell and cover with basil leaves. Layer with tomato confit and goat cheese and season. Bake at 160° Celsius for 10 minutes.

Garnish with arugula and balsamic dressing.

TOMATO AND EGGPLANT PARMESAN

FOR THE EGGPLANT AND TOMATOES

3 pc	sliced eggplant in bread crumbs mixed with parmesan cheese
3 pc	parmesan cheese, sliced
3 pc	tomatoes, sliced
1 pc	mozzarella cheese, sliced
15 ml	tomato stew
	salt and pepper

Deep-fry the eggplant until golden brown and pat dry with paper towels. Layer the Parmesan cheese on top of fried eggplant and place under a salamander to melt. Season the sliced tomatoes with salt and pepper and pan-fry quickly on each side. Layer the eggplant with tomatoes and finish with a slice mozzarella. Melt under a salamander.

FOR THE TOMATO STEW

1 kg	tomatoes diced
280 gr	onions, diced
40 gr	basil, chopped
50 gr	red wine vinegar
40 gr	olive oil
	salt and pepper

Merge all ingredients together and serve at room temperature.

PURÉED TOMATO SAUCE

100 gr	tomatoes, peeled and chopped
10 gr	onions, chopped
2 pc	whole garlic cloves
5 ml	oregano
5 ml	thyme
50 ml	olive oil
10 ml	fresh basil, chopped

Sautee onions and garlic in olive oil and add remaining components. Simmer slowly over low heat for 20 minutes. Remove garlic and puree.

ASSEMBLY

Spoon tomato sauce on a plate and place the eggplant and tomato stacks on top. Spoon a little tomato stew on to the stacks.

Garnish with crispy eggplant and sprouts.

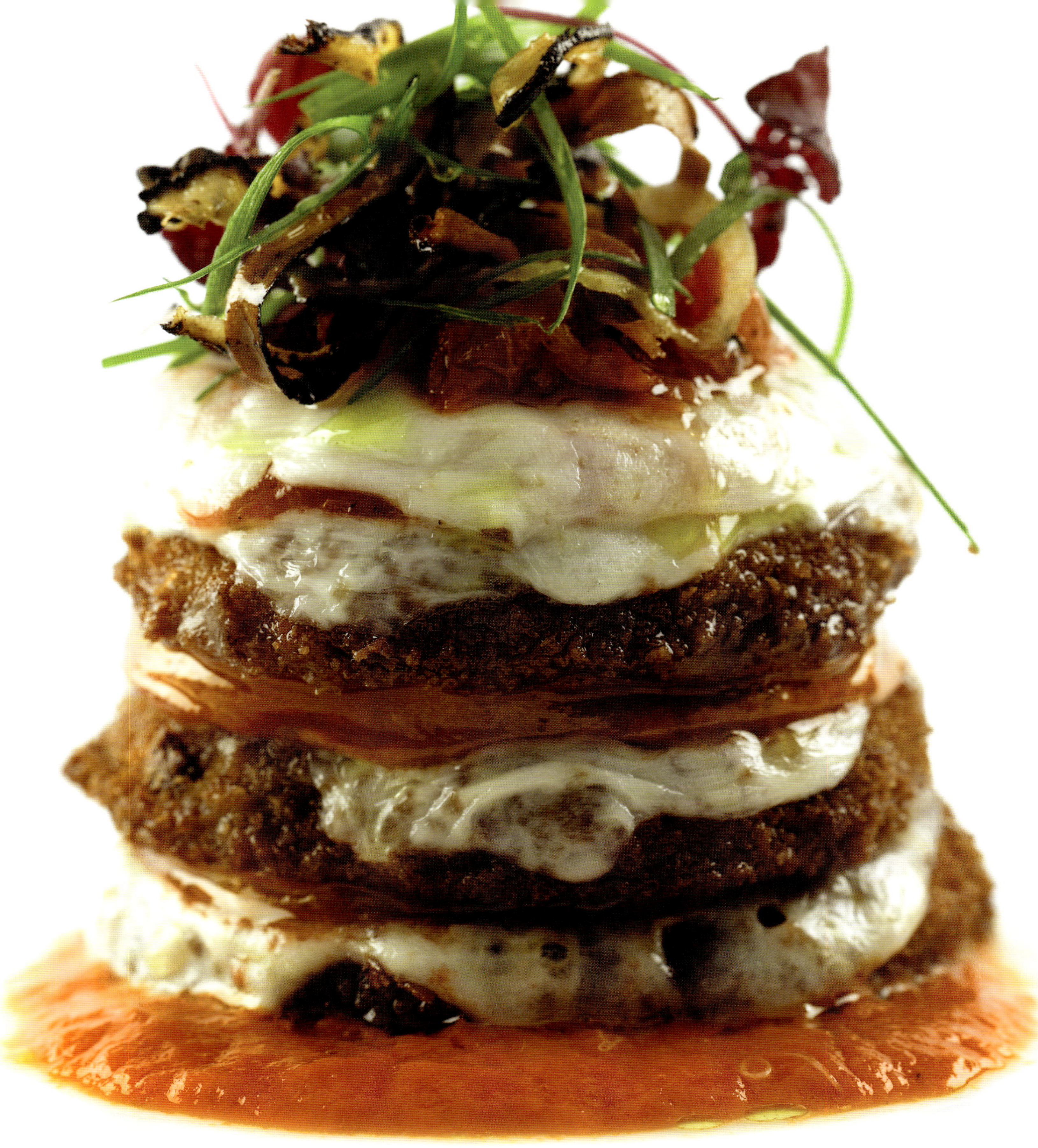

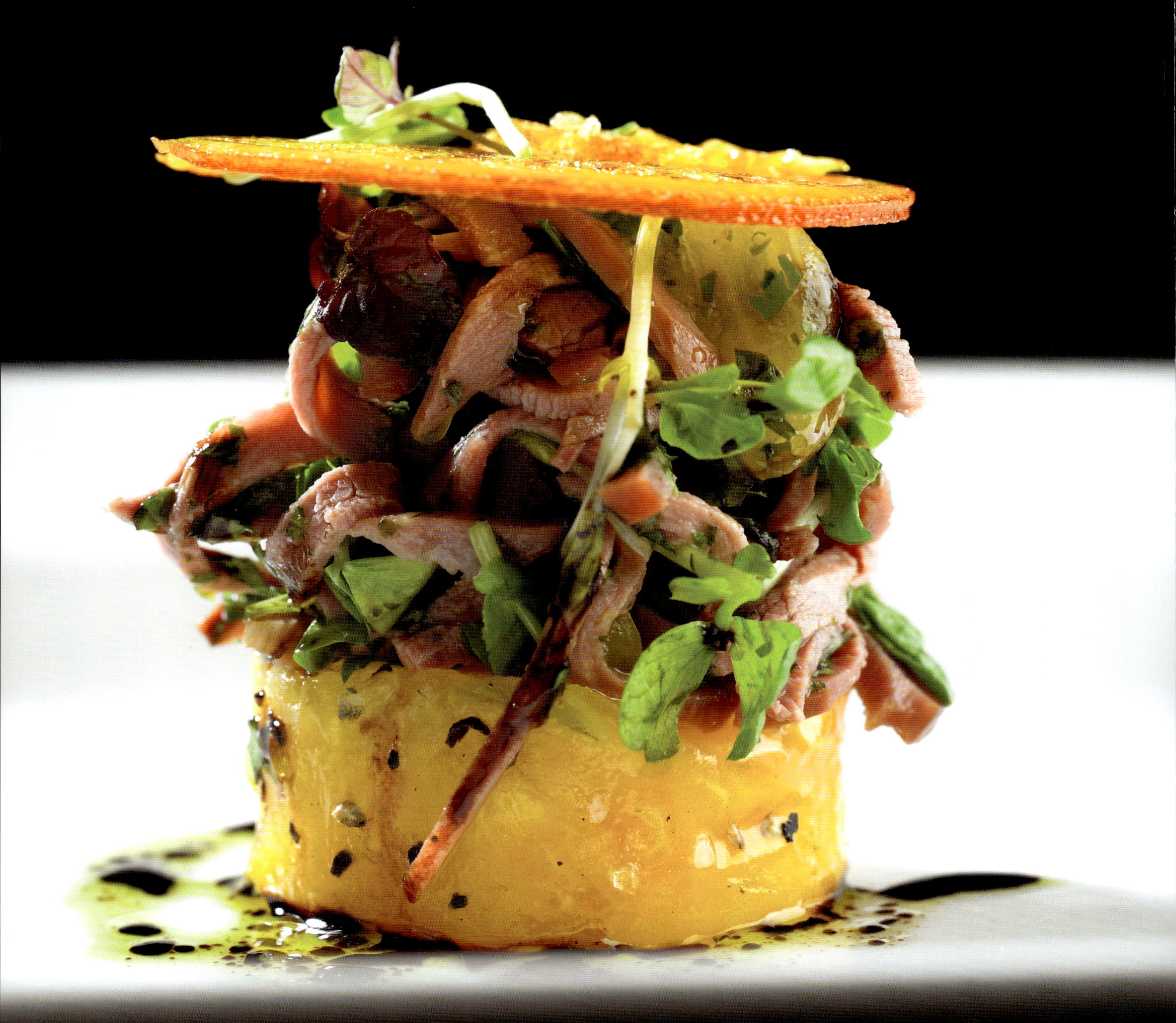

HEIRLOOM TOMATO WITH SMOKED DUCK AND CANDIED ORANGE

FOR THE HEIRLOOM TOMATOES

1 kg	heirloom tomatoes
350 gr	smoked duck, julienne
150 gr	candied oranges diced
100 gr	green pea sprouts
100 ml	candied orange dressing

Blanch the tomatoes in boiling salted water for 10 seconds and plunge into ice water. Remove the skins. Cut the tomatoes into cylinder shapes using a round cutter and season with salt and pepper.
Mix the smoked duck julienne, candied oranges and sprouts. Add the dressing and toss. Place the smoked duck salad on top of the tomatoes and garnish with the dried oranges.

FOR THE CANDIED ORANGES

100 ml	orange juice
200 gr	sugar
100 ml	vinegar
300 ml	water
5 gr	salt
300 gr	orange skins

Bring liquid components and salt to a boil, add orange skins and simmer for 1 hour. Remove from heat and allow to cool down.
Remove orange skins and dice.

FOR THE CANDIED ORANGE DRESSING

25 gr	candied orange skins
100 gr	shallots
50 gr	sugar
100 ml	sherry vinegar
100 ml	olive oil
	salt and pepper

FOR THE DRIED ORANGE GARNISH

200 gr	thinly sliced orange skins
50 gr	icing sugar
5 gr	salt

Lay sliced orange skins on a non-stick baking tray and sprinkle with icing sugar and salt.
Dry in 70° Celsius oven for 5 hours.

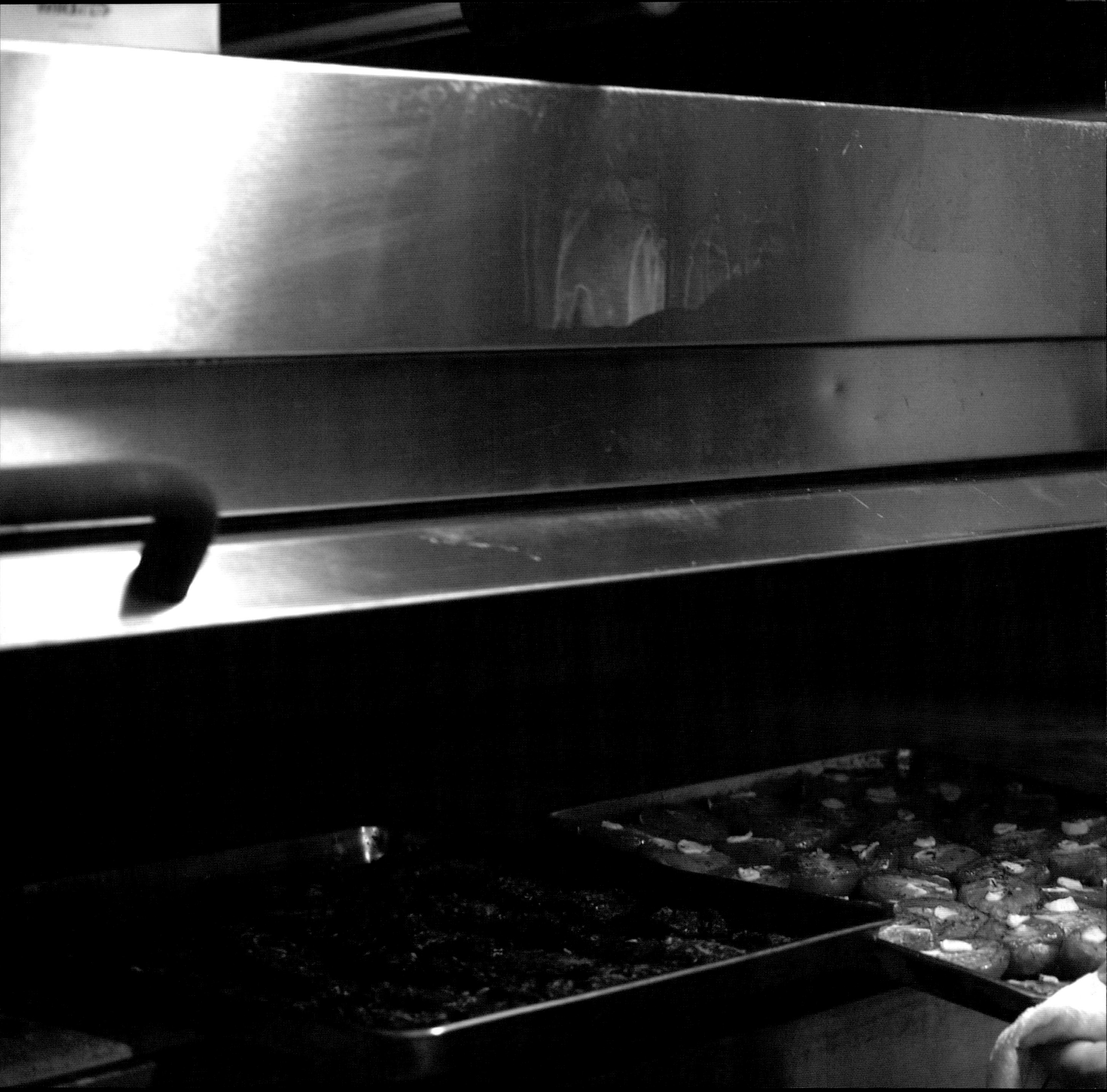

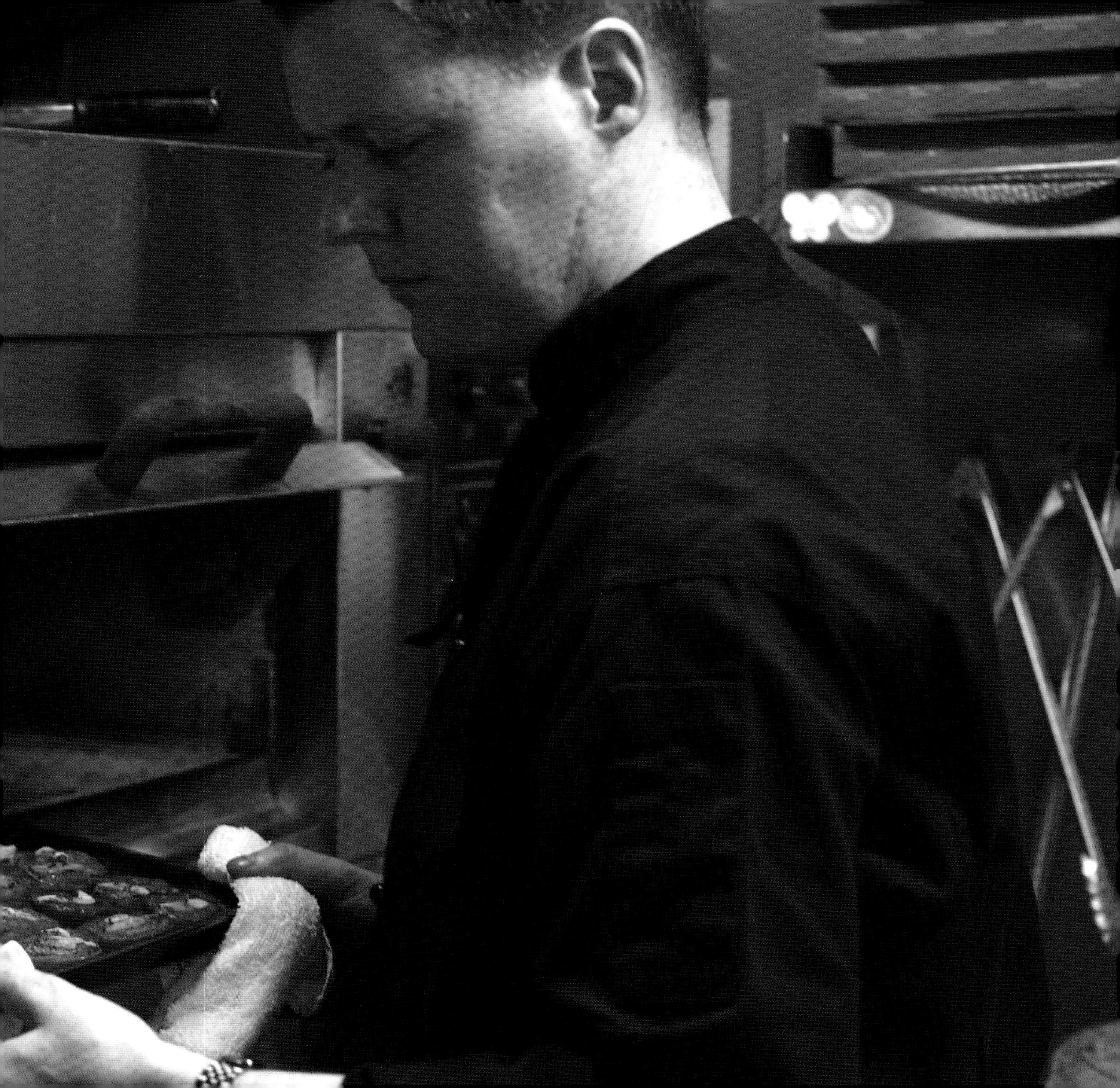

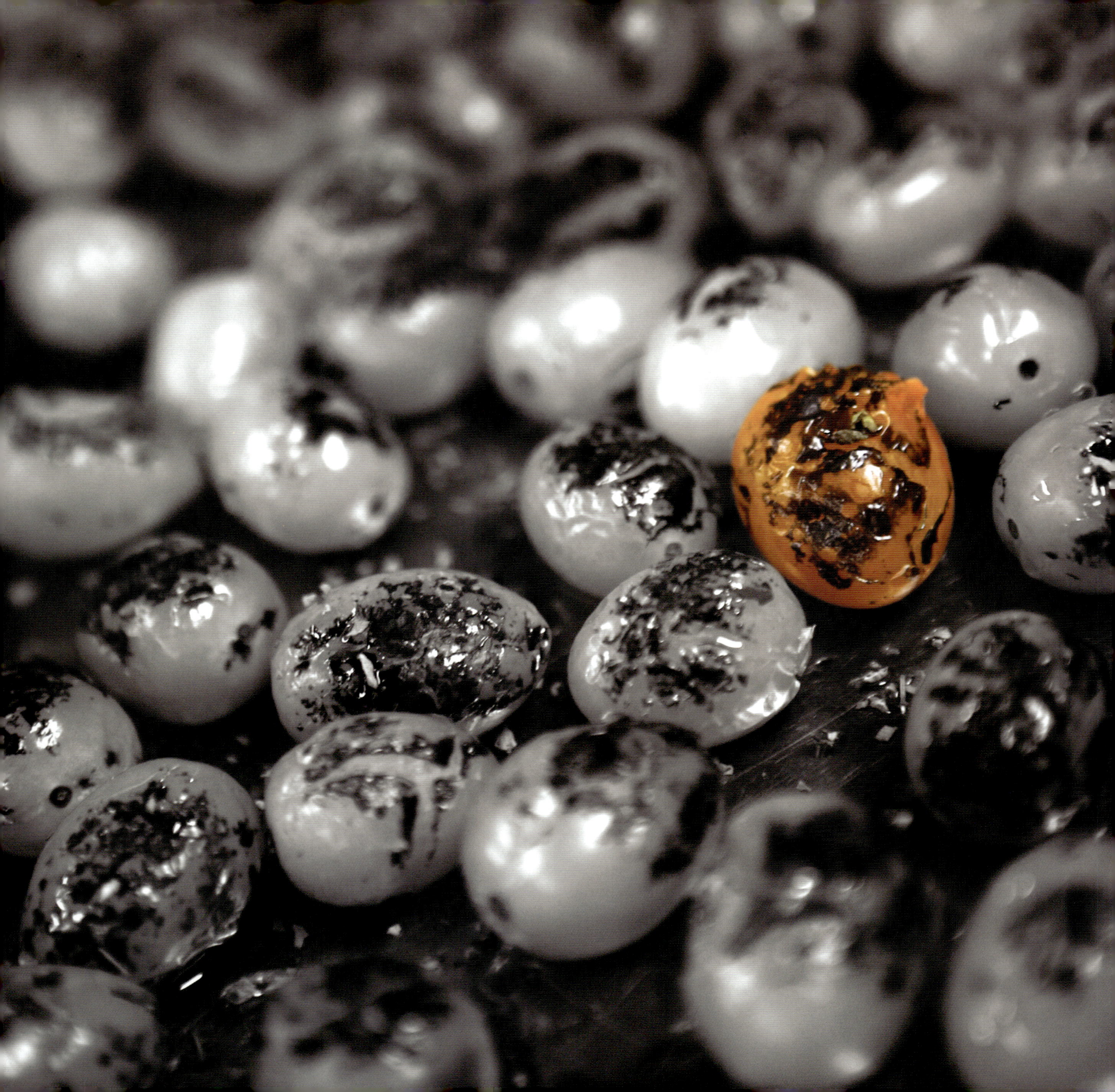

```
              *** COPY *** 3
           Table No. : 51
       No of Guest : 1
       Order No.   : 831
       Staff       : David
       Term ID     : 3
       Start Time  : 08/06/17 12:17
       ─────────────────────────────
       1 PACKAGE A
       1 Chicken wing
       1 Shrimp
       1 Clear Soup
       1 Hot wet tea
         Soda Up
         Up 3/2
```

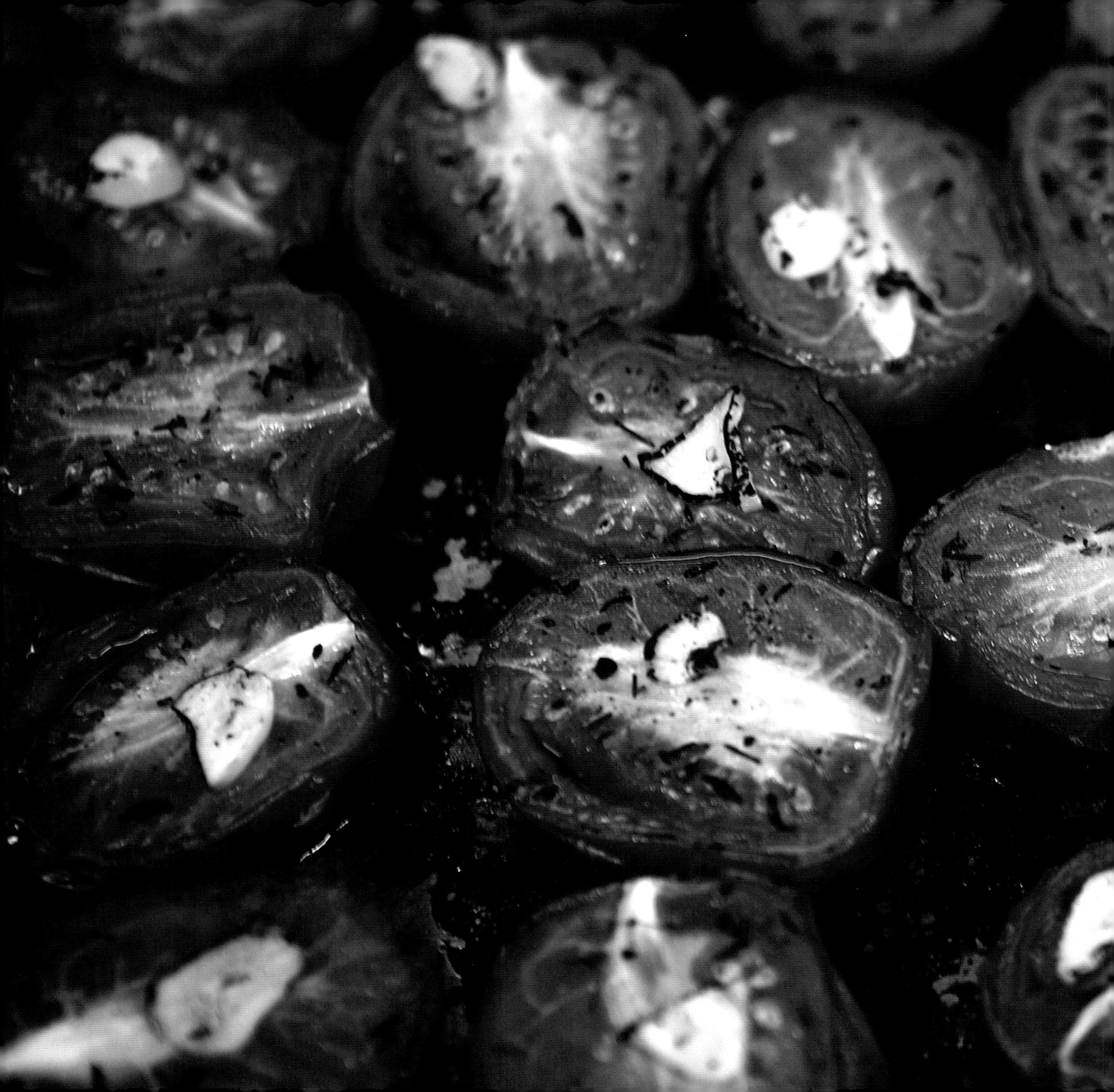

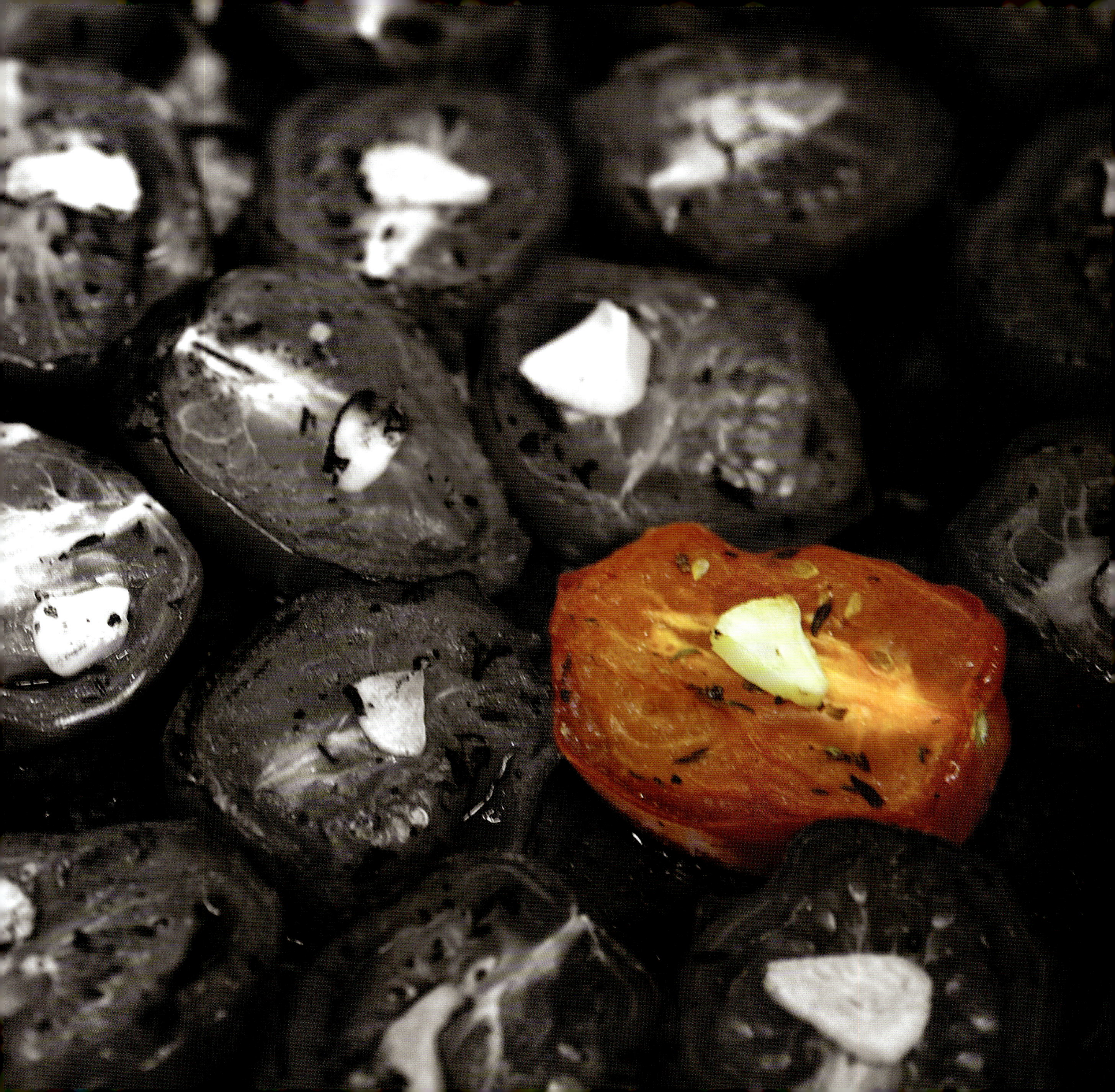

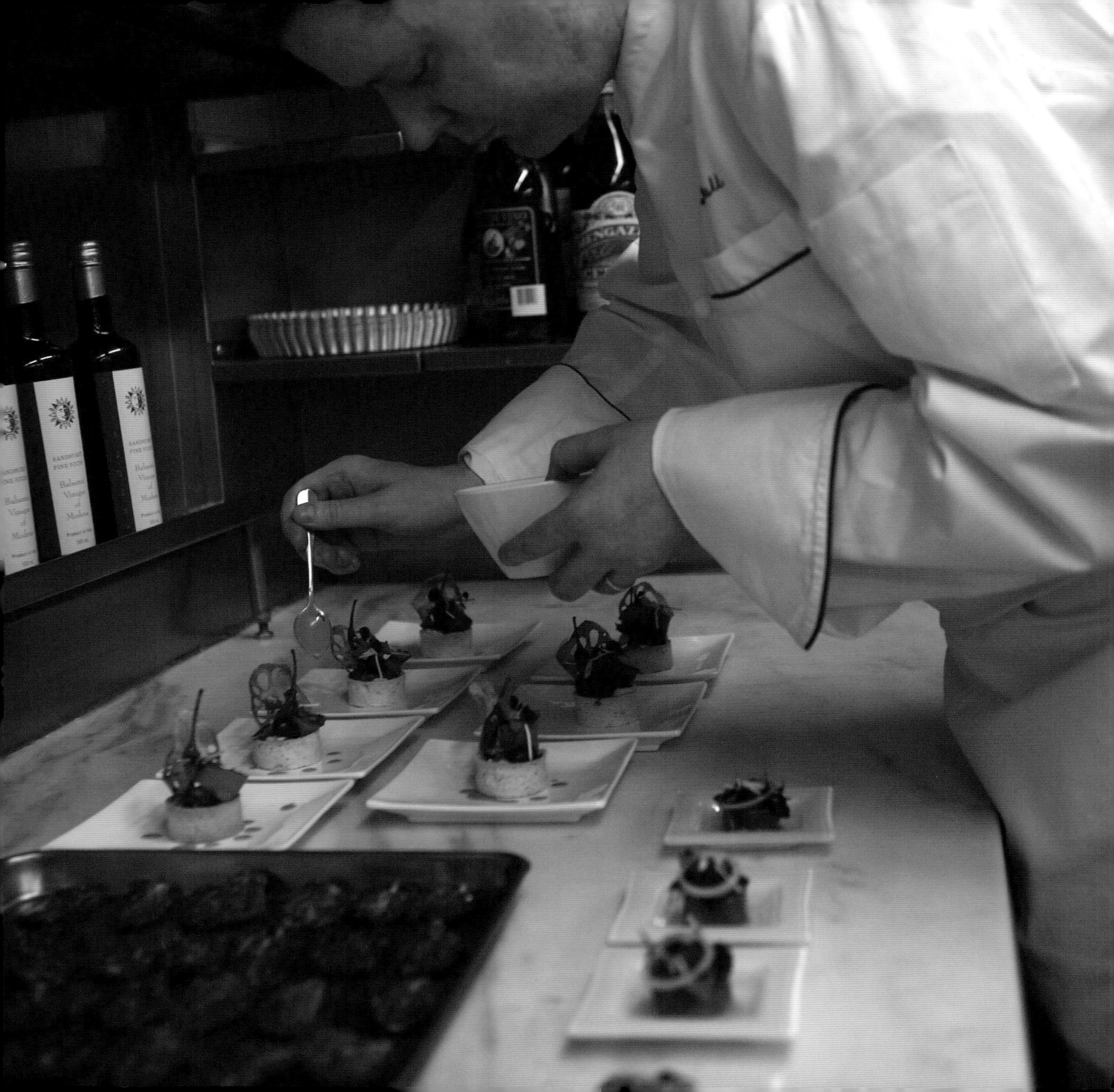

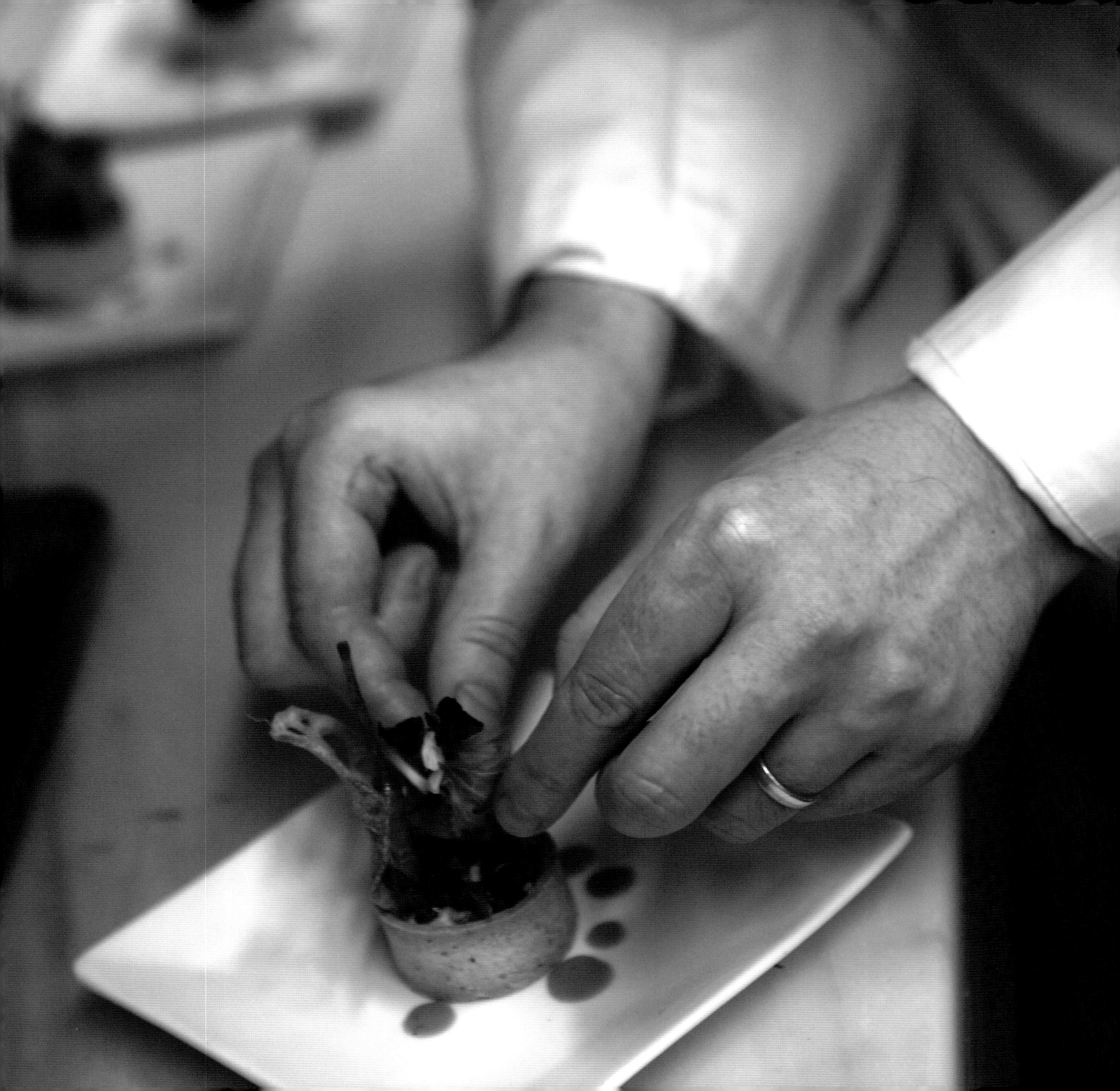

TOMATO AND BUFFALO MOZZARELLA RAVIOLI WITH ROCKET PESTO

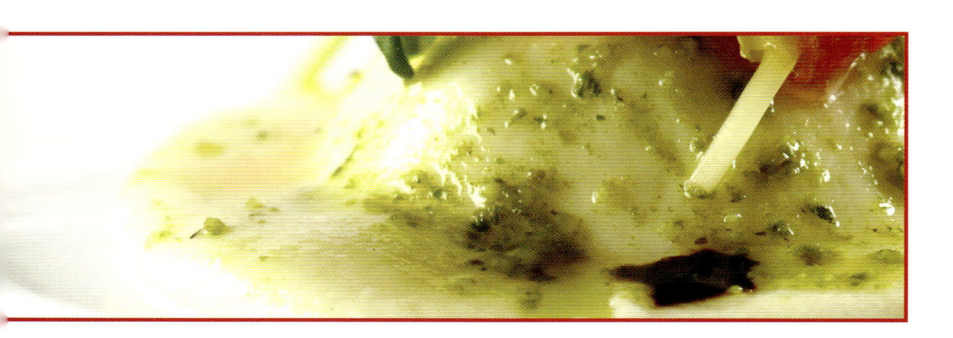

FOR THE RAVIOLIS
300 gr   semi-dried tomatoes
400 gr   buffalo mozzarella
50 gr   onion, chopped
10 gr   fresh basil
            salt and pepper

Slice the mozzarella and lay out half of the slices on a baking tray. Place the tray under a salamander and allow the cheese to begin to melt.
Toss the tomatoes with onions, basil, salt and pepper. Spoon the tomato mixture into the center of each mozzarella slice. Place the remaining slices of mozzarella on top to form ravioli pocket. Return to salamander and allow cheese to begin to melt.
Cut with a circular cutter to form equal ravioli sized pockets.

ROCKET PESTO
100 gr   rocket lettuce
10 gr   italian parsley chopped
10 gr   fresh basil
10 gr   garlic
200 ml   olive oil
50 gr   roasted pine nuts
50 gr   parmesan cheese
            salt and pepper

Blend rocket, basil and garlic with olive oil in a high speed blender. Add the pine nuts and parmesan cheese and blend. Season.

BALSAMIC DRESSING
500 ml   balsamic vinegar
300 ml   red wine
100 gr   sugar

Bring to a boil and reduce to 100 ml.

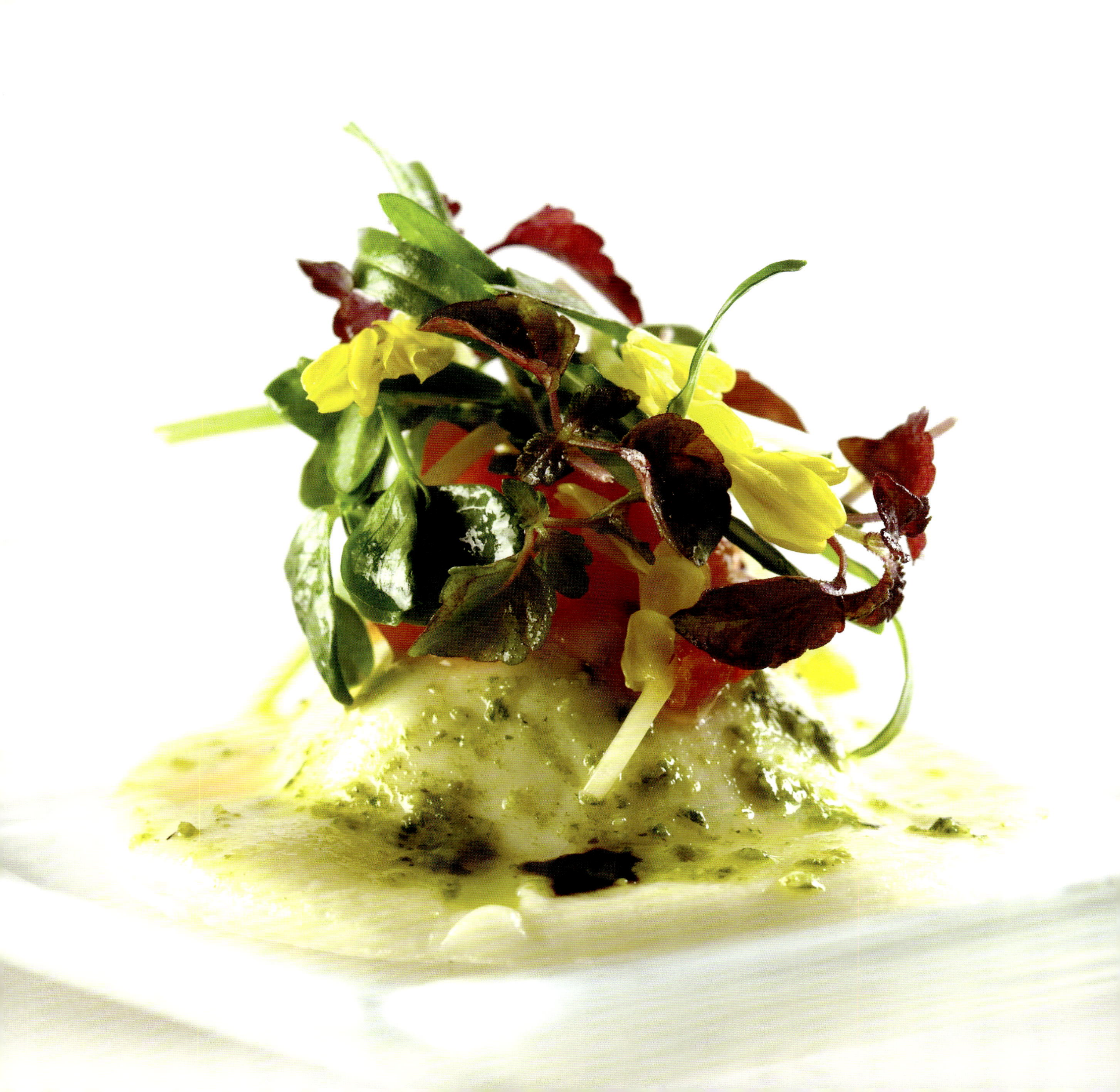

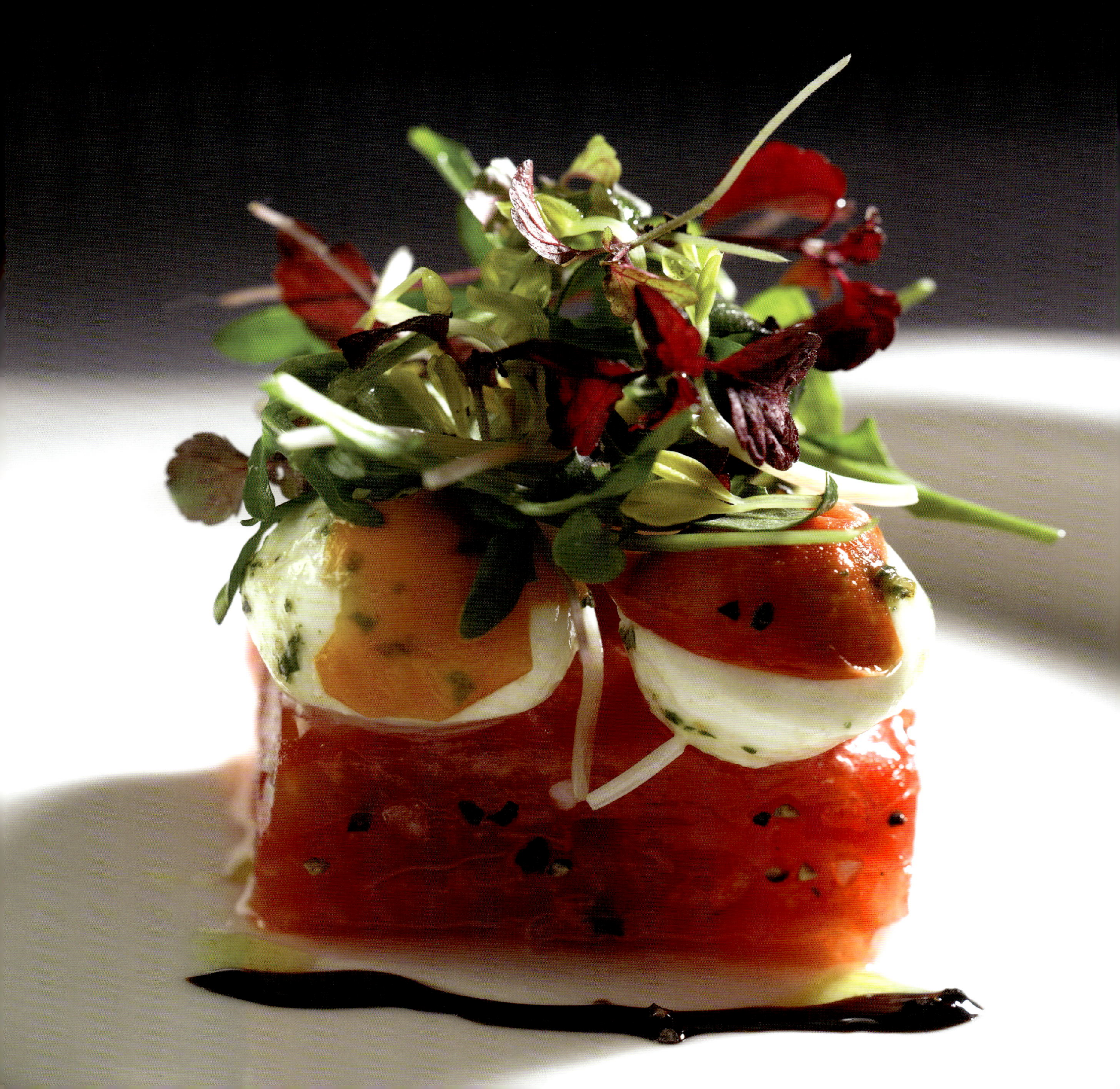

SMOKED PLUM TOMATO PAVÉ WITH BOCCONCINI

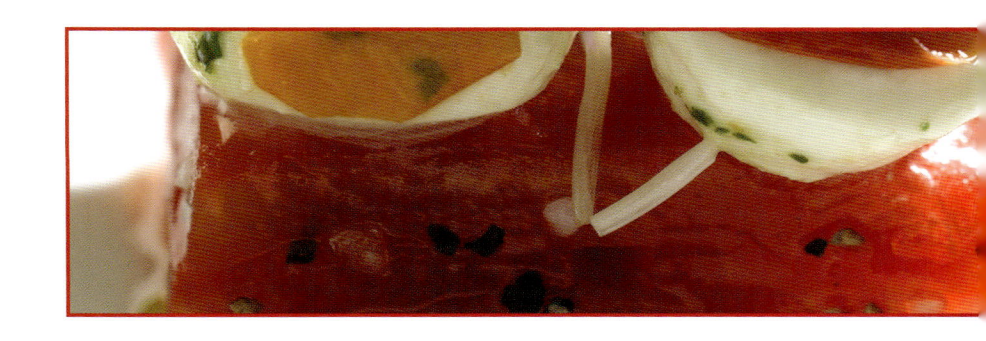

FOR THE TOMATOES
200 gr	plum tomatoes, peeled and seeded
30 ml	fresh thyme
30 ml	olive oil
	rock salt

Lay the tomatoes on a baking tray and brush with olive oil. Liberally season with salt and sprinkle with thyme leaves.
Place tomatoes in a 'hot smoker' with apple wood chips for 15 minutes. Remove and while still warm layer into a rectangular mold until full. Press tomatoes to condense.
Cover with plastic film and refrigerate for 5 hours.

FOR THE MOZZARELLA
4 pc	bocconcini cheese
10 gr	arugula
5 gr	cress
15 ml	balsamic reduction (see recipe index)
10 ml	basil oil
	salt and pepper

Season the mozzarella with salt and fresh black pepper and place on top of tomato pave.
Place cress and arugula leaves over mozzarella and drizzle with balsamic reduction and basil oil.

KING SCALLOPS WITH TOMATO CRUST ON RICH SHELLFISH CREAM

FOR THE TOMATO CRUST

50 gr	parmesan cheese
50 gr	white bread crumbs
50 gr	sun-dried tomatoes, chopped
5 ml	rosemary, chopped
1 pc	egg yolk
20 gr	soft butter
	salt and pepper

Merge all components to form a paste.

FOR THE KING SCALLOPS

4 pc	king scallops
	salt and pepper

Season the scallops and sear in hot pan. Remove from pan and cover the scallops with the tomato crust.
Finish the scallops under a hot salamander.

TOMATO SHELLFISH CREAM

50 gr	tomato juice
20 gr	sun-dried tomatoes
50 gr	whipping cream
30 gr	white wine
20 gr	shellfish stock
	salt and pepper

Bring to a boil and simmer 10 minutes. Blend and strain.

Garnish with crispy rosemary.

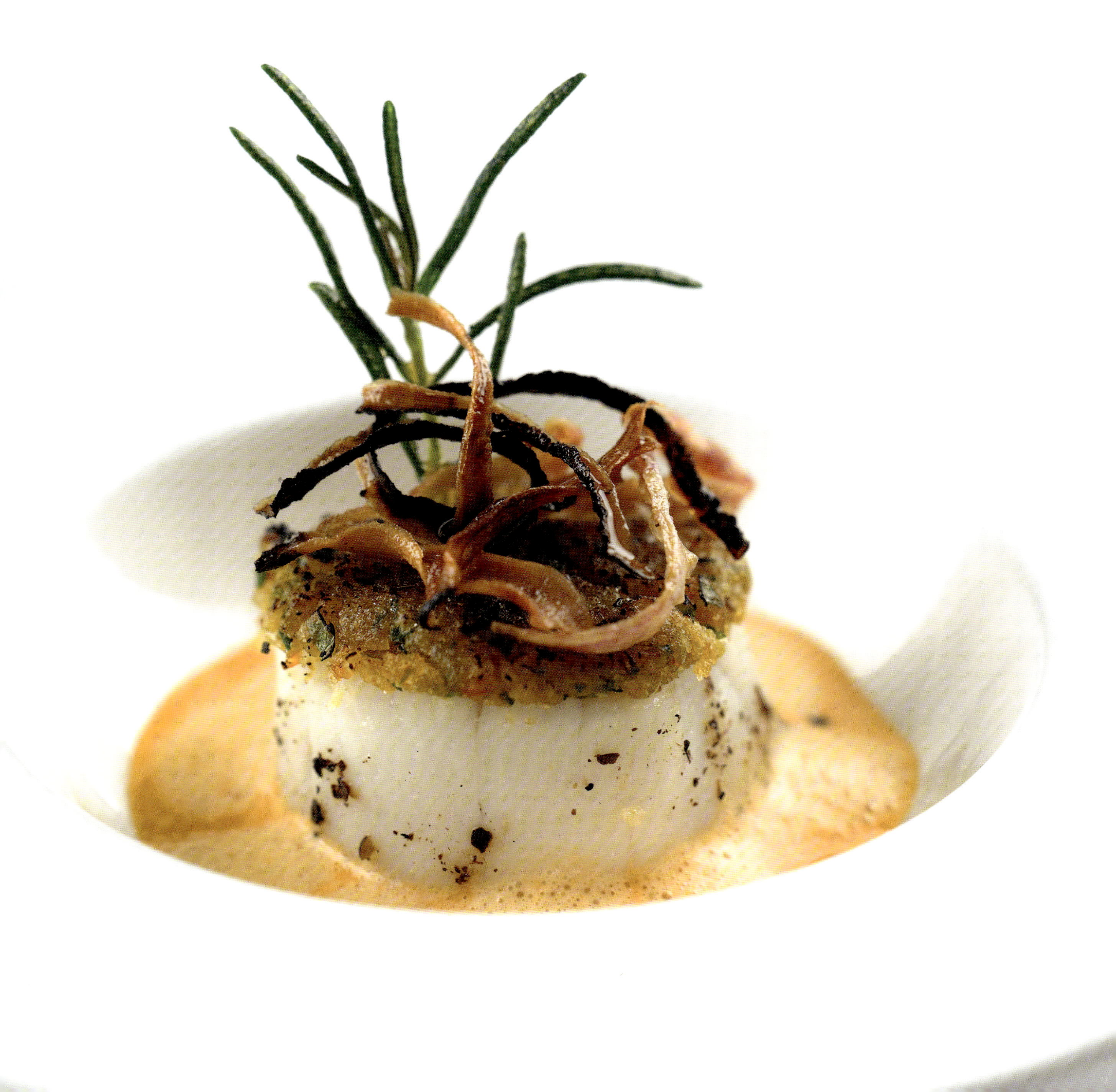

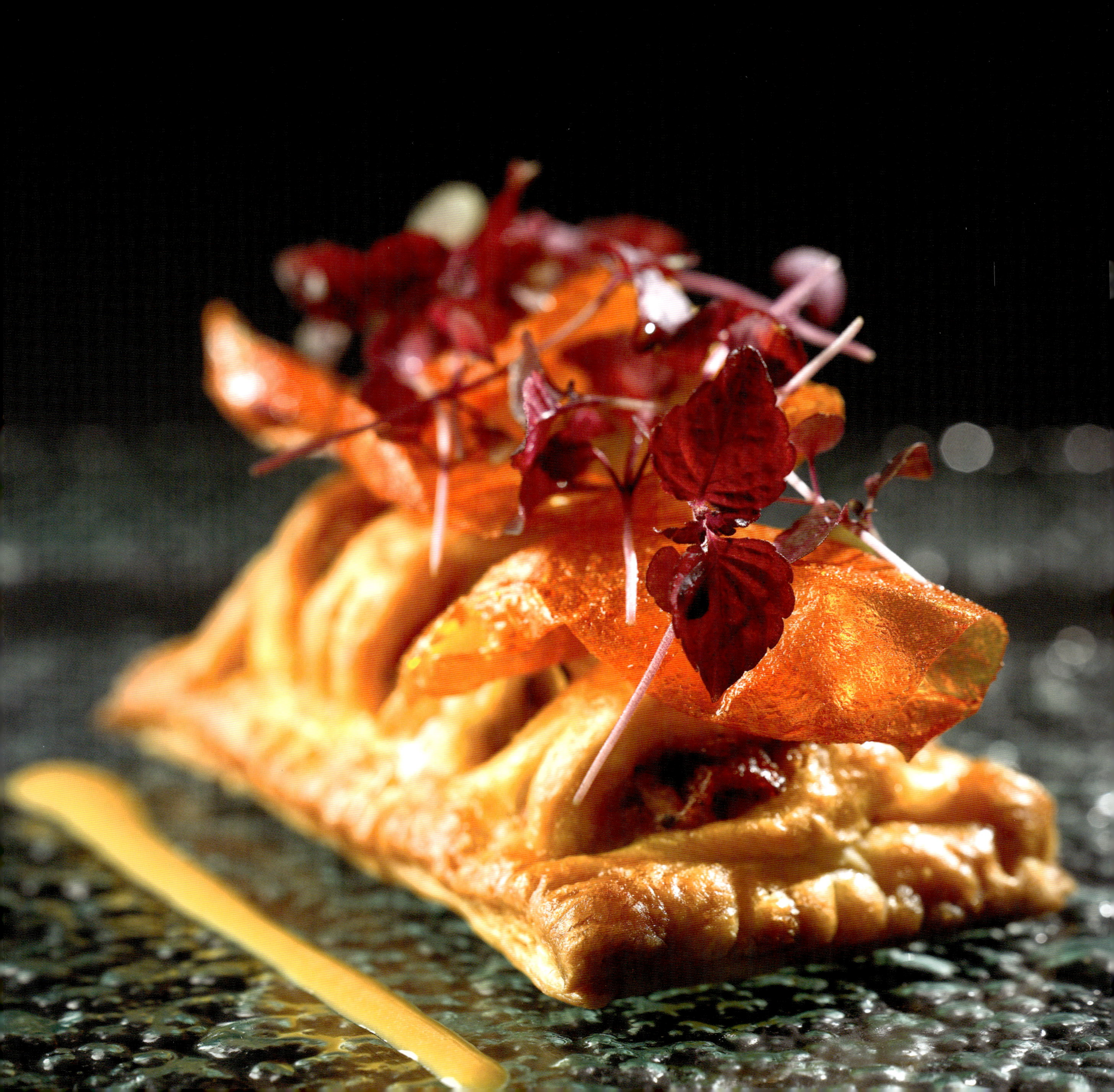

COUSTRALEE TOMATO AND ZUCCHINI JALOUSIE

FOR THE COUSTRALEE TOMATOES

Blanch tomatoes in salted water for 10 seconds and plunge into ice water. Peel tomatoes, cut into quarter segments and remove the seeds. Season with rock salt and fresh black pepper.
Dry tomatoes in the oven at 80° Celsius for 30 minutes, (this will help prevent the pastry from becoming soggy).

FOR THE ZUCCHINI RELISH

100 gr	zucchini, diced
100 gr	onions, chopped
10 gr	capers, chopped
5 gr	sugar
1 pc	garlic clove, roasted
50 ml	white wine
50 gr	olive oil
15 ml	basil, chopped
	salt and pepper

Pan-fry the zucchini quickly in olive oil and drain. Using the same oil, sauté the onions and garlic for 2 minutes and add capers and sugar. Deglaze with white wine and return zucchini to the pan. Cook over low heat for 15 minutes. Finish with the basil and cook for an additional 1 minute.

FOR THE SEMI-DRIED TOMATO CREAM

50 gr	tomatoes
100 ml	whipping cream
30 ml	white wine
	salt and pepper

Cook all components for 5 minutes and blend.

FOR THE PUFF PASTRY

Roll out puff pastry to a rectangular strip and spike with a fork. Spoon a layer of zucchini relish onto puff pastry and cover with a layer of dried tomato segments. Place another layer of pastry over tomatoes to cover.
Using a sharp knife make incisions on the top layer of pastry from across the center. Brush with egg wash and bake at 180° Celsius for 10 minutes.

Top with micro purple basil, crispy tomato skins and serve with semi-dried tomato cream.

CLEAR PACHINO TOMATO GAZPACHO WITH FRIED KALAMATA OLIVES

CLEAR PACHINO GAZPACHO

300 ml	chicken broth
	juice from one lime
300 gr	pachino tomatoes, pureed
5 ml	garlic, chopped
30 ml	red wine vinegar
100 gr	red bell peppers, roasted and diced
10 ml	tobasco
4 pc	egg whites
	salt and pepper

Merge all components (except egg whites, salt and pepper) and place in the refrigerator for 24 hours.
The next day, remove chilled mixture from refrigerator, beat egg whites to slightly stiff and vigorously mix together. Season with salt and pepper. Pour mixture into a heavy bottom pot and bring to a boil slowly. Stir the soup occasionally to ensure the eggs whites have not stuck to the bottom of the pot. Once it begins to boil, reduce the heat to a simmer and do not stir again. Allow the soup to simmer for 1 hour until it clears. Strain and cool down.

FRIED KALAMATA OLIVES

10 pc	olives
1 pc	whole eggs
250 ml	ice water
65 ml	all purpose flour

Merge eggs, ice water and flour. Dip olives into batter and deep fry.

GARNISH

30 gr	spring onions, chopped
100 gr	cucumber, diced, peeled and seeded
30 gr	sugar lump tomatoes, blanched, peeled and seeded
1 pc	sprig of tarragon, leaves only
1 pc	sprig of thyme, leaves only
30 gr	red onions, diced
10 gr	baby capers

ASSEMBLY

Place all garnishes into the soup and allow to rest for 2 hours.
Serve with black olive tempura.

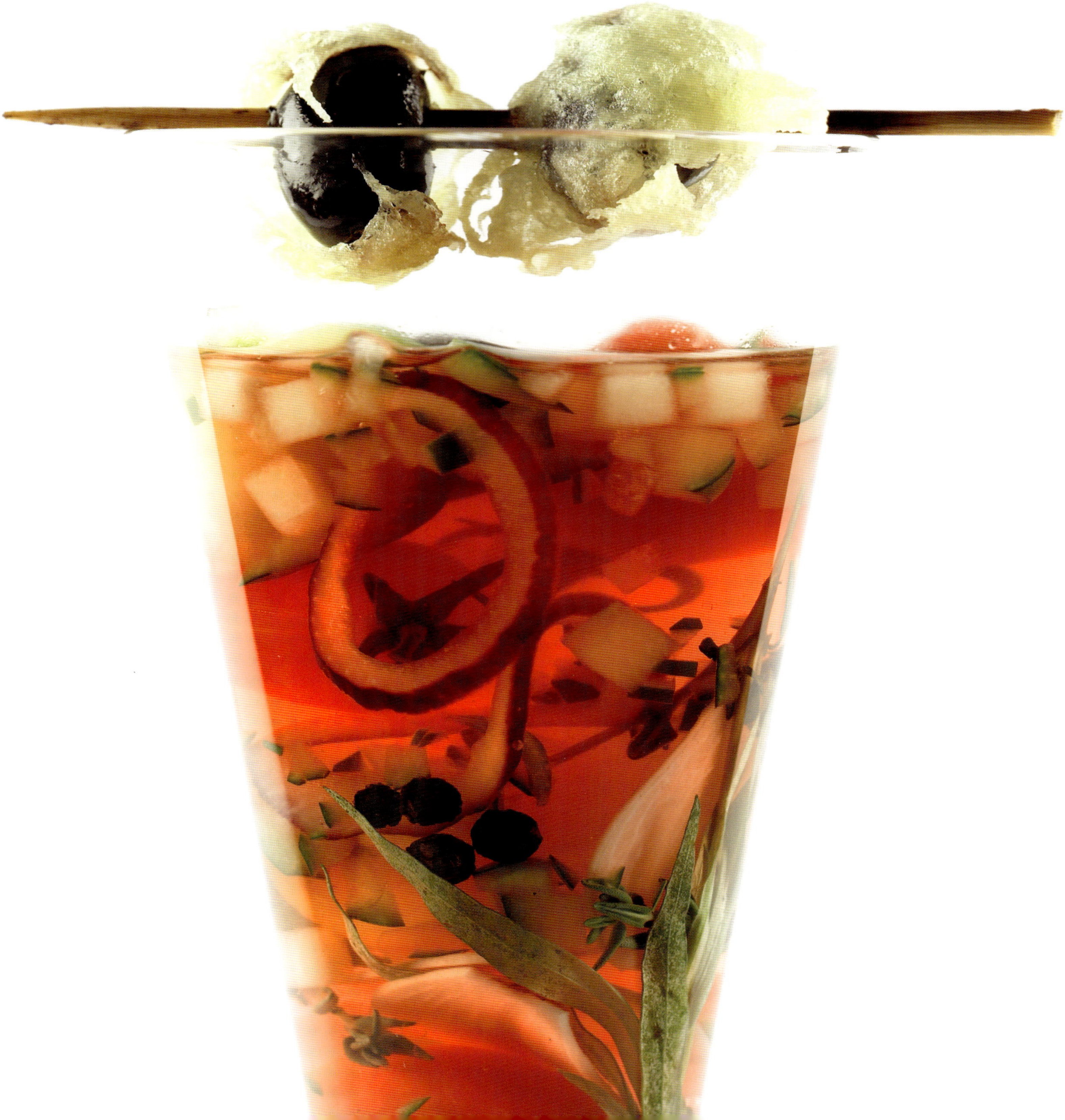

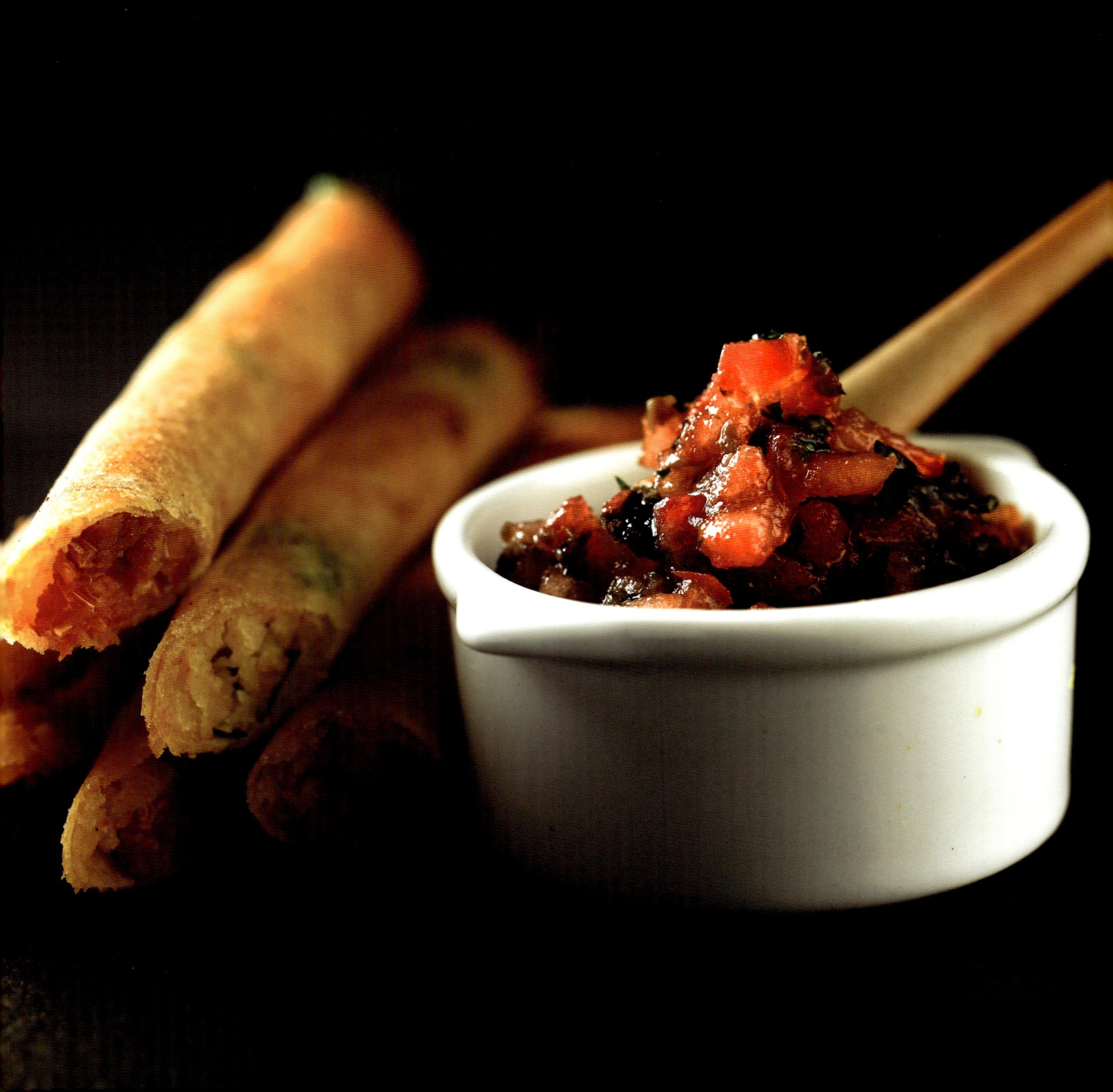

CHEESE AND TOMATO BRICKS WITH WOOD FIRED TOMATO CHUTNEY

FOR THE FILLING
100 gr	feta cheese, diced
100 gr	oven- dried tomatoes, diced
20 gr	olives, diced
20 gr	roasted peppers, diced
5 gr	italian parsley, chopped
	salt and pepper
5 pc	feuille de brick
1 pc	egg yolk

Merge all components for the filling. Lay out the feuille de brick and spoon the filling into the middle. Roll up tightly as if making a spring roll. Seal edges with egg yolk. Brush with a little olive oil and bake in a 160° Celsius oven for 5 minutes until golden brown.

TOMATO CHUTNEY
150 gr	tomatoes
30 gr	onions, chopped
10 gr	garlic, chopped
5 ml	olive oil
20 gr	sugar
10 ml	white balsamic

Blanch the tomatoes in boiling salted water for 10 seconds and plunge into ice water. Remove skins.
Place peeled tomatoes in an iron skillet and roast in a wood fired oven for 10 minutes.
Cool down and dice.
Sauté the onions and garlic in the olive oil. Add the sugar and vinegar and cook for 1 minute. Add the tomatoes and cook slowly for 5 minutes,

The chutney should be served warm.

MOMOTARO TOMATO AND ROSE JELLY WITH ROASTED SOY BEAN FLOUR

COMPONENTS
- 200 gr momotaro tomatoes
- 1 lt tomato water (see recipe index)
- 20 gr rose petal jam
- 70 gr sugar
- 8 pc gelatin leaves

DYNAMICS
Blanch tomatoes in boiling salted water for 10 seconds and plunge into ice water. Peel and deseed. Blend to a fine puree.

Merge tomato puree with tomato water, rose petal jam and sugar and cook for 15 minutes over medium heat. Remove from heat and stir in soaked gelatin leaves. Strain and pour into a mold. Refrigerate for 12 hours.
Cut in to squares and dip in roasted soy bean flour, (see recipe index).

Momotaro tomatoes are sweet, succulent and superb for making jams, jellies or iced desserts.

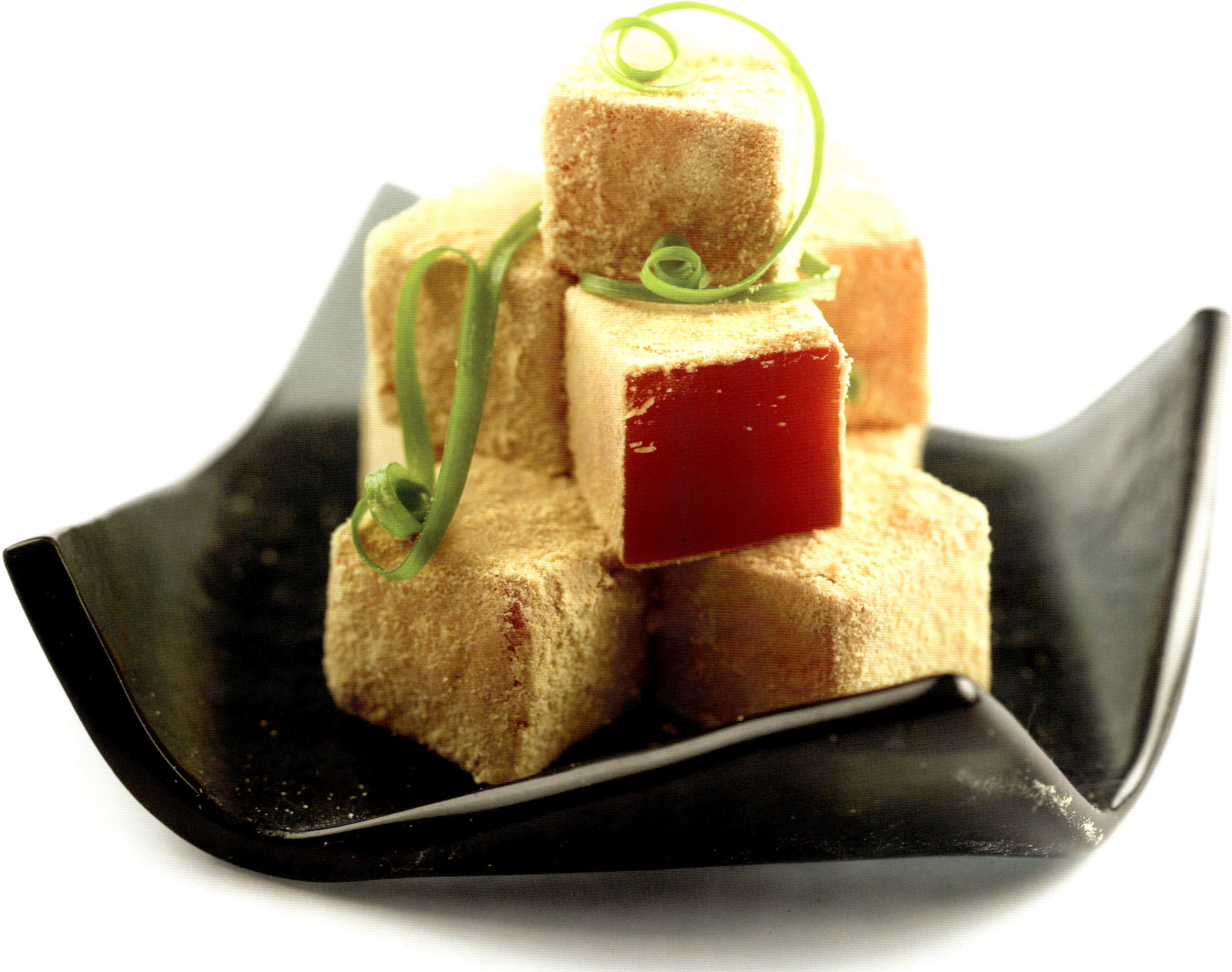

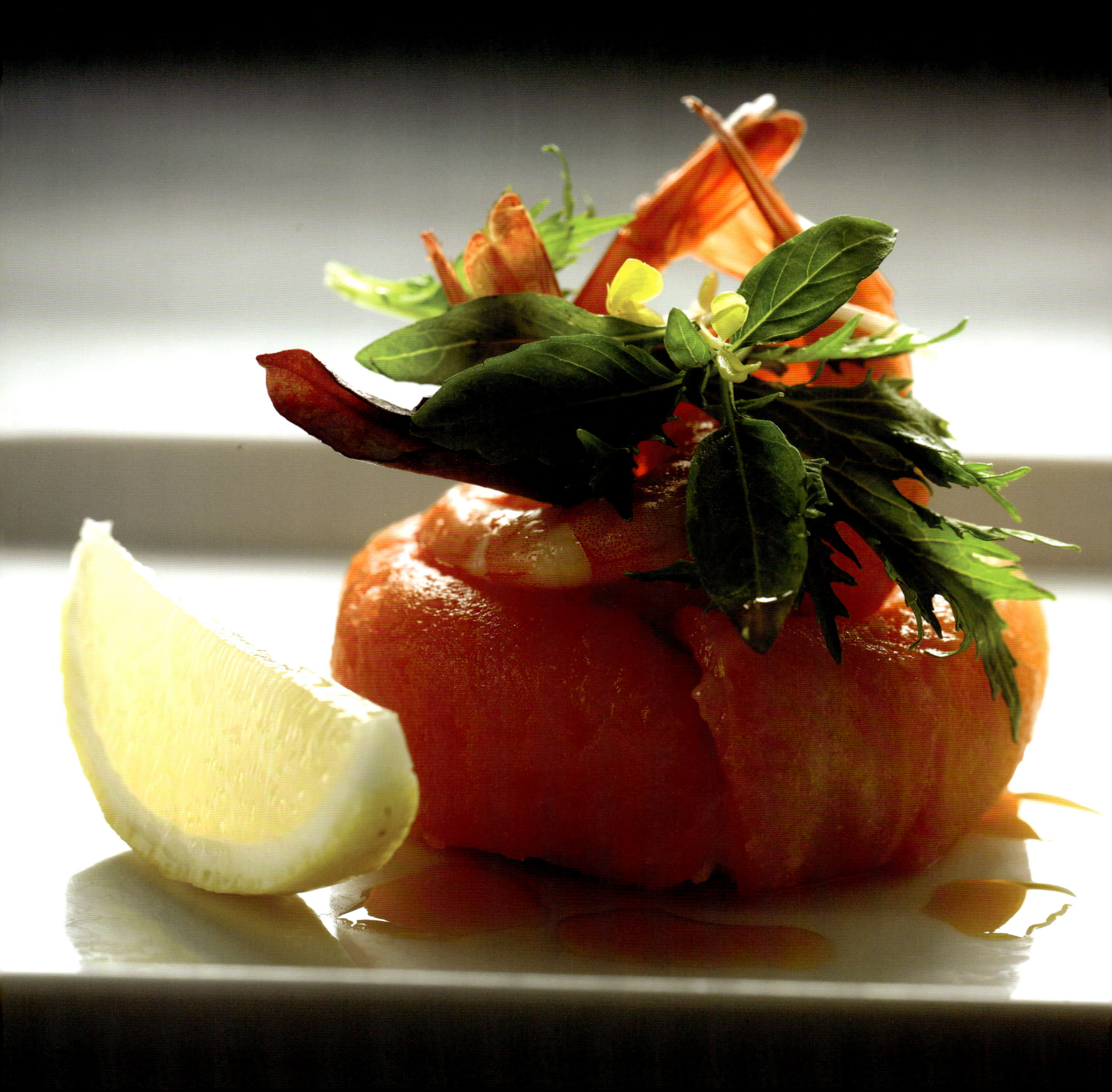

ORGANIC TOMATO CROWN WITH PRAWNS AND MICRO GREENS

FOR THE TOMATOES
500 g	organic beef steak tomatoes
	rock salt and pepper

Blanch the tomatoes in boiling salted water for 10 secondd and plunge into ice water. Peel and deseed the tomatoes. Cut tomatoes into quarter sections and lay on a non-stick baking tray. Season with rock salt and pepper and bake at 160° Celsius for 5 minutes.
Allow tomatoes to cool.

FOR THE PRAWN FILLING
100 gr	poached tiger prawns, diced
20 gr	onions, chopped
15 ml	parsley, chopped
30 ml	aioli
	salt and pepper

Merge all components.

ASSEMBLY
Line a 'savarin' ring mold with the dried tomatoes. Fill mold with prawn filling and finish with another layer of dried tomatoes.
Refrigerate for 1 hour.
Invert and remove from mold.

Garnish with poached prawns and micro greens.

HOMEMADE KETCHUP

COMPONENTS
500 ml	white vinegar
30 ml	molasses
90 ml	sugar
2 kg	tomatoes, skinless and seedless
100 gr	white onions, chopped
10 ml	celery salt
10 ml	salt
500 ml	water
20 ml	mustard powder
8 pc	garlic cloves, roasted
30 ml	worcestershire
20 ml	tobasco
60 ml	tomato paste
2 pc	bay leaf
2 pc	cinnamon stick
10 ml	coriander powder
6 pc	fresh basil leaves

DYNAMICS
Merge all components and cook over low heat for 1 hour. Remove cinnamon stick and bay leaf. Puree and pass through a fine sieve. Return to stove and cook for an additional 10 minutes.

To make green tomato ketchup, use green tomatoes and double the amount of sugar.

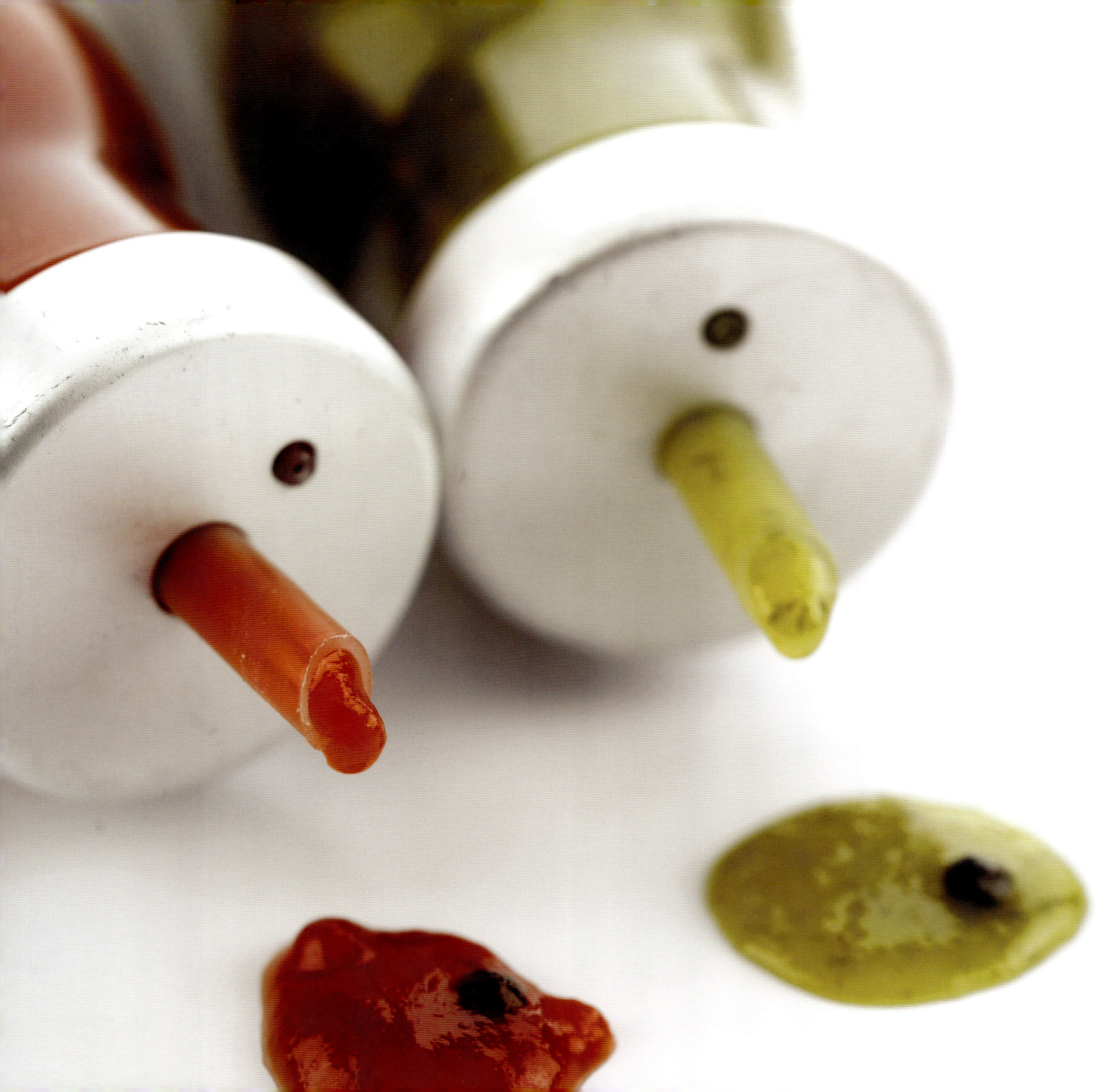

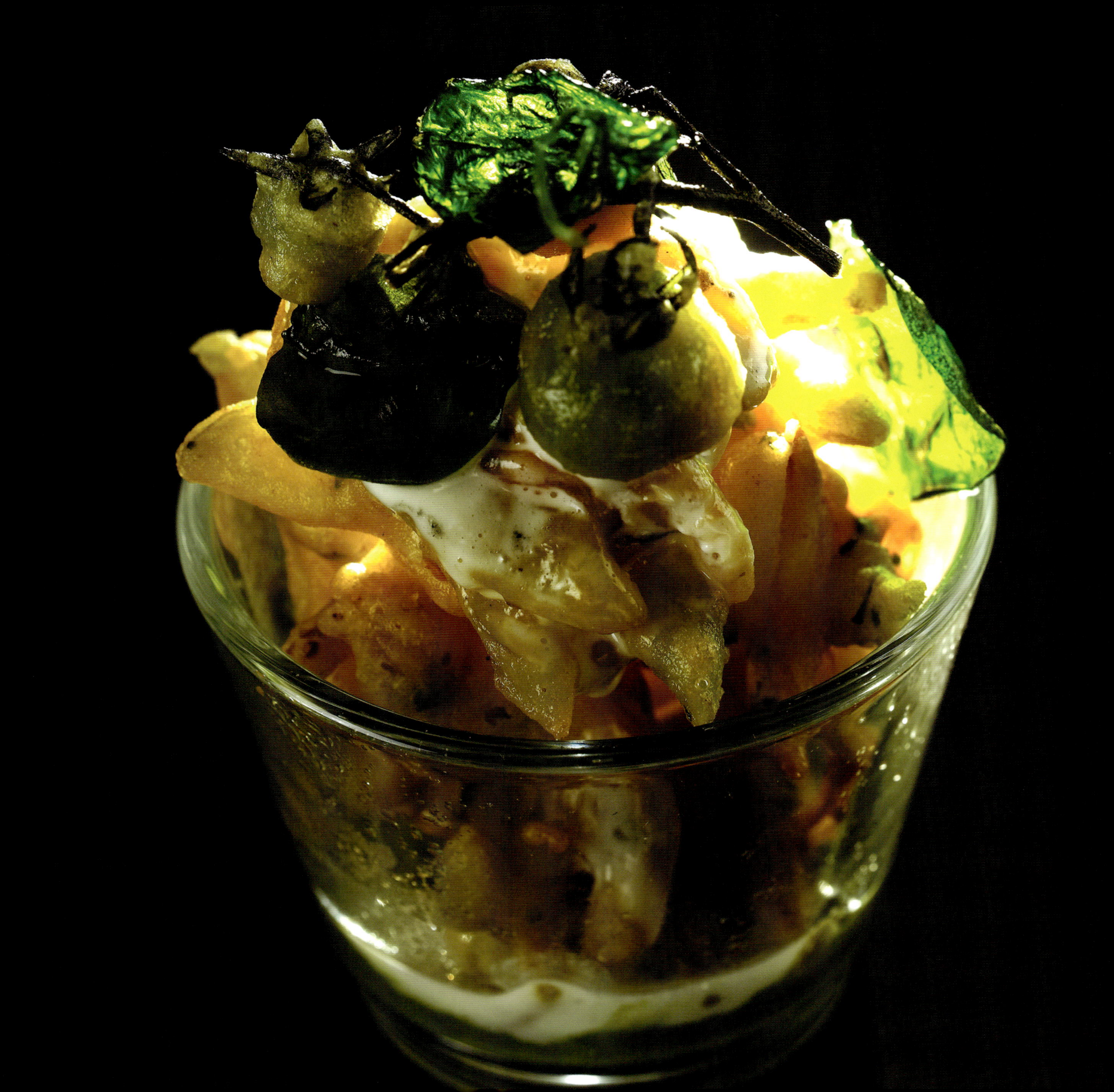

FRIED EVERGREEN TOMATO BHAGIS WITH BRUCCIO CREAM

FOR THE TOMATOES
100 gr	peeled and seeded green tomatoes, sliced lengthwise
20 gr	red onions, sliced lengthwise

FOR THE BATTER
30 gr	chick pea flour (see recipe index)
30 gr	water
3 ml	baking powder
1 pc	whole egg, beaten
3 ml	fenugreek powder
	salt and pepper

Merge all ingredients to form a batter.

Season the tomatoes and onions with salt and pepper Dust with chick pea flour and add to batter. Form into little clusters and deep fry until golden brown.

BRUCCIO CREAM
50 ml	whipping cream
30 ml	chicken stock
50 gr	bruccio cheese (see recipe index)
10 ml	fresh coriander, chopped
3 ml	coriander powder
	salt and pepper

Bring the cream and stock to a boil. When boiling, add the cheese. Add fresh coriander and coriander powder. Season and simmer for 1 minute.

Garnish with oven-dried baby tomatoes on the vine.

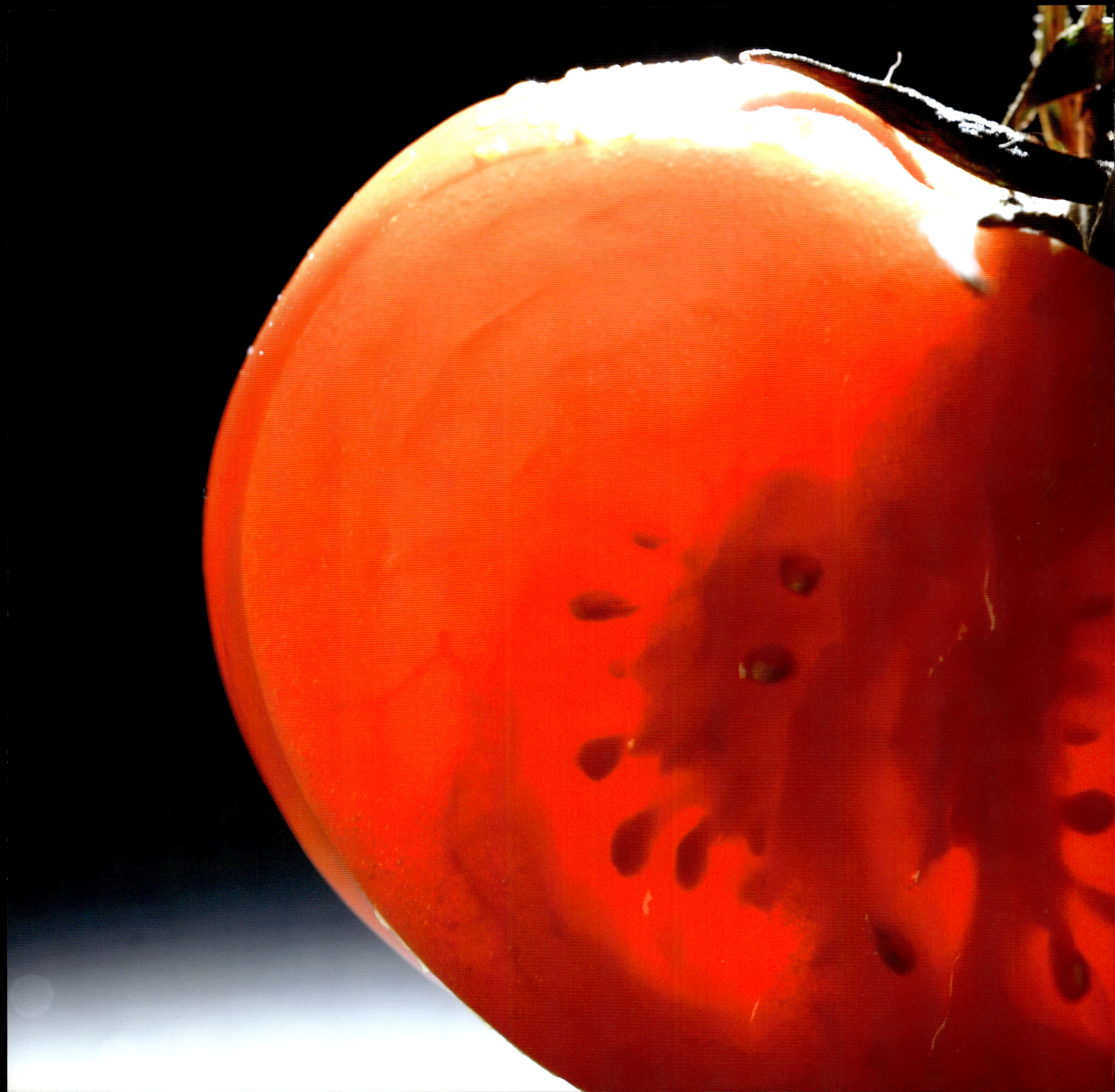

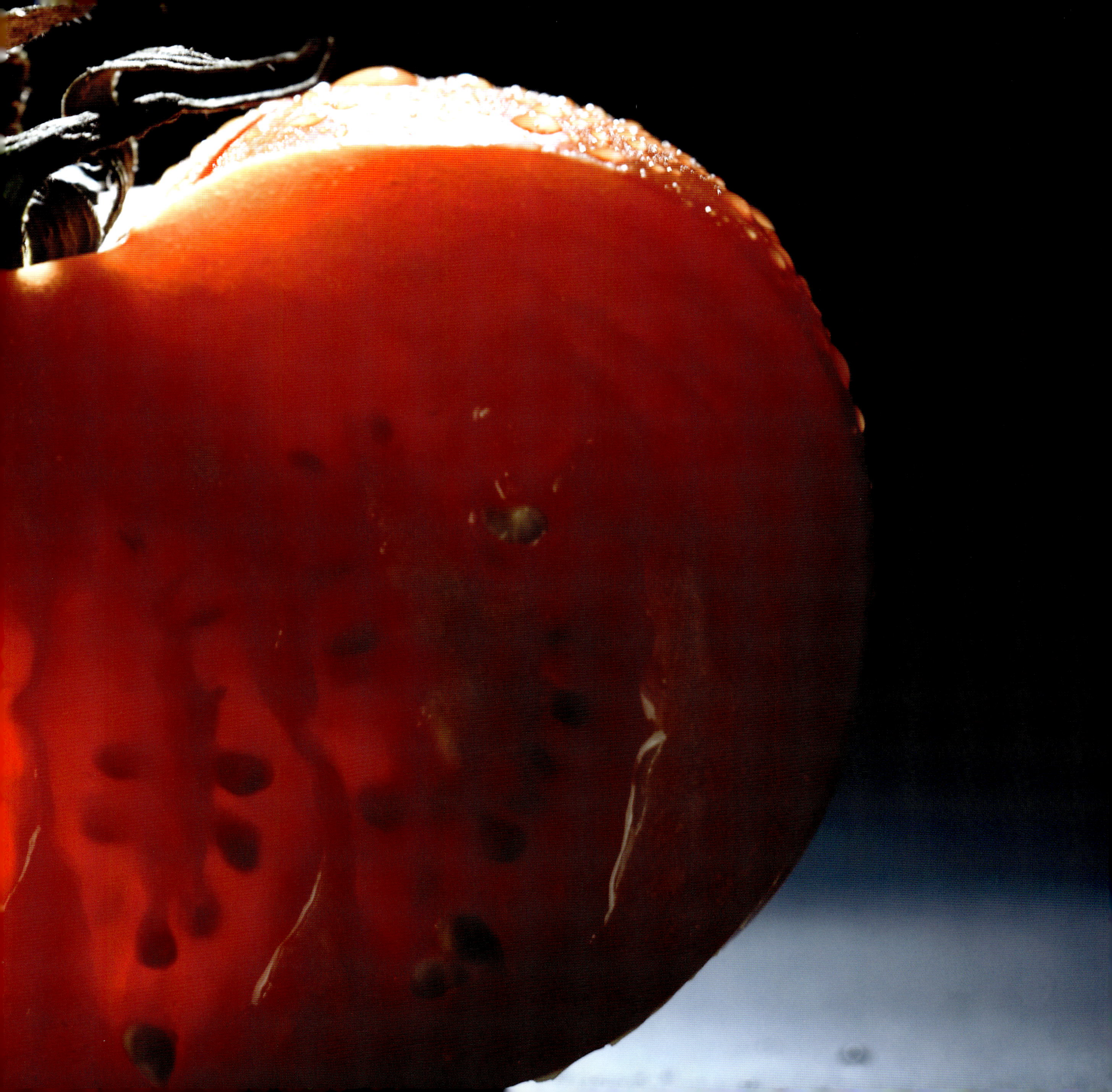

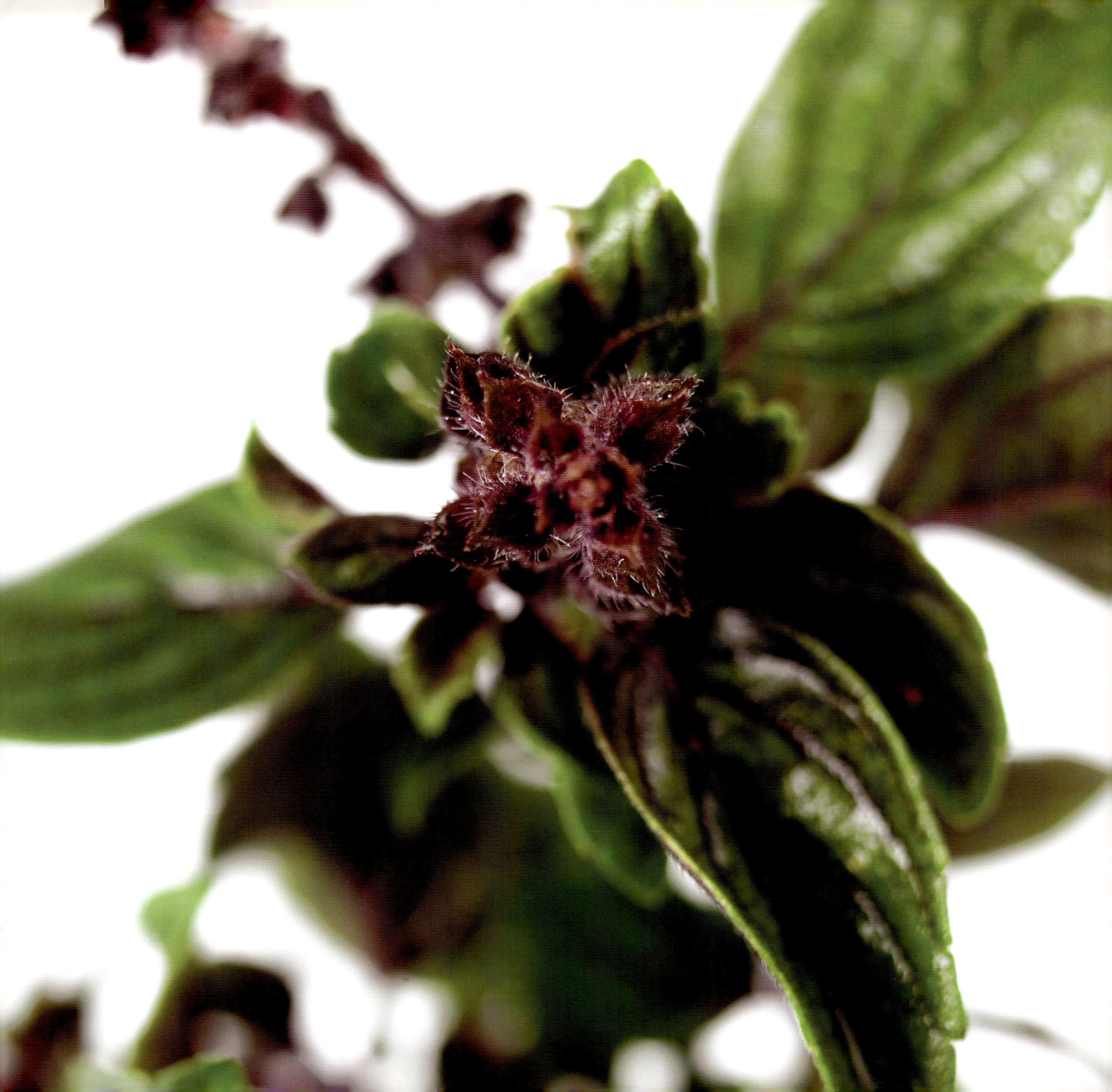

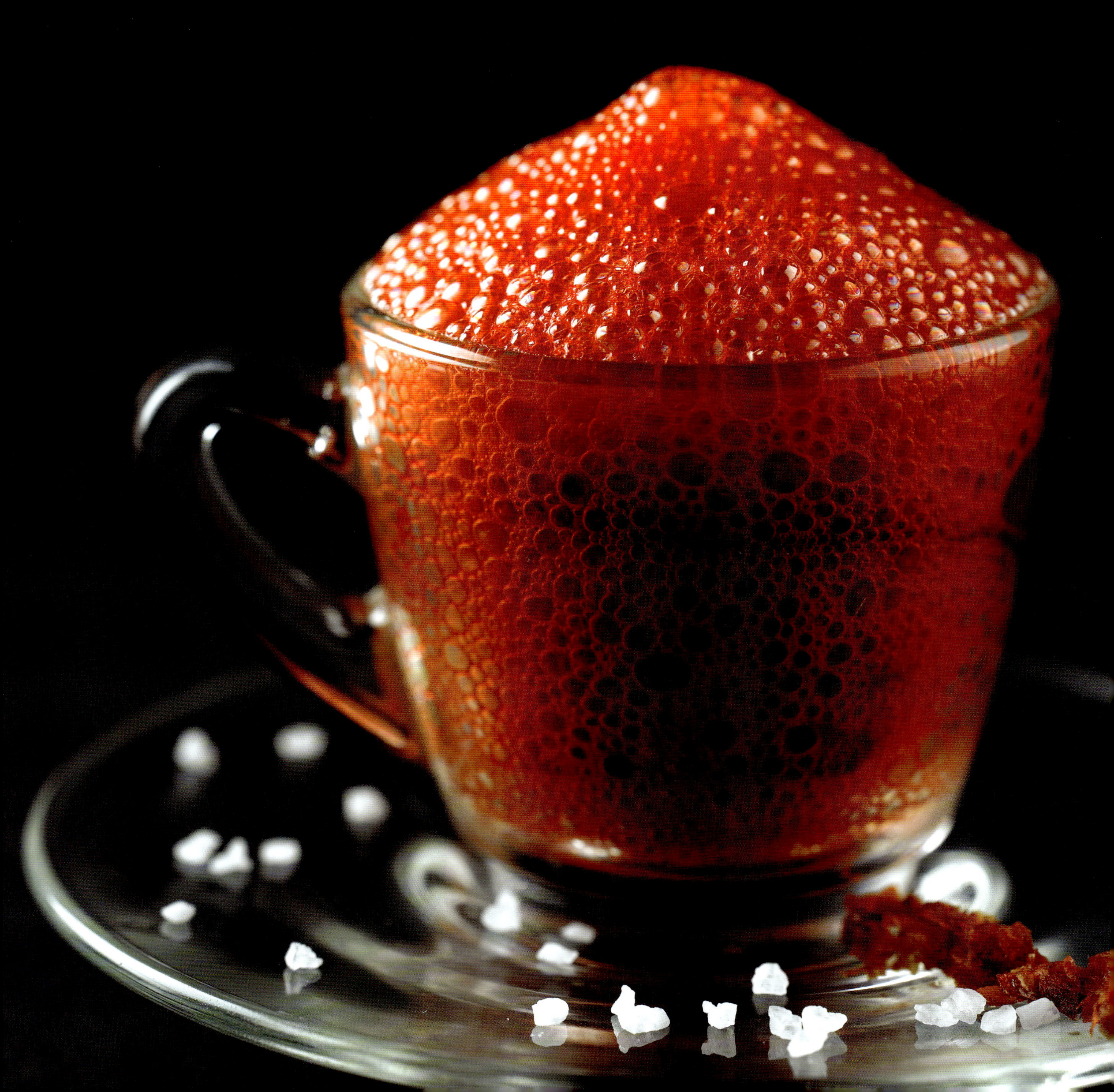

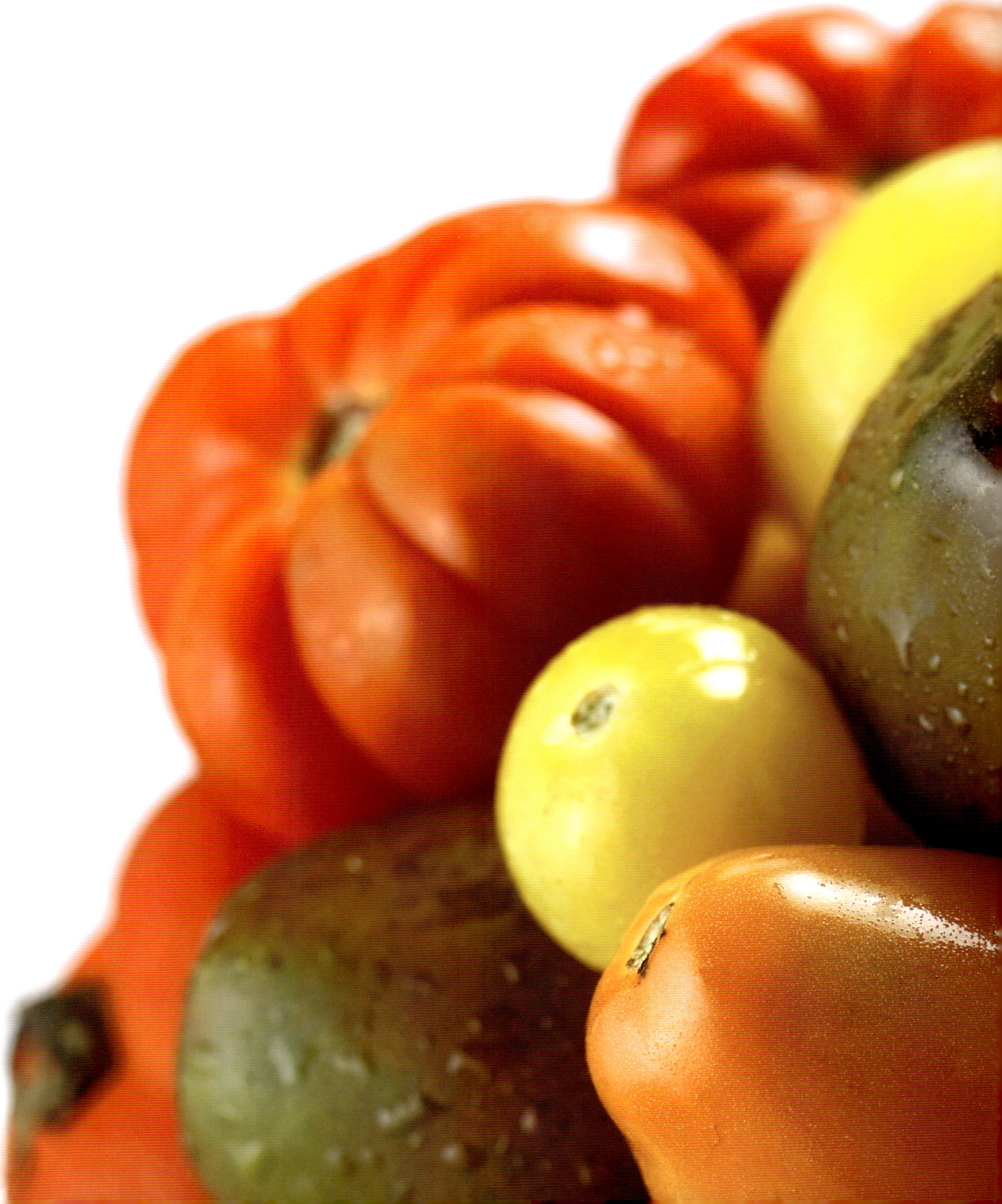

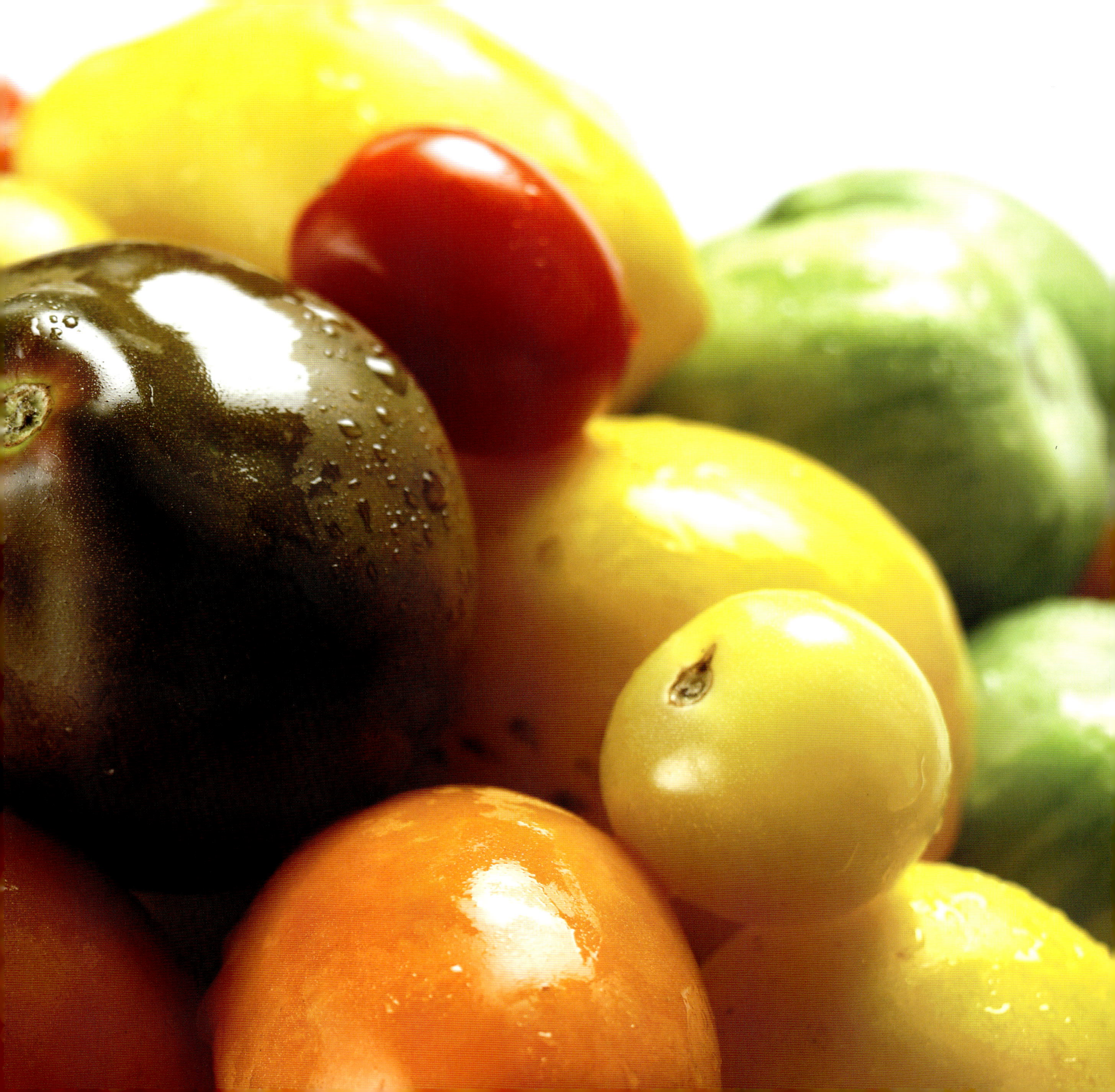

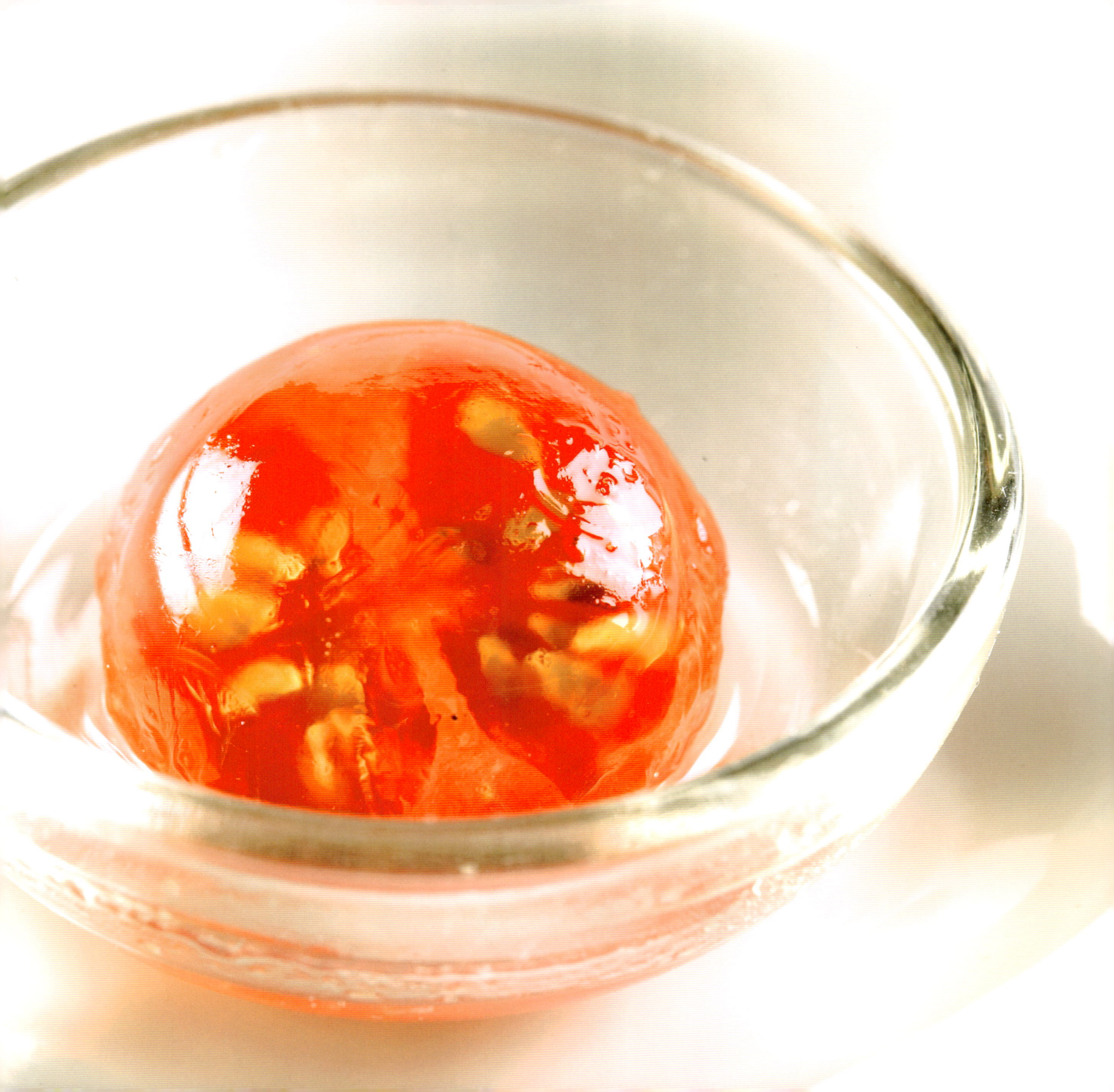

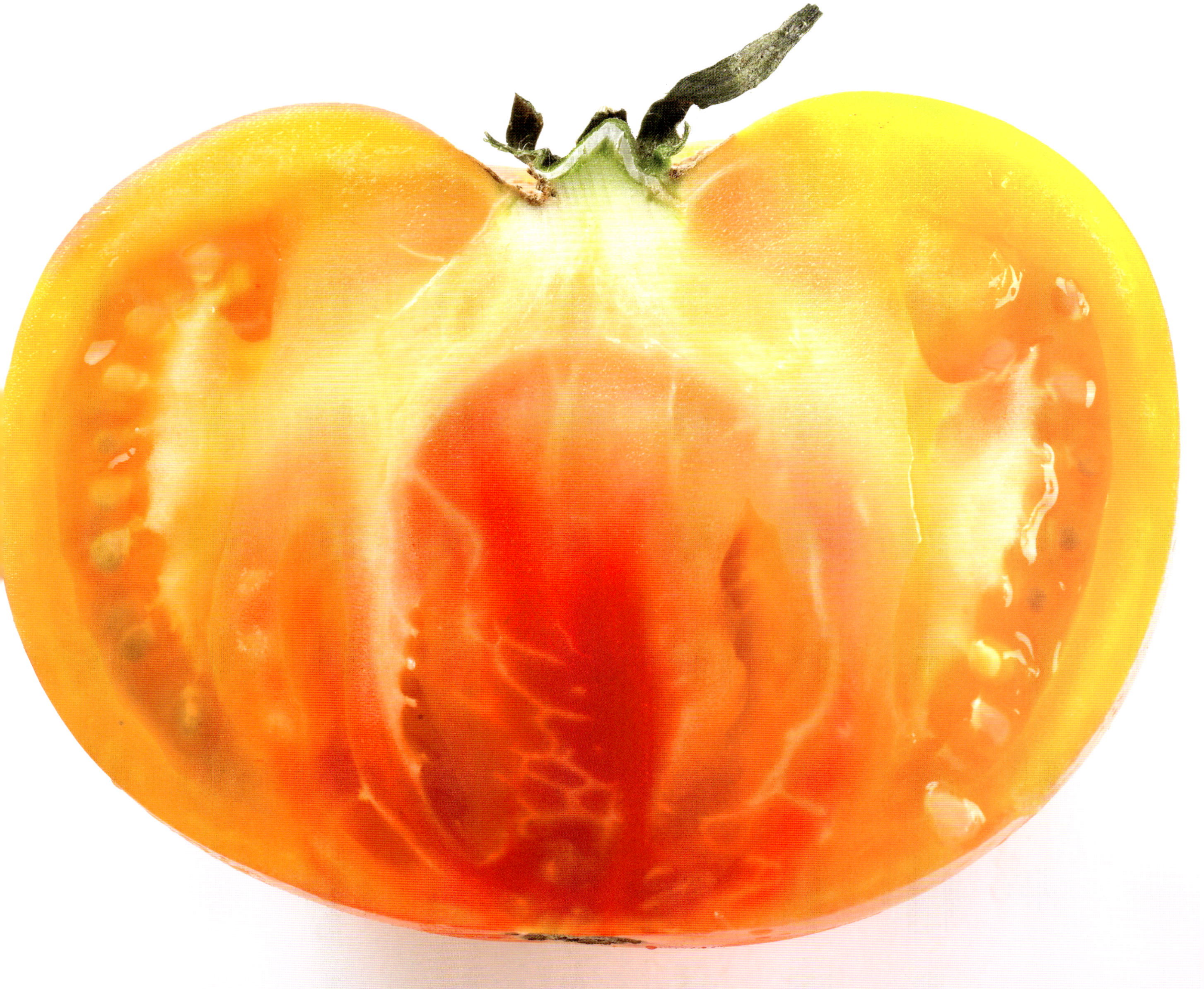

GOAT CHEESE WITH SAN MARZANO TOMATOES AND TRUFFLES

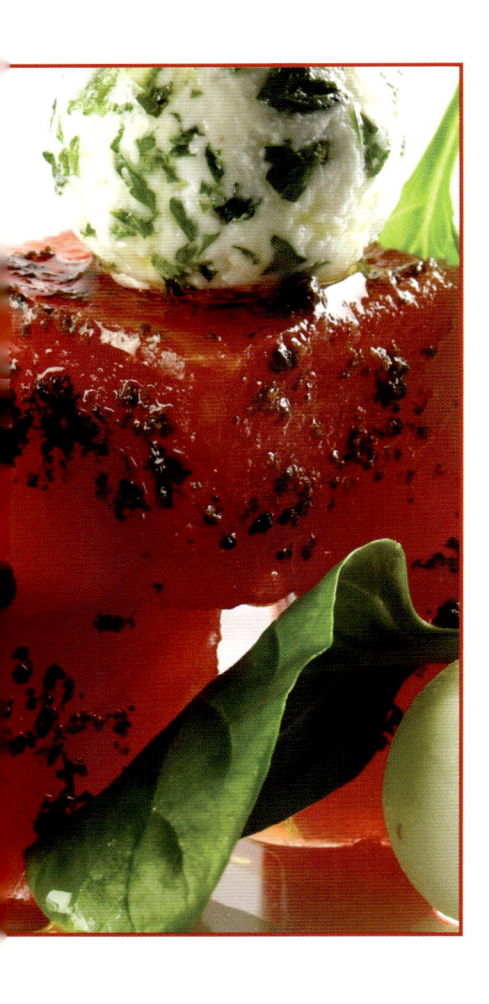

FOR THE TOMATO CONFIT
- 200 gr tomatoes
- 30 ml olive oil
- salt and pepper

Blanch tomatoes in boiling salted water for 10 seconds and plunge into ice water. Remove skins and seeds. Slice and lay the tomatoes on a greased tray. Liberally brush tomatoes with olive oil. Season with salt and pepper and dry at 70° Celsius for 1 hour. Remove from oven and place in a square mold for 30 minutes.
Remove from the mold and place on plate. Drizzle with olive oil and chopped truffles. Finish with goat cheese.

FOR THE GOAT CHEESE
- 50 gr goat cheese
- 5 gr truffles, chopped
- 5 ml truffle oil
- 10 ml parsley chopped
- black pepper

Form goat cheese into different sized balls. Using 2/3rd of the cheese, alternate rolling the balls in parsley and chopped truffle.

Serve with baby spinach tossed with sherry vinaigrette.

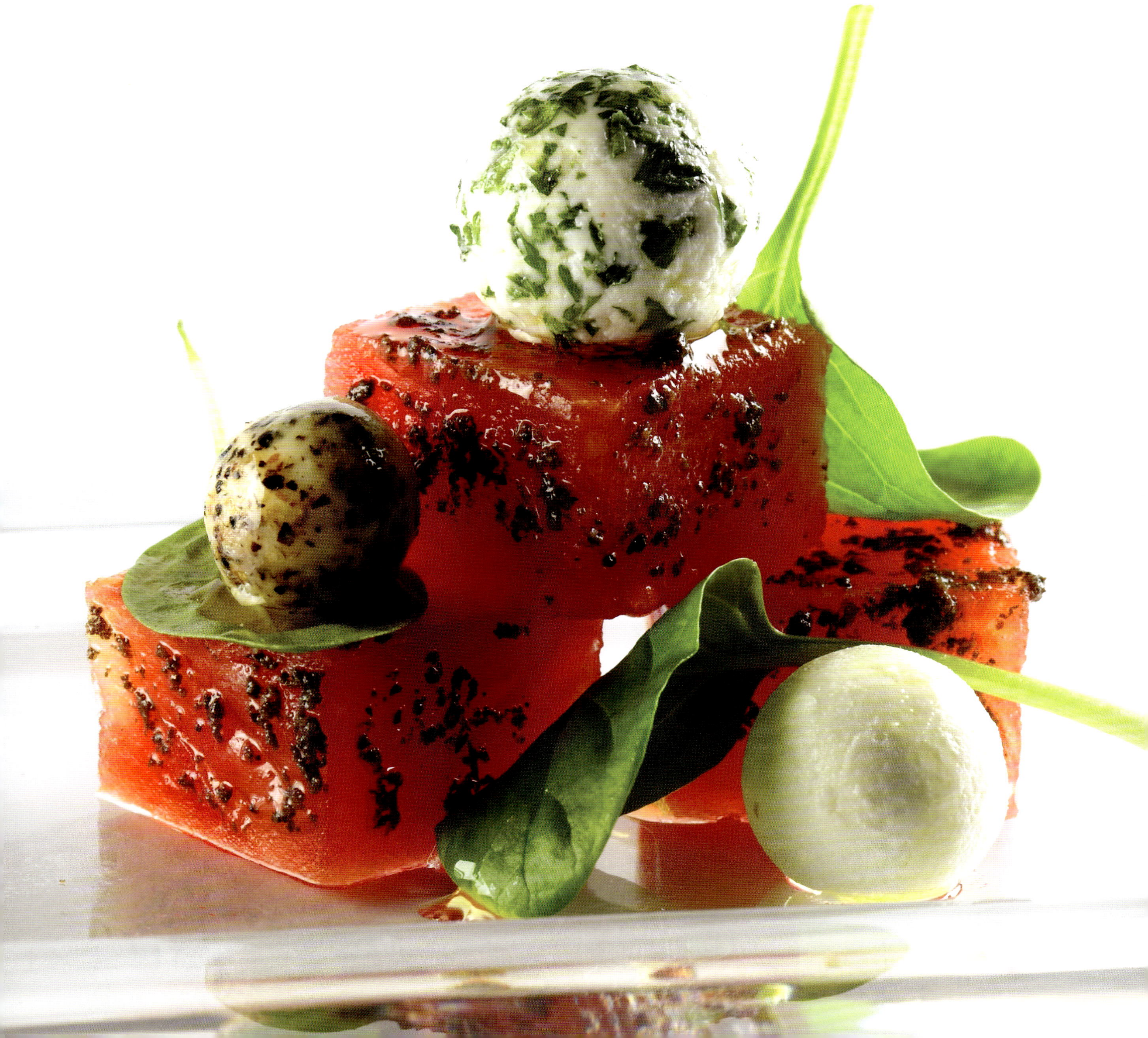

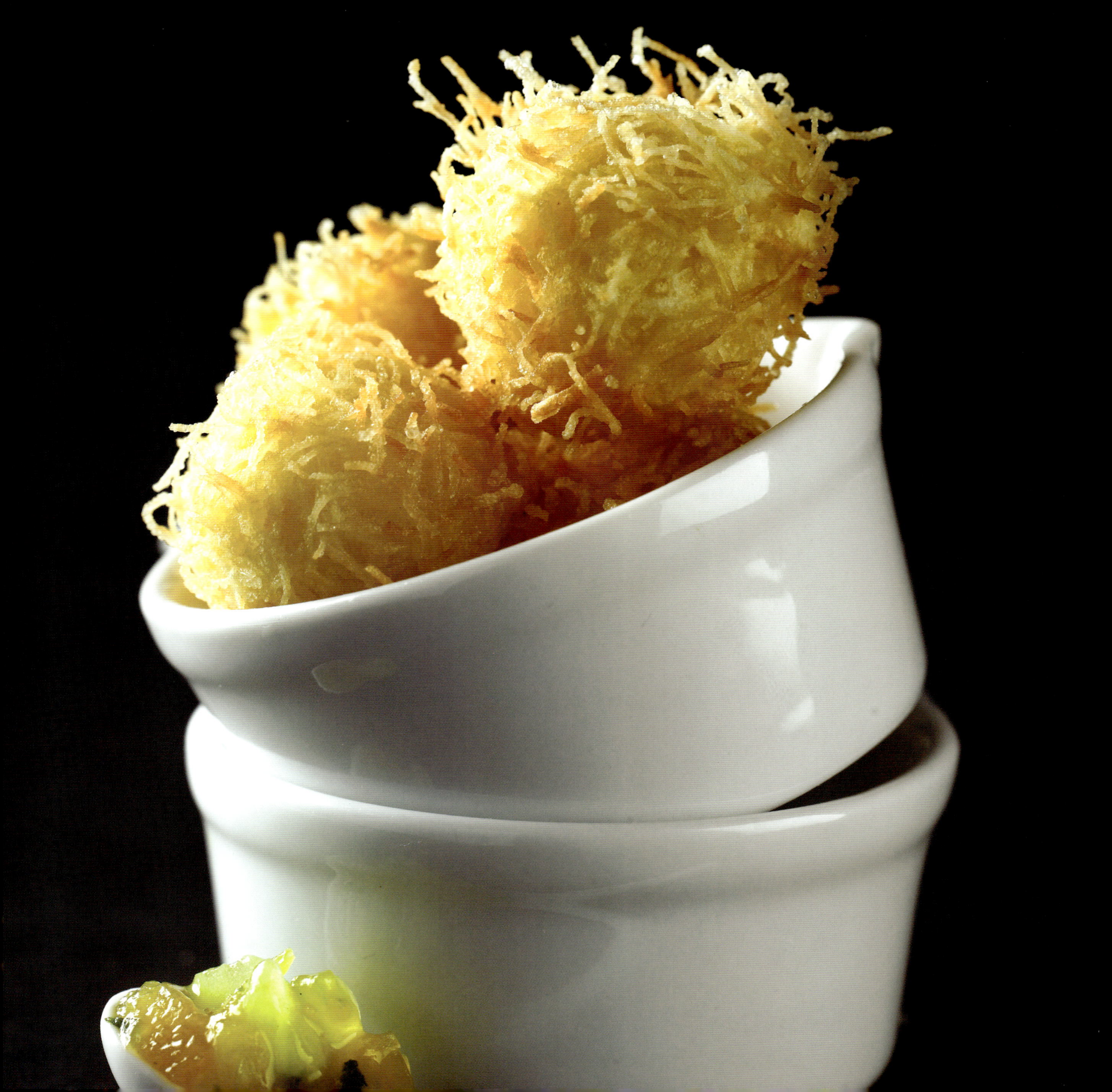

GOAT CHEESE FRITTERS WITH ZEBRA TOMATO COULIS

FOR THE FRITTERS

250 ml	goat cheese, room temperature
2 pc	egg whites
250 ml	semolina
15 ml	baking powder
30 ml	zebra tomatoes, diced
5 gr	salt
10 ml	sugar
125 ml	milk
15 ml	italian parsley, chopped
20 gr	kataifi pastry

Whip egg whites and fold in all remaining ingredients. Form the mixture into round dumplings.
Roll the dumplings in kataifi pastry and deep fry for 2 minutes.

FOR THE TOMATO COULIS

100 gr	zebra tomatoes, diced
10 gr	garlic chopped
20 gr	onions chopped
	salt and pepper

Merge all components in a pot and bring to a boil. Reduce heat and simmer for 5 minutes to infuse flavors.

TOMATO POPCORN POLENTA WITH SARDINES

FOR THE SARDINES

200 gr	fresh sardines, gutted and cleaned

Carefully de-scale the skin of sardines without bruising the flesh.
Cut off the heads and tails. Season with salt, pepper and lemon juice and pan-fry in olive oil.

POPCORN POLENTA

100 gr	corn meal
15 ml	fresh tomato paste
400 gr	water
5 gr	salt
40 gr	parmesan cheese, shredded
20 gr	butter

Simmer water, corn meal, salt, and tomato paste for 15 minutes. Add the Parmesan cheese and butter and mix with a whip. Cool. Roll the mixture into small balls and dredge in corn meal.
Deep fry until golden brown.

FOR THE TOMATO FONDUE

100 gr	tomatoes, diced
20 gr	onions, chopped
10 gr	garlic, chopped
30 ml	butter
	salt and pepper

Merge all components and simmer for 10 minutes.

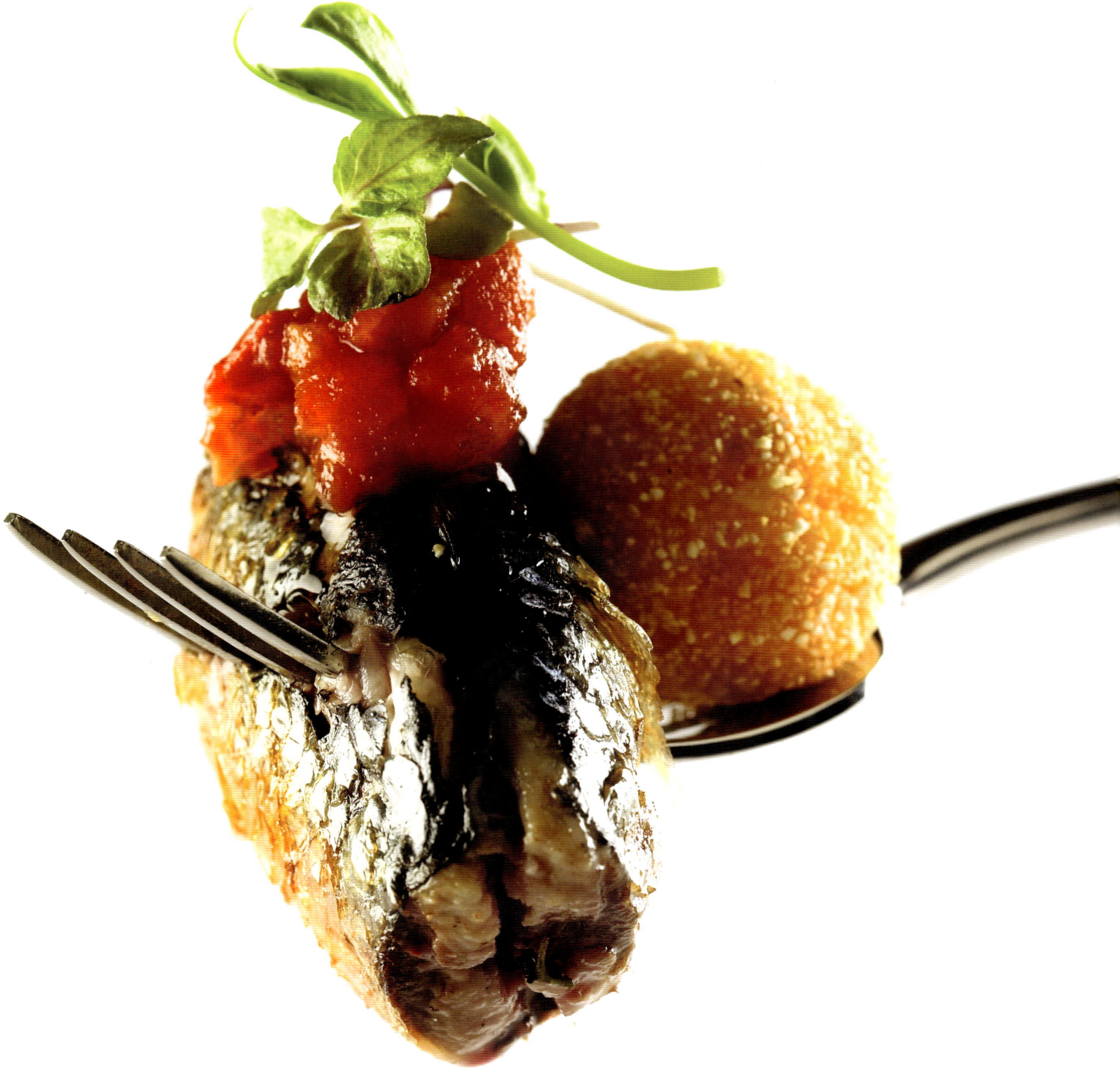

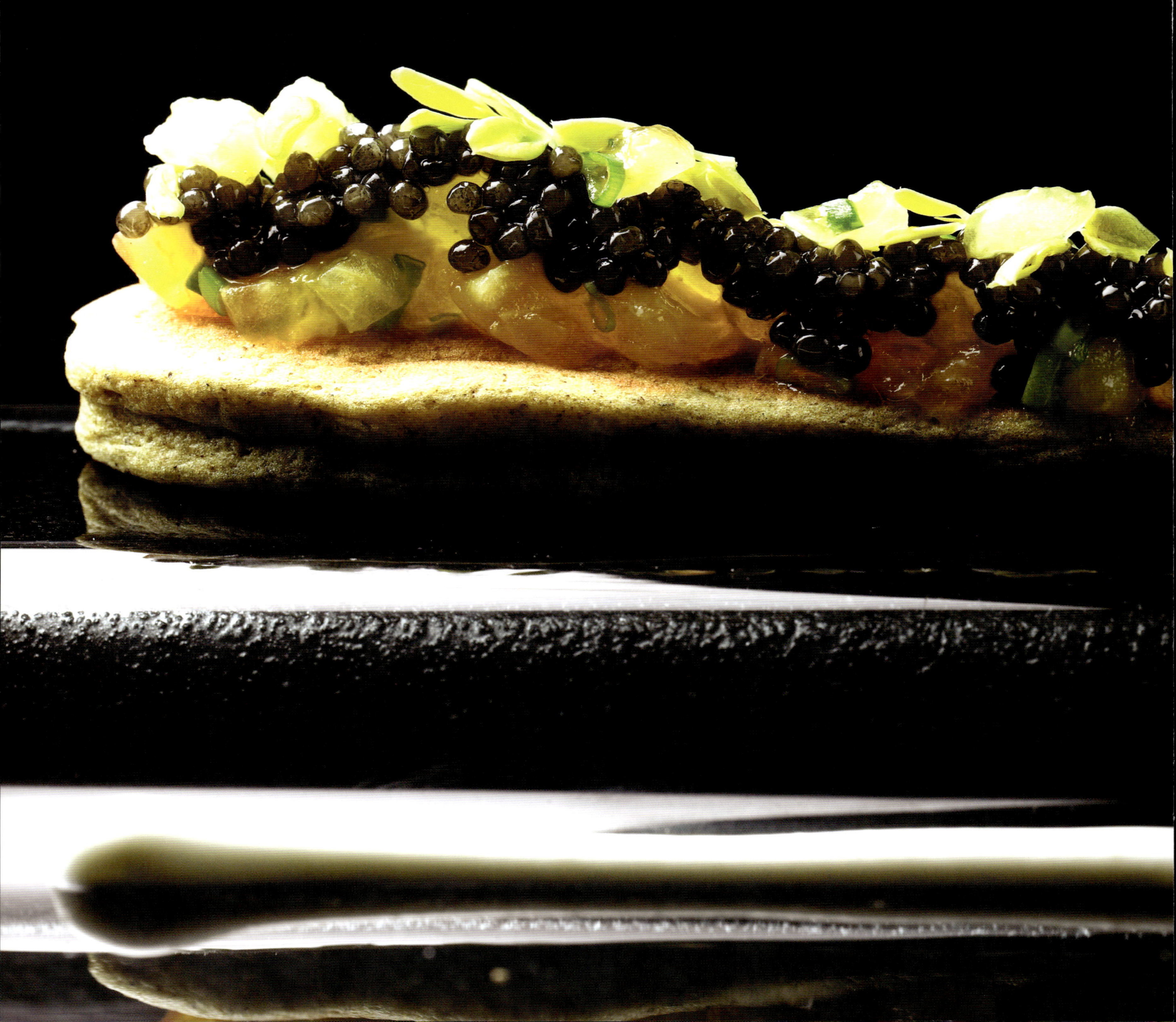

GARDEN PEACH TOMATO BLINIS WITH CAVIAR AND SOUR CREAM

FOR THE GARDEN PEACH TOMATO BLINIS

140 gr	buckwheat flour
2 pc	eggs yolks
10 gr	dried yeast powder
250 ml	warm water
50 gr	garden peach tomato puree
	salt and pepper
2 pc	egg whites

Merge buckwheat flour, egg yolks, dried yeast, water and tomato puree. Season and allow to rest for 2 hours.
Whip egg whites to stiff peaks and fold in.

Pan-fry blinis in non-stick frying pan.

FOR THE GARNISH

30 gr	garden peach tomatoes, diced
10 gr	red onions, chopped
5 ml	parsley, chopped
	salt and pepper

ASSEMBLY

10 gr	beluga caviar
10 ml	sour cream
10 ml	chives chopped
10 gr	yellow pea sprouts

Place the blinis on a plate and top with the tomato garnish, caviar, chives and sprouts. Pipe the sour cream.

LAMB CHOP WITH DRIED TOMATO CRUST ON BALSAMIC TOMATOES

FOR THE CRUST
- 50 gr   oven-dried cherry tomatoes, chopped
- 50 gr   parmesan cheese
- 1 pc   egg yolk
- 30 gr   soft butter
- 10 ml   dijon mustard
- salt and pepper

Merge all components to form a rough paste.

BALSAMIC CHERRY TOMATOES
- 30 ml   balsamic
- 20 gr   onions, chopped
- 50 gr   cherry tomatoes
- 5 ml   garlic, chopped
- 5 ml   basil, chopped
- 30 ml   olive oil
- 5 ml   sugar
- salt and pepper

Heat the olive oil and add the tomatoes, cook for two minutes. Add the onions and garlic and cook for 1 minute. Add the balsamic, salt, sugar and pepper. Finish with basil.

FOR THE LAMB
Season the lamb chops and sear on both sides. Cover one side of the lamb with the crust paste and place in the oven to finish.

ASSEMBLY
Spoon the cherry tomatoes on plate and top with the lamb.

Garnish with crispy parsley and deep-fried orange tomato ring.

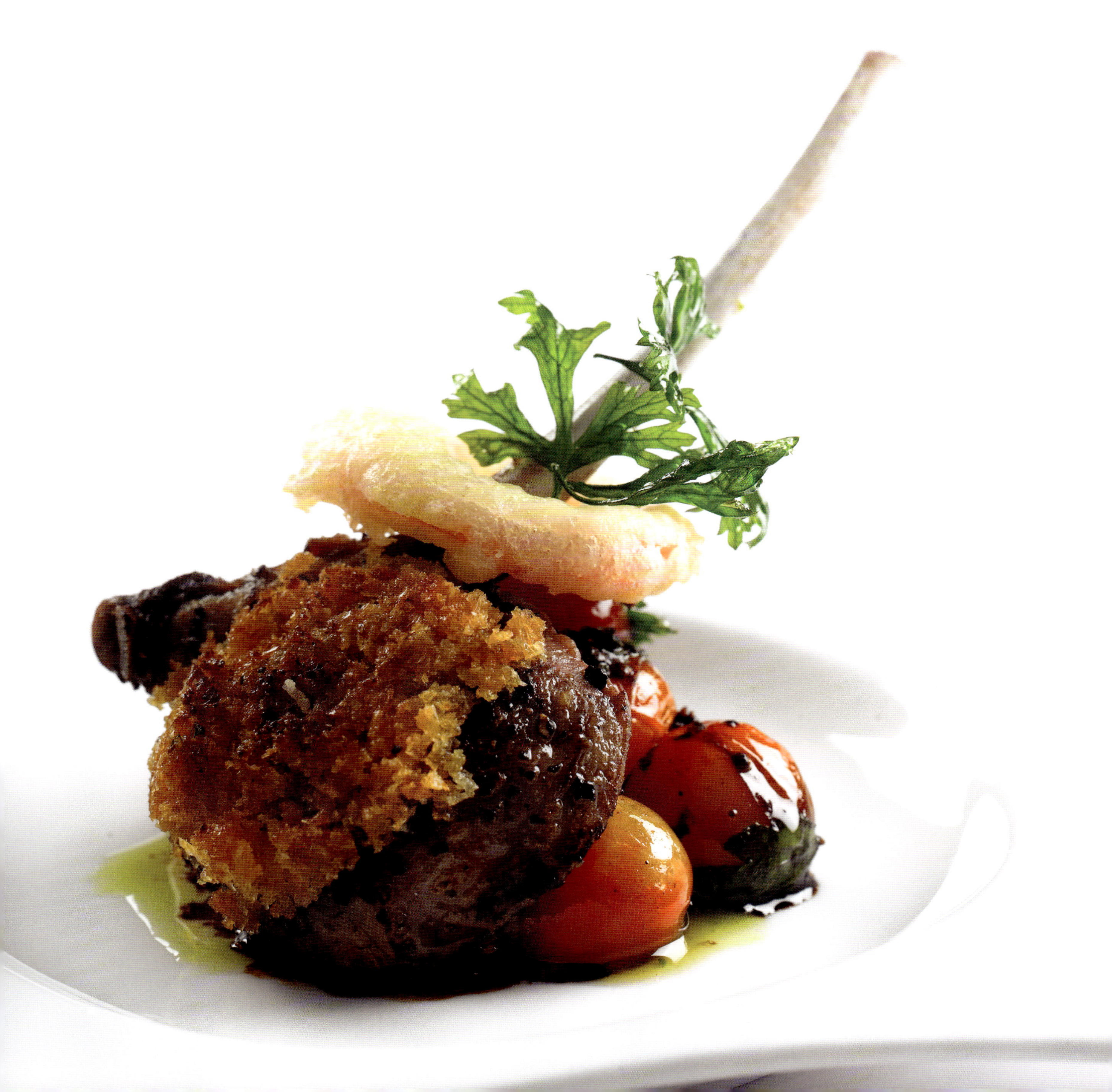

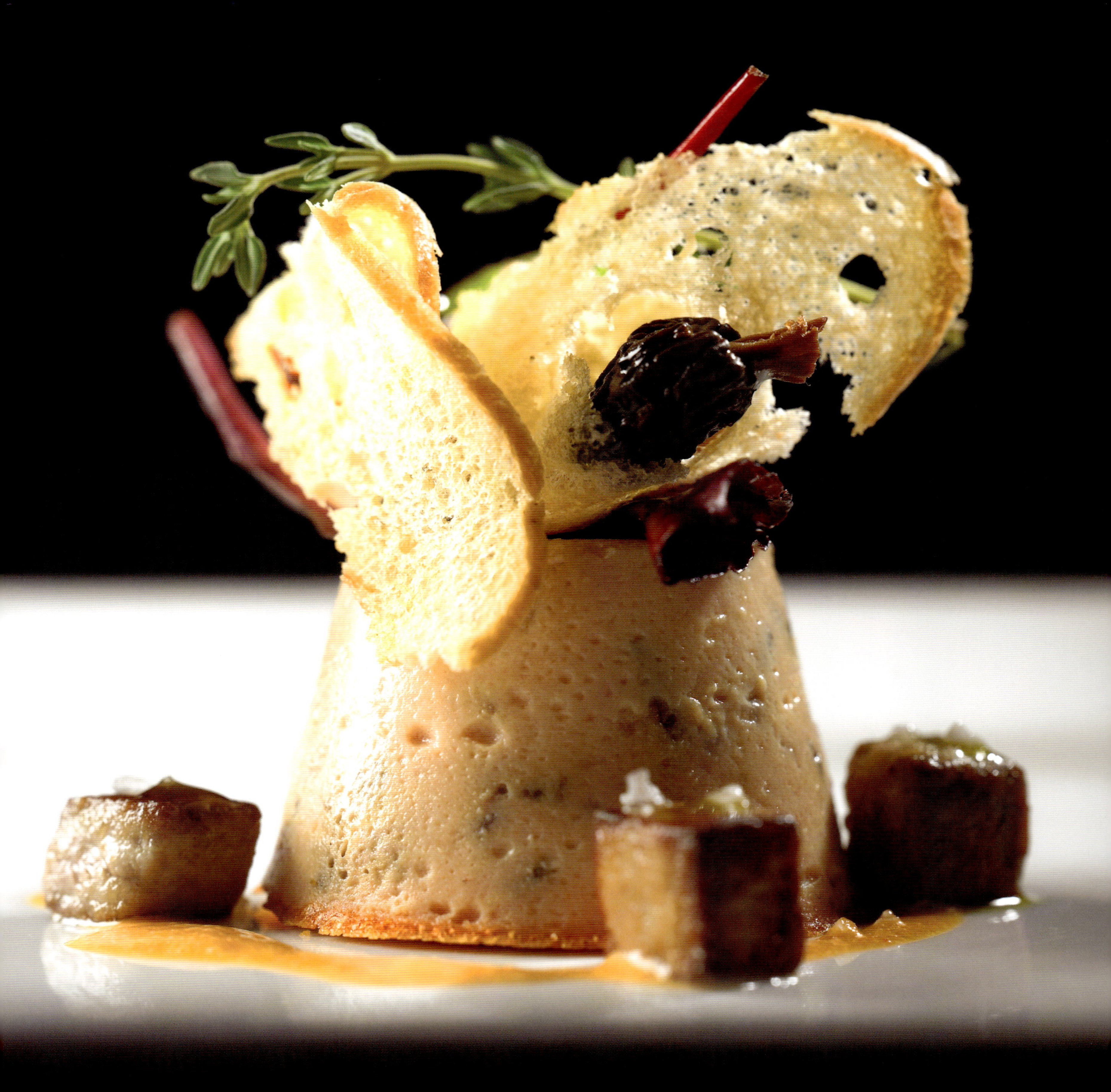

TOMATO AND MOREL TIMBALE WITH FOIE GRAS AND TOMATO MELBA

FOIE GRAS TIMBALE

150 gr	foie gras
5 pc	whole eggs
150 ml	whipping cream
50 gr	fresh tomato paste
	salt and pepper

Merge all components, blend and strain. Pour into timbale molds with sautéed morel mushrooms.
Poach in bain marie inside an oven at 150° Celsius for 20 minutes.

FOR THE SAUTÉED MOREL MUSHROOMS

50 gr	morel mushrooms
50 gr	onions
1 pc	bay leaf
1 pc	sprig of rosemary
2 pc	garlic, chopped
30 ml	soft butter
50 ml	white wine
120 ml	chicken stock

Sauté morel mushrooms, onions, bay leaf, rosemary and garlic in butter. Deglaze with white wine and add the stock. Reduce to a dry consistency. Remove herbs.

Blend slightly and merge with foie gras timbale mixture.

MELBA

1 pc	thinly sliced ciabatta bread
5 ml	olive oil

Brush the bread with the oil and dry under salamander.

FOR SERVING

5 pc	baby oak leaf and dried thyme
30 gr	pan-fried foie gras

FOR THE TOMATO CREAM

50 gr	seedless and skinless tomatoes, diced
15 ml	soft butter
50 ml	whipping cream
30 ml	white wine
	salt and pepper

Sweat the tomatoes in the butter for 1 minute. Add the wine and cream and cook for 2 minutes until thick. Season and blend.

Spoon the tomato cream on the plate and place the timbale on top.
Add the sautéed foie gras and melba toast.

TOMATO AND BUFFALO MOZZARELLA SALAD

COMPONENTS

100 gr	buffalo mozzarella
100 gr	plum tomatoes
6 pc	basil leaves
20 gr	arugula
30 ml	olive oil
15 ml	balsamic vinegar
4 pc	kalamata olives
	red onion
	yellow pea sprouts
	salt and pepper

DYNAMICS

Slice the tomatoes and cheese and season with salt and pepper. Layer the tomato and mozzarella with the basil. Place arugula on top and drizzle with balsamic and olive oil.

Garnish with sliced red onions and yellow pea sprouts.

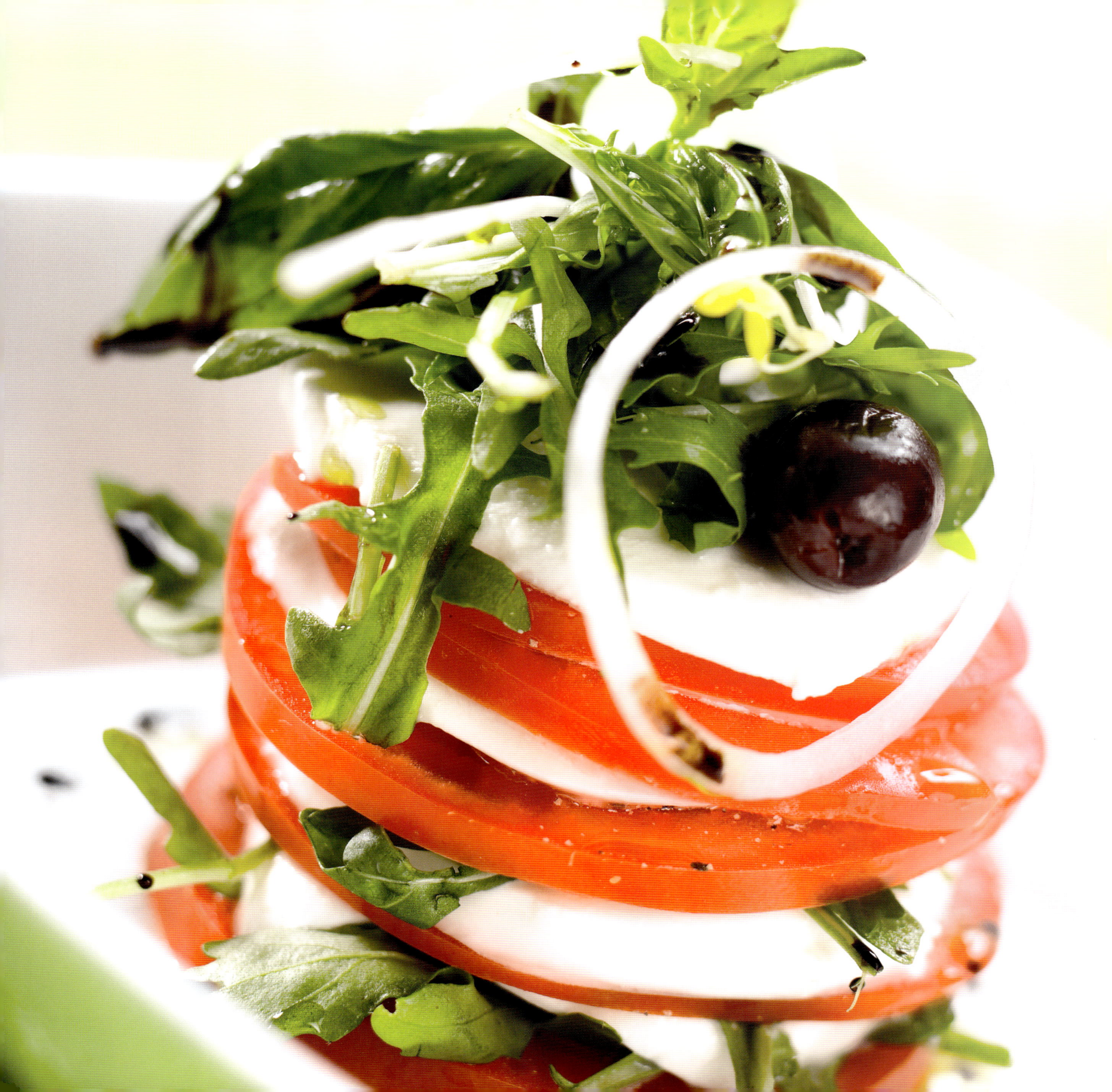

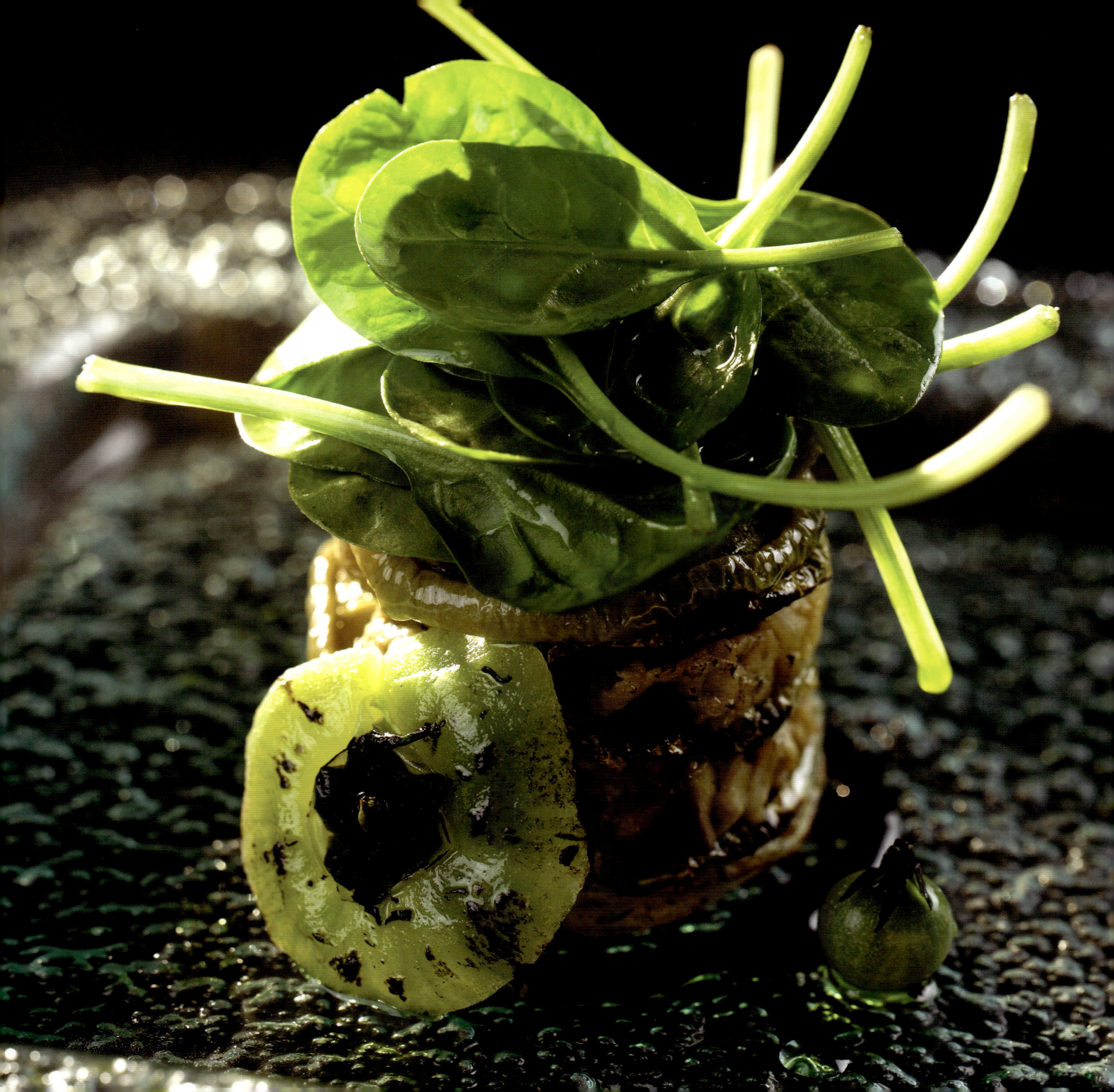

EMERALD GREEN TOMATOES AND EGGPLANT WITH BABY SPINACH

FOR THE EMERALD TOMATOES

200 gr	emerald tomatoes
	salt and pepper

Slice tomatoes and season with salt and pepper. Dry the tomatoes in an 80° Celsius oven for 1 hour. After, grill the dried tomatoes quickly and arrange in layers with the eggplant paste and finish with fresh baby spinach drizzled with balsamic dressing.

FOR THE EGGPLANT PASTE

500 gr	eggplant
100 gr	tomatoes
3 pc	garlic cloves, sliced
	zest and juice from 2 lemons
15 ml	thyme leaves
100 gr	olive oil

Cut eggplant in half and lay on a baking tray. Season the eggplant with salt and pepper and leave at room temperature for 1 hour.
Slice tomatoes and layer on top of the seasoned eggplant. Add the sliced garlic. Sprinkle with lemon zest, juice, olive oil and thyme leaves.
Bake in a 170° Celsius oven for 20 minutes. Remove from oven and cool slightly. Peel skin from the eggplant and mash with a fork.

BALSAMIC DRESSING

30 ml	balsamic vinegar
1 pc	egg yolk
10 ml	dijon mustard
100 ml	olive oil
1 pc	garlic clove
1 pc	basil leaf
	salt and pepper

Blend the egg yolk, mustard and garlic. Add the olive oil slowly and finish fresh basil.

Garnish with baby spinach tossed with balsamic dressing.

CHORIZO AND BREAD KNÖDEL WITH TOMATO JAM

FOR THE CHORIZO KNÖDEL

10 pc	crusty tomato ciabatta rolls
350 ml	warm milk
5 gr	salt
80 gr	butter
40 ml	tomato paste
3 pc	eggs, lightly beaten
30 ml	fresh parsley, chopped
50 gr	onions, finely chopped
45 ml	semolina flour
100 gr	raw chirizo

Cut the tomato rolls and cover with warm milk. Sauté the chorizo for 2 minutes and strain, reserve oil from pan.
Merge all components and refrigerate for 10 minutes. Form the mass into small ball shapes and poach in boiling salted water for eight minutes.
Heat the chorizo oil in a frying pan and toss the knödel balls in the pan for 1 minute.

FOR THE TOMATO JAM

100 gr	brandyvine tomatoes, diced
30 ml	green peppers, diced
50 gr	onions, diced
15 gr	sugar
30 ml	white wine vinegar
1	sprig rosemary, chopped
45 ml	olive oil
	salt and pepper

Sweat the onions and peppers in the olive oil. Add the sugar, vinegar and rosemary and cook for 1 minute. Add the remaining components and cook an additional 15 minutes.
Spoon jam into serving dish. Spear the knödel on a bamboo skewer.

Garnish with crispy chorizo, basil leaves and tomato skins.

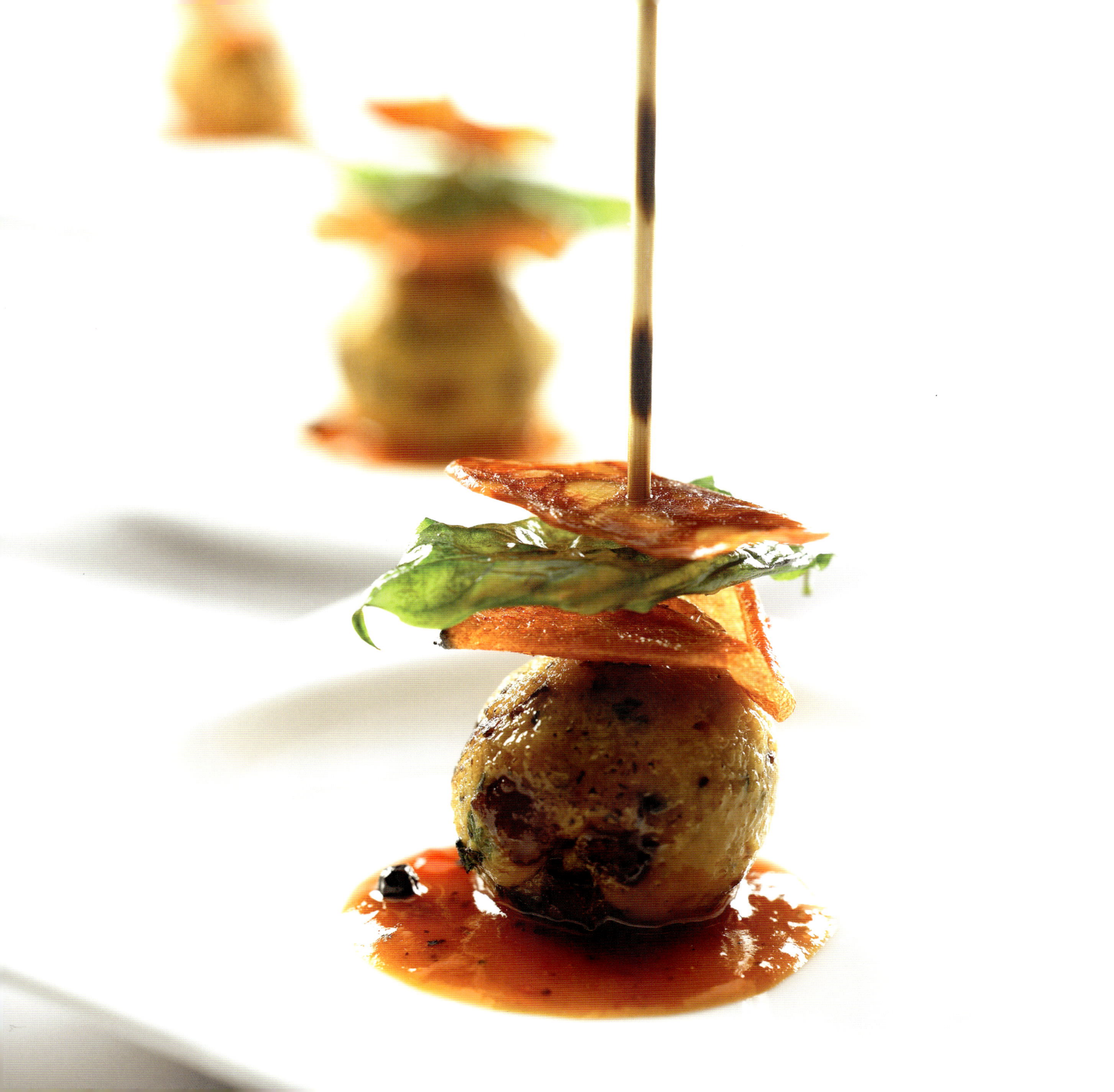

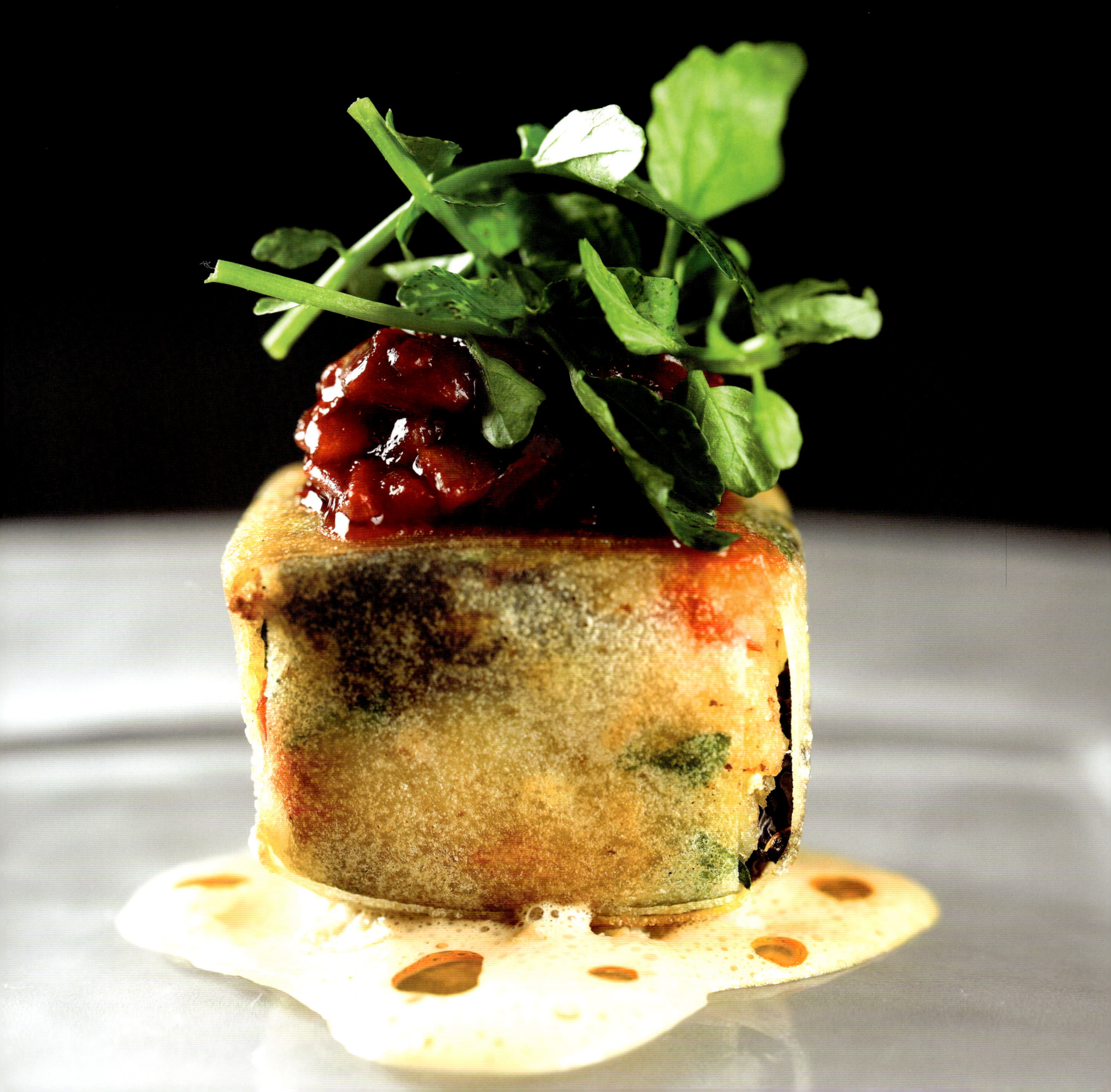

SWEETBREADS AND CHEROKEE PURPLE TOMATO PARCEL

FOR THE PARCEL FILLING
1 pc	feuille de brick
80 gr	sweetbreads, blanched
20 gr	cepe mushrooms, diced
10 ml	italian parsley
15 ml	cherokee tomato, diced
10 ml	onions, chopped
30 ml	veal glaze
	egg yolk
	salt and pepper

Clean sweetbreads and cut into small pieces. Sauté cepe mushrooms, onions and sweetbreads in olive oil for 2 minutes. Add veal glaze and tomatoes. Finish with the parsley.
Lay out feuille de brick and spoon the sweetbread mixture into the center. Fold over and secure ends with egg yolk. Pan-fry on both sides to golden brown.

FOR THE CHEROKEE TOMATOES STEW
50 gr	cherokee tomatoes, peeled and seeded
10 gr	red onions, chopped
5 gr	garlic, chopped
30 ml	olive oil
15 ml	port wine
	salt and pepper

Sweat the onions and garlic in olive oil. Add the tomatoes and cook over low heat for 10 minutes. Season.

FOR THE DIJON CREAM
15 ml	dijon mustard
50 gr	whipping cream
30 ml	chicken stock
15 ml	white wine
	salt and pepper

Bring all components to a boil and simmer for 5 minutes to reduce while whisking vigorously.

Garnish with watercress and drizzle sherry vinaigrette over top.

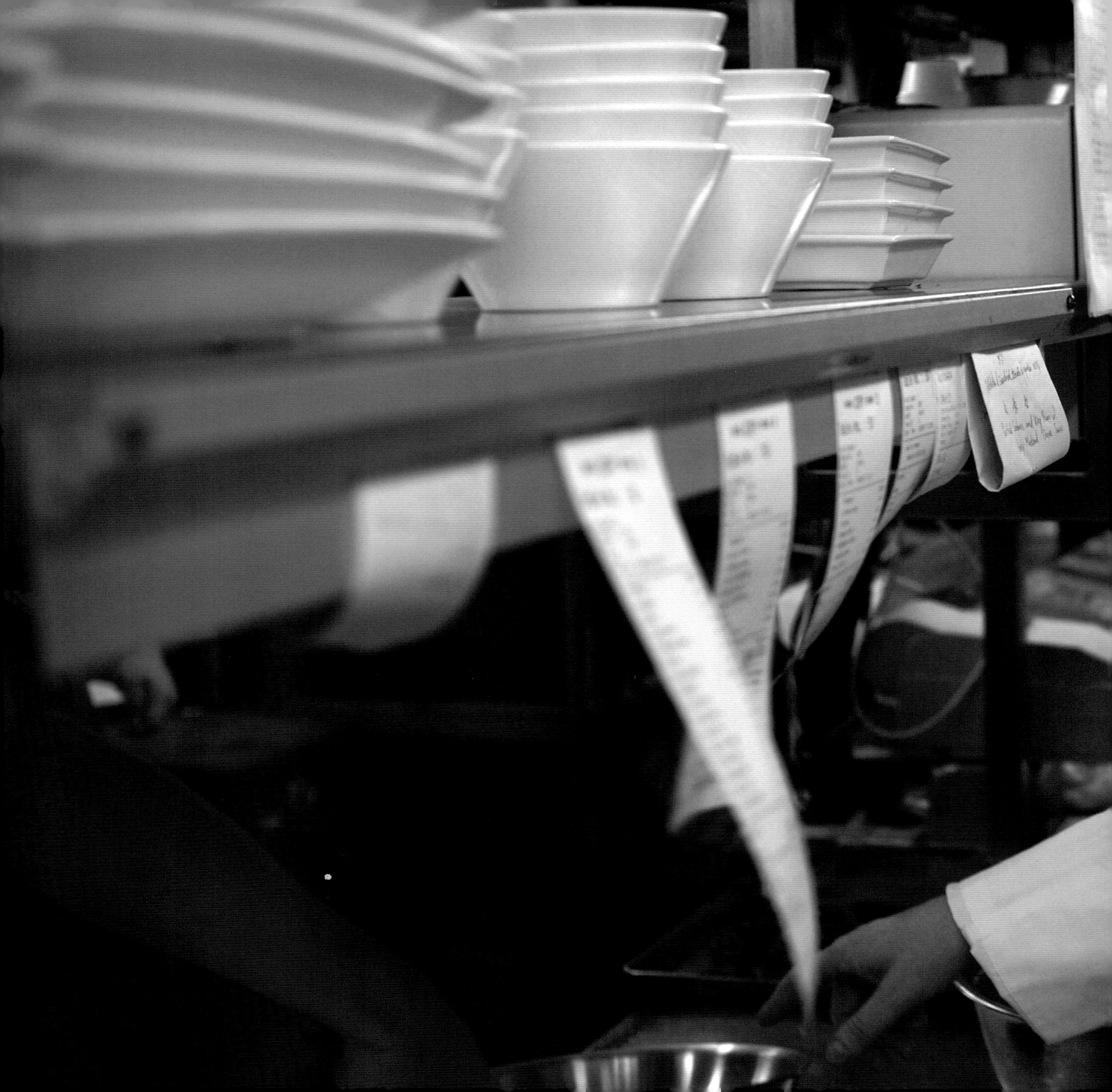

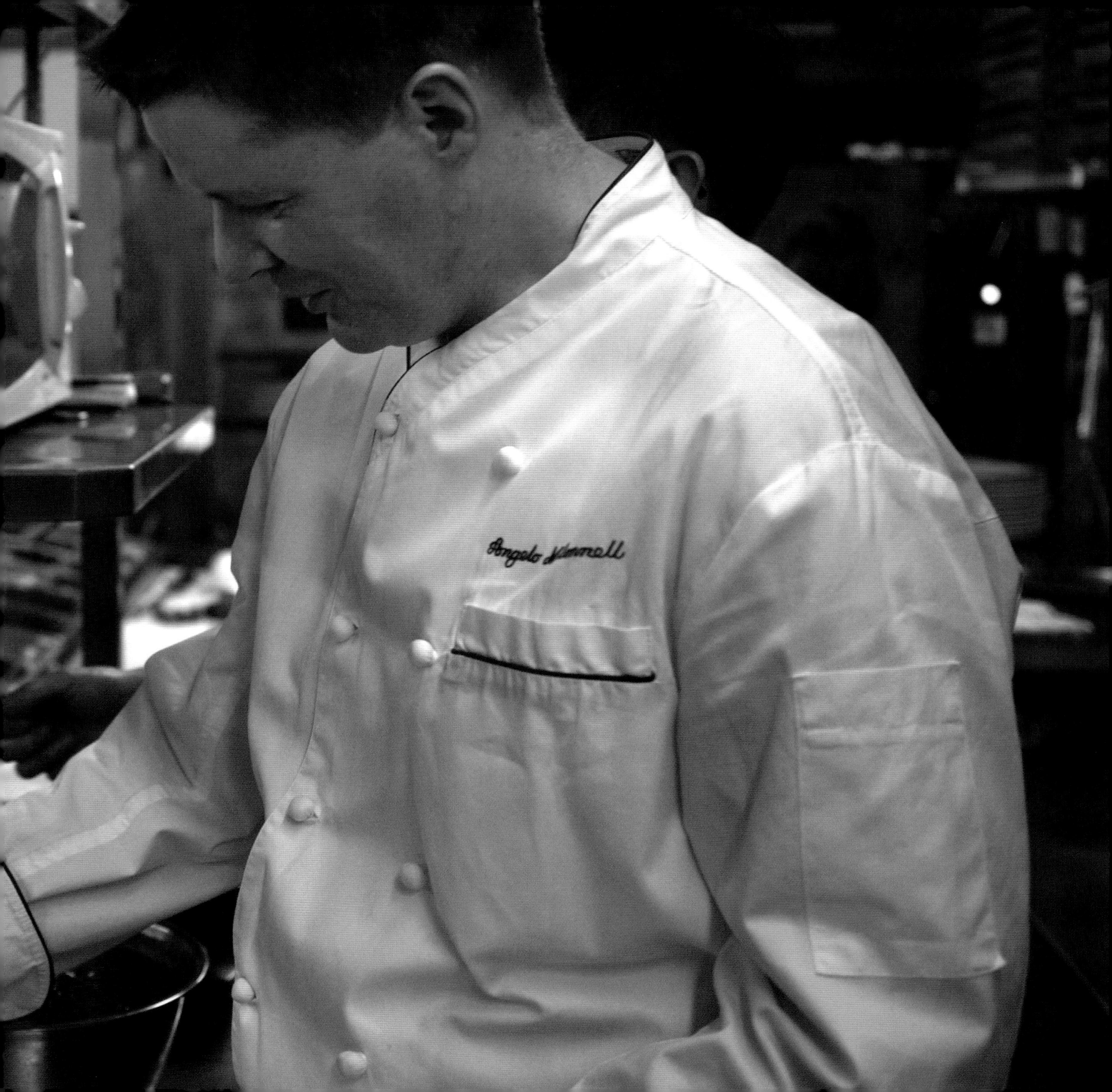

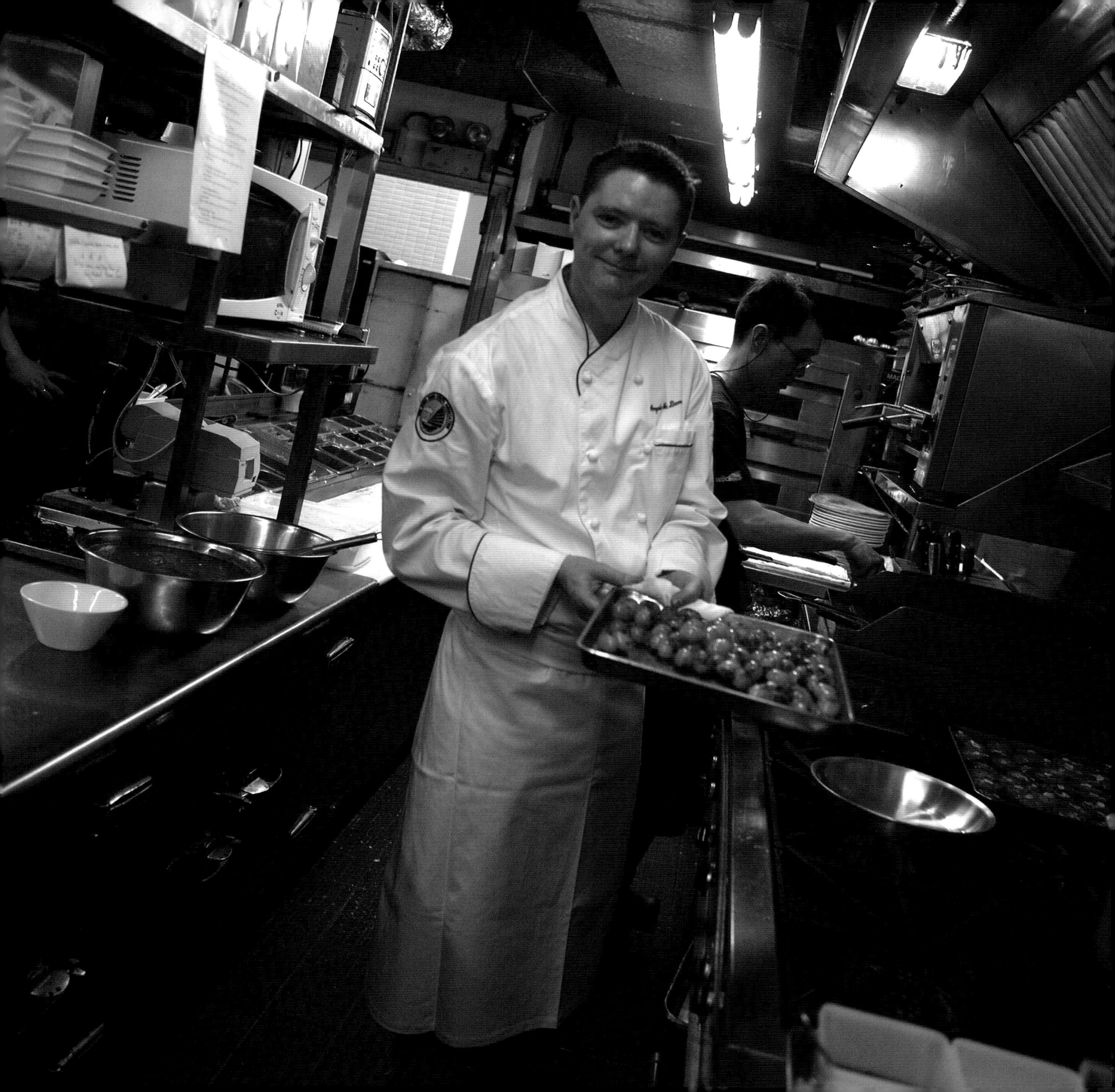

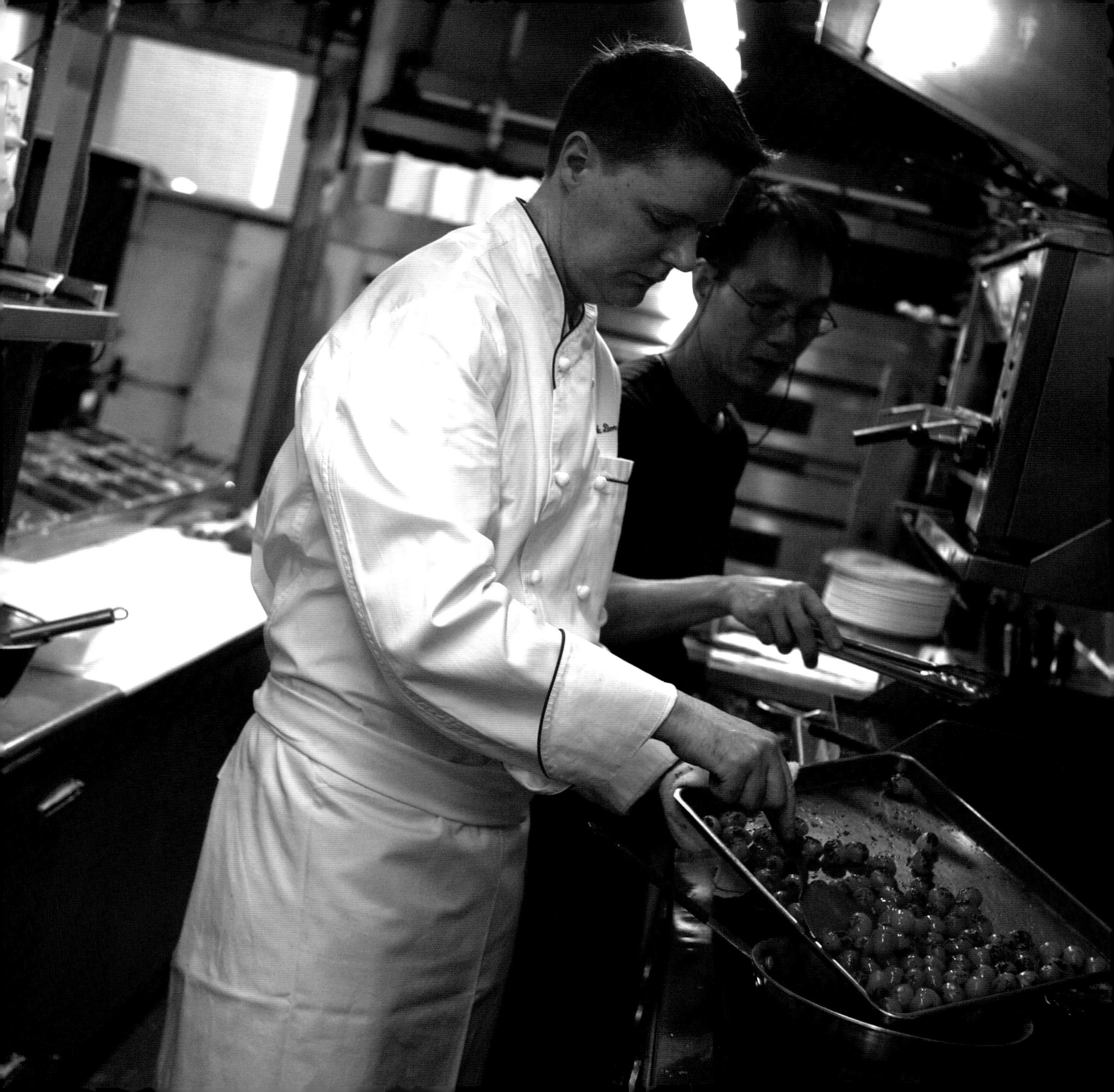

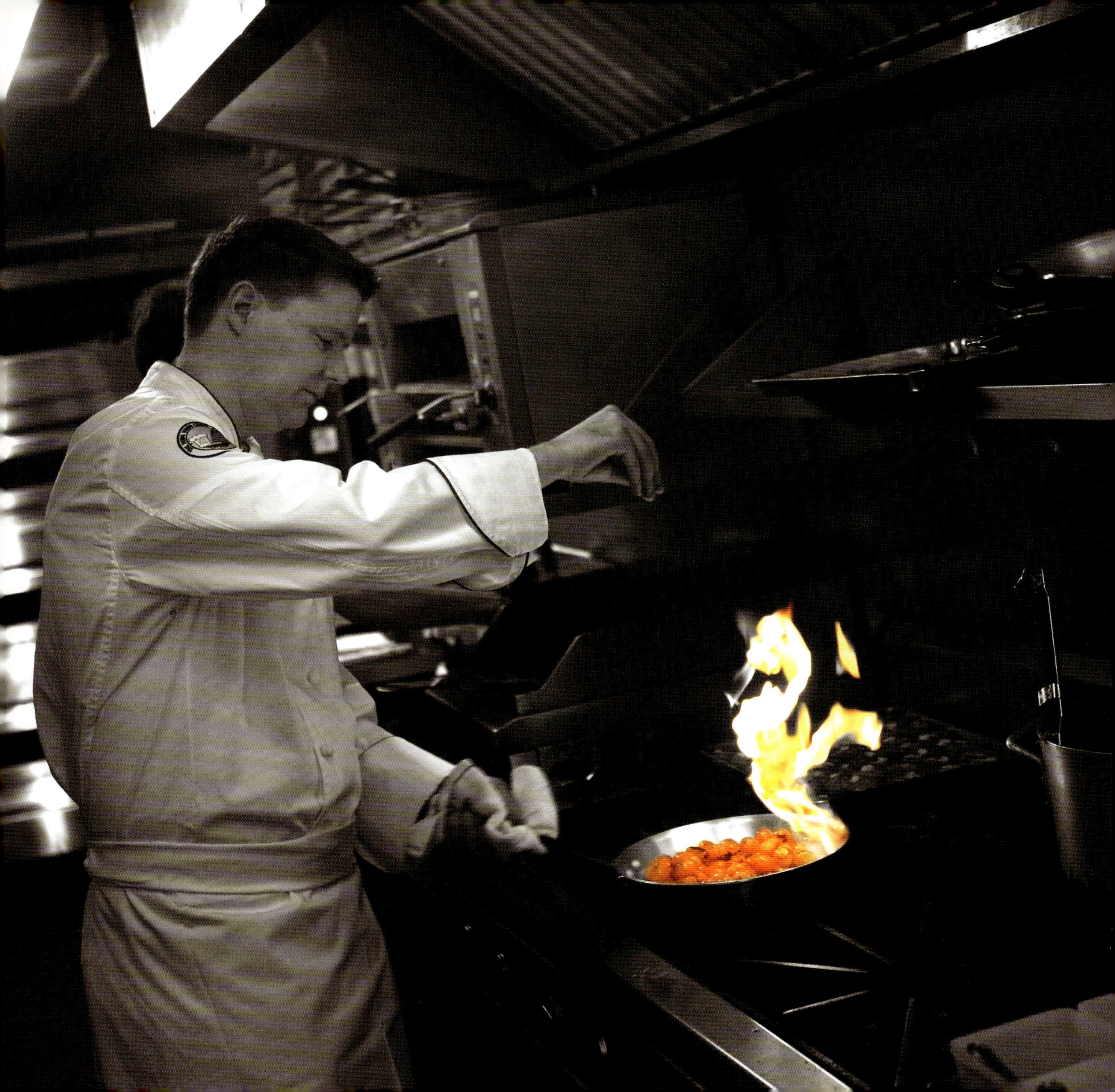

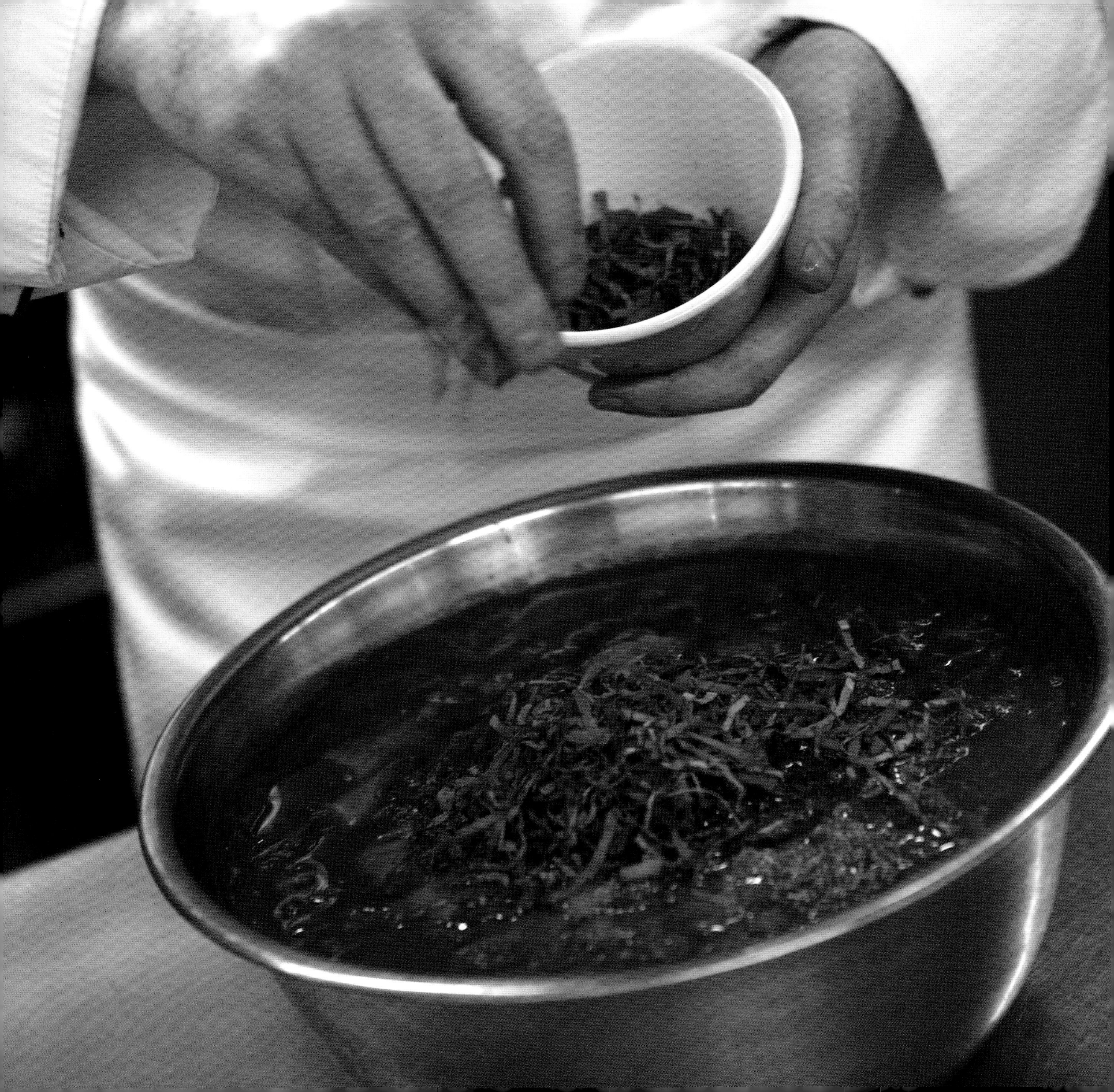

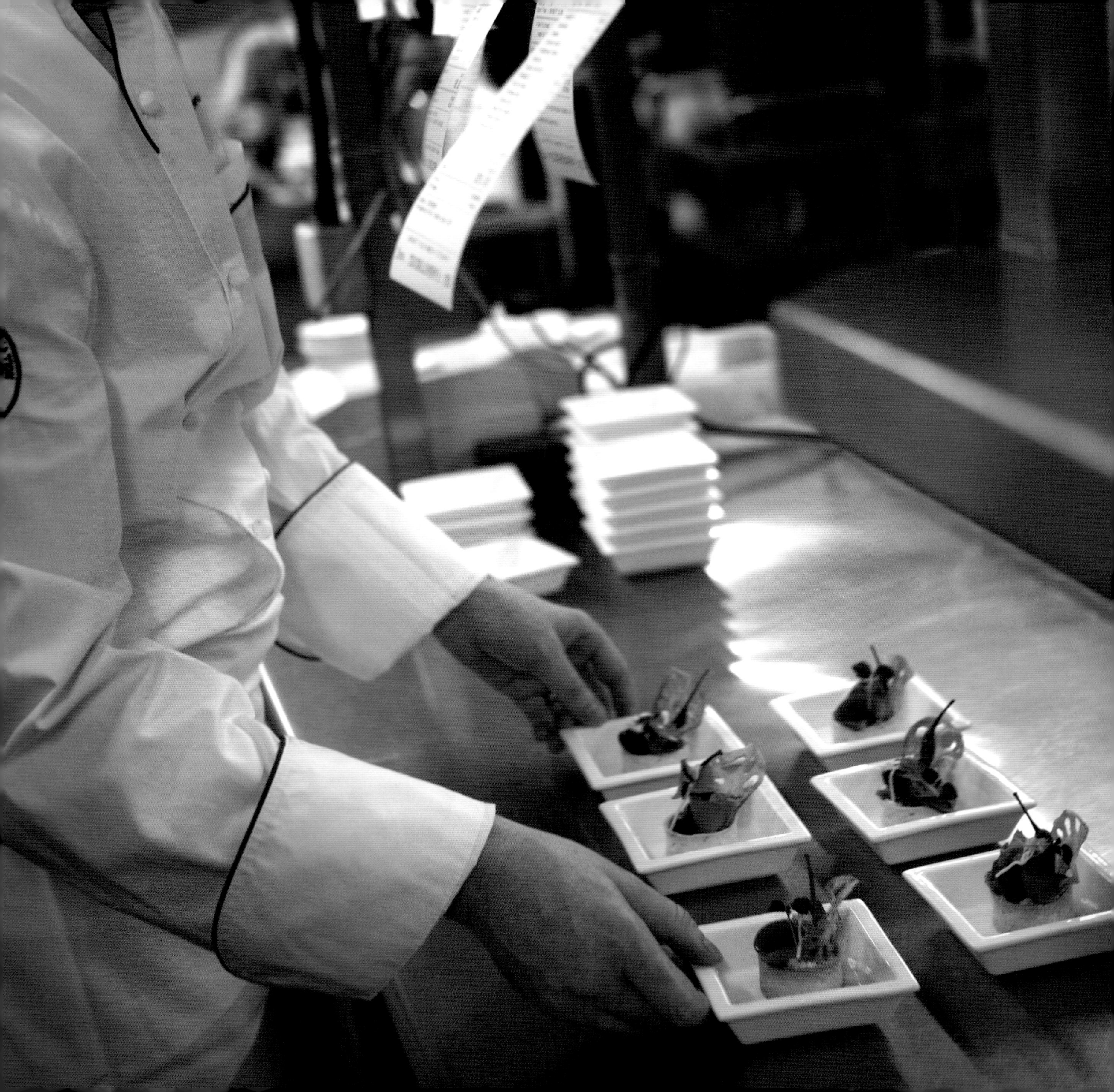

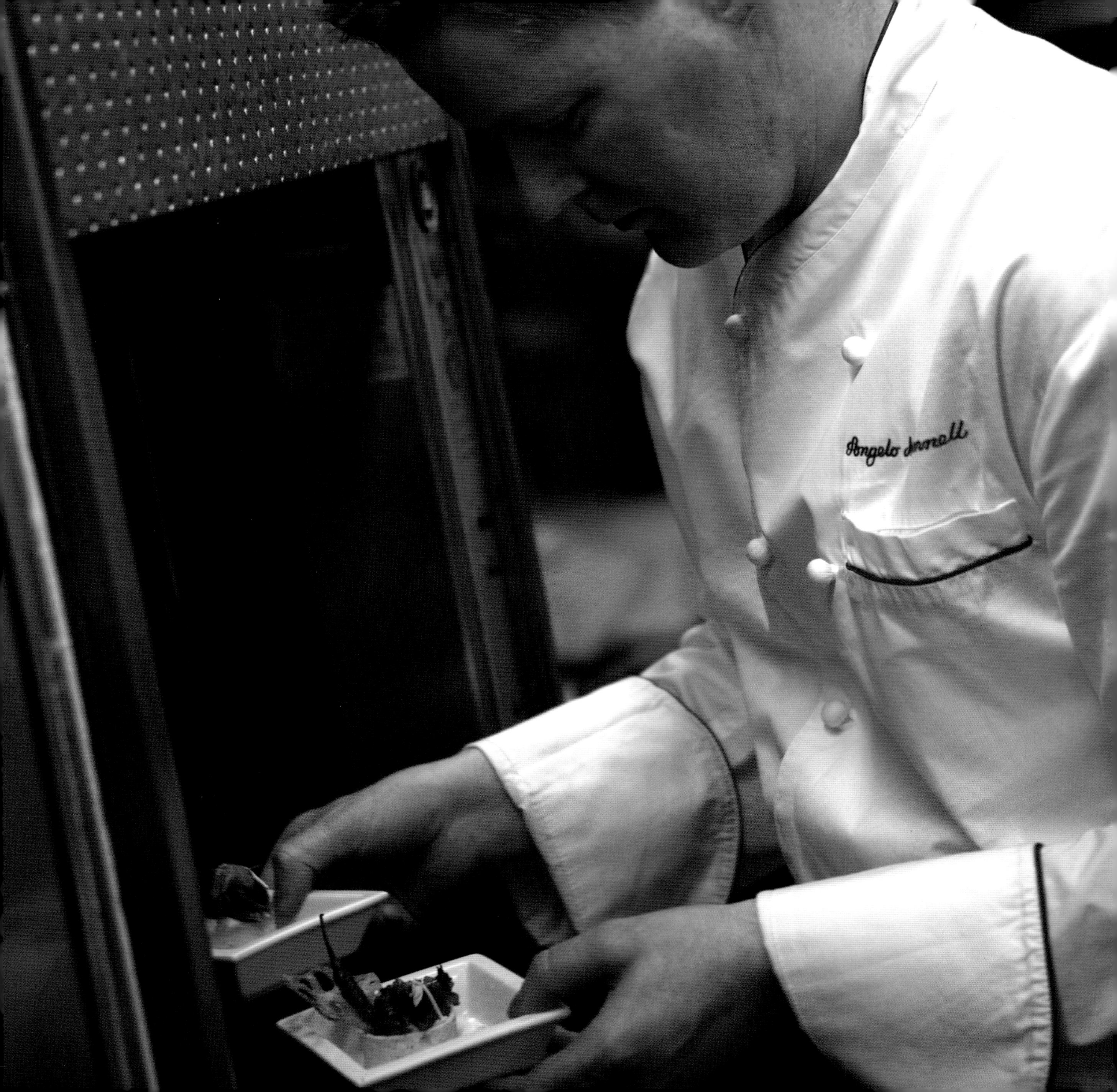

VINE TOMATO AND PAPAYA TARTAR WITH ANCHOVIES

FOR THE TARTAR
200 gr	vine tomatoes, diced
200 gr	papaya, diced
20 ml	italian parsley, chopped
20 ml	tarragon, chopped
80 gr	onions, diced
25 ml	lemon juice
30 ml	olive oil
	salt and pepper

Merge all components.

FOR THE ANCHOVIES
200 gr	fresh boneless anchovies
10 ml	all spice
15 ml	thyme
5 ml	black pepper
5 ml	cayenne
3 ml	cinnamon
15 ml	sugar
75 ml	olive oil
1 pc	clove garlic, chopped
30 ml	cider vinegar
30 ml	soy sauce
5 ml	nutmeg
	juice from 1 lime

Merge all components and marinate the anchovies for 3 hours. Remove from marinade and place on a greased tray. Roast anchovies in a 160° Celsius oven for 10 minutes.
Slice anchovies.

PAPAYA SEED DRESSING
75 ml	white wine vinegar
15 ml	onion, grated
10 ml	dijon mustard
30 ml	sugar
5 ml	salt
10 ml	tabasco
150 ml	olive oil
30 ml	papaya seeds

Blend vinegar, onion, mustard, sugar and salt. Slowly incorporate the olive oil. Whiles still blending, add tobasco and finish by adding papaya seeds until coarsely chopped.

FOR THE PAPAYA PAVÉ
200 gr	papaya, sliced
200 gr	tomato fillets, sliced and oven-dried for 1 hour

Line the bottom of stainless steel mold with sliced papaya. Spoon in a layer of tomato-papaya tartar. Place roasted sliced anchovies on top. Place a layer of oven dried-dried tomato fillets on top. Add another layer and tomato-papaya tartar and finish with sliced papaya.
Place a weight on top and refrigerate for 3 hours.

Slice and place on a plate, top with fresh watercress and drizzle with papaya seed dressing.

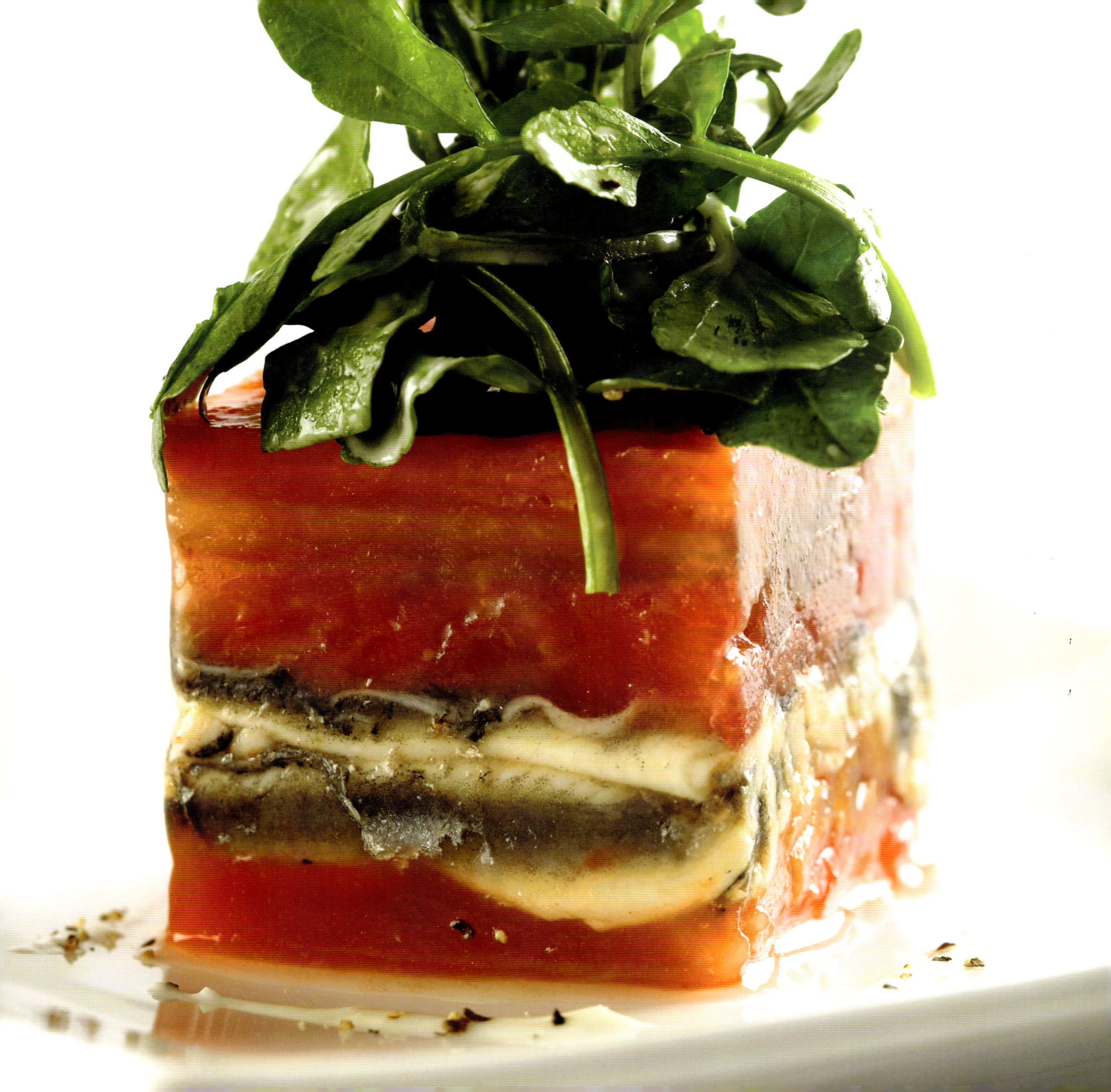

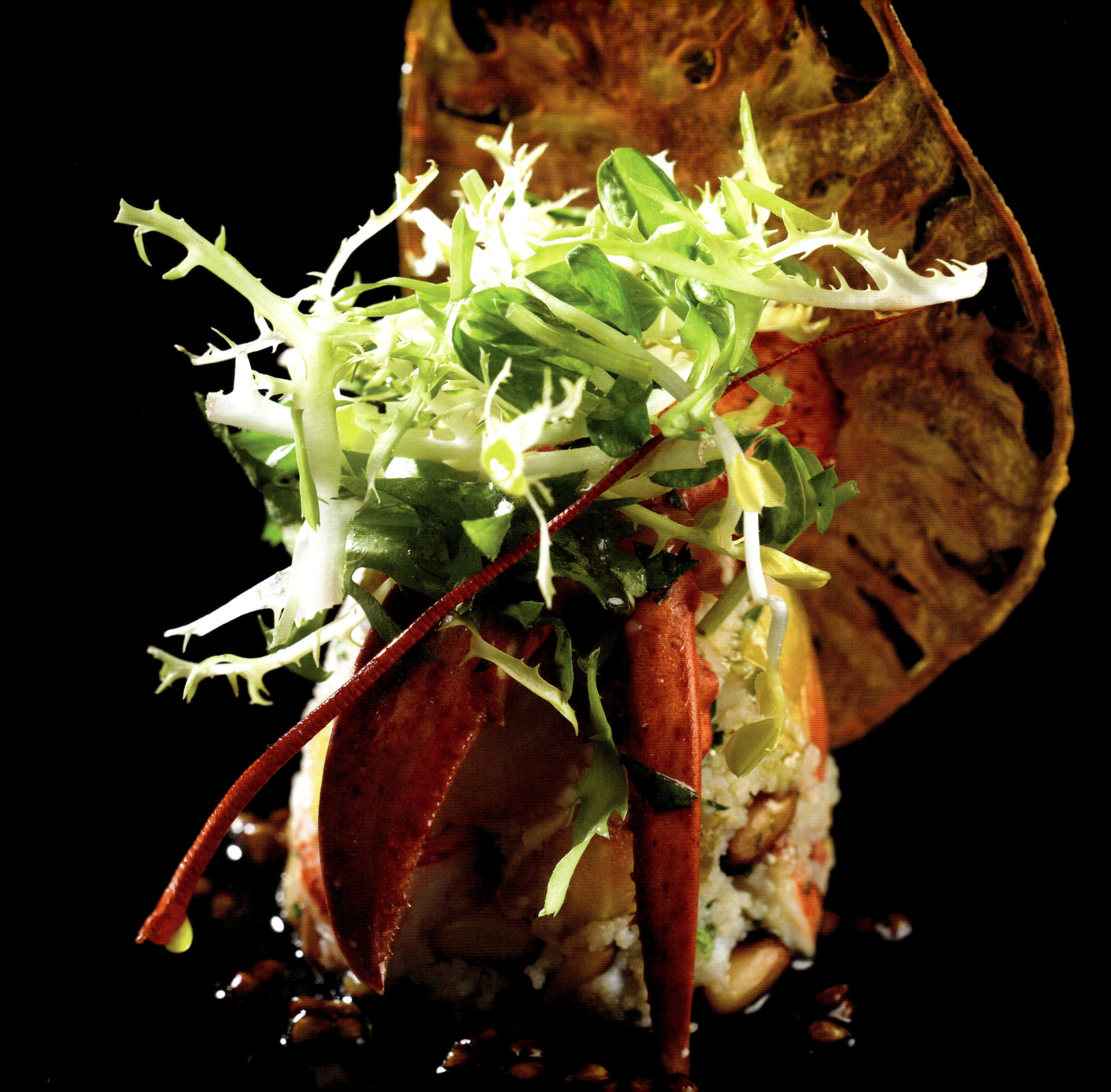

PINEAPPLE HEIRLOOM TOMATO WITH LOBSTER TABOULEH

DRIED HEIRLOOM TOMATO CHIPS

Slice an heirloom tomato very thin and lay on a greased baking tray. Brush with olive oil and season with salt and pepper. Place in preheated oven at 80 ° Celsius for 4 hours.

FOR THE TABOULEH

15 ml	butter
250 ml	barley cous cous
125 ml	fish stock
125 ml	coconut milk
1 pc	bay leaf
30 gr	yellow bell peppers, roasted and diced
5 ml	parsley, chopped
5 ml	coriander, chopped
	zest of one lime
	salt and pepper

Melt the butter in a heavy pot. Add the cous cous and stir to coat grains. Add coconut milk, stock and bay leaf and bring to a boil. When the liquid reaches a boil, turn off the heat and cover the pot. When the cous cous has cooled, spread the grains using a fork to loosen. Add the coriander, parsley, lime and yellow peppers.

FOR THE PINEAPPLE HERILOOM TOMATOES

Blanch the tomatoes in salted water for 10 seconds and plunge into ice water. Remove skin and seeds. Dice and set aside.

LOBSTER SALAD

250 gr	lobster meat
60 gr	coconut milk
40 gr	cucumber, diced
40 gr	red bell pepper, diced
40 gr	heirloom tomatoes, diced
60 gr	aioli
	coriander, chopped
	salt and pepper

Poach a 600-700 gr. live lobster in boiling heavily salted water. Plunge into ice water. Remove claws from shells and set aside. Remove tail meat from the shell and dice. Merge with all remaining components except lobster claws.

Toss lobster salad with tabouleh and aioli.

AIOLI

2 pc	egg yolks
2 pc	garlic cloves, chopped
90 ml	olive oil
15 ml	lime juice
	salt and pepper

Blend yolks with garlic. Slowly add the olive oil while whisking briskly. Add the lime juice and season.

ASSEMBLY

On a plate, place a ring mold in the center. Spoon in lobster salad and tabouleh Press lightly with the back of a spoon. Remove the ring and top with poached lobster claw and frisée lettuce.

Garnish with dried tomato chips and drizzle with tomato seed oil, (see recipe index).

TOMATO CRUSTED SEARED TUNA WITH PACHINO TOMATO SALSA

ACHIOTE MARINADE
- 40 gr   achiote paste
- 60 gr   orange juice
- 5 gr   fresh ginger, chopped
- 5 gr   fresh cilantro, chopped
- 10 gr   sugar

Mix all ingredients in a high speed blender until smooth

FOR THE TUNA
- 120 gr   tuna loin
- 40 gr   achiote paste
- salt
- cracked black pepper

Season the tuna with salt. Submerge in the achiote marinade for 2 hours.
Remove from marinade and season with cracked black pepper. Sear the tuna in a hot frying pan to rare.
Roll in tomato flakes before serving.

TOMATO FLAKES
- 200 gr   tomato skins
- 30 ml   olive oil
- salt and pepper

Lay the tomato skins on a flat baking tray. Brush olive oil over the skins and sprinkle salt and fresh ground pepper. Place in a 70° Celsius oven and dry for three hours. Crush between sheets of grease-proof paper to a powder.
The whole dried leaves can be kept in an air tight container overnight and crushed at the last minute.

TOMATO SALSA
- 10 gr   garlic, chopped
- 100 gr   onions, chopped
- 1 pc   chili, chopped
- 5 gr   cilantro, chopped
- 450 gr   pachino tomatoes, diced
- 30 ml   olive oil
- juice of one lime
- salt and pepper

Mix all ingredients together and allow flavors to infuse for 30 minutes before serving.

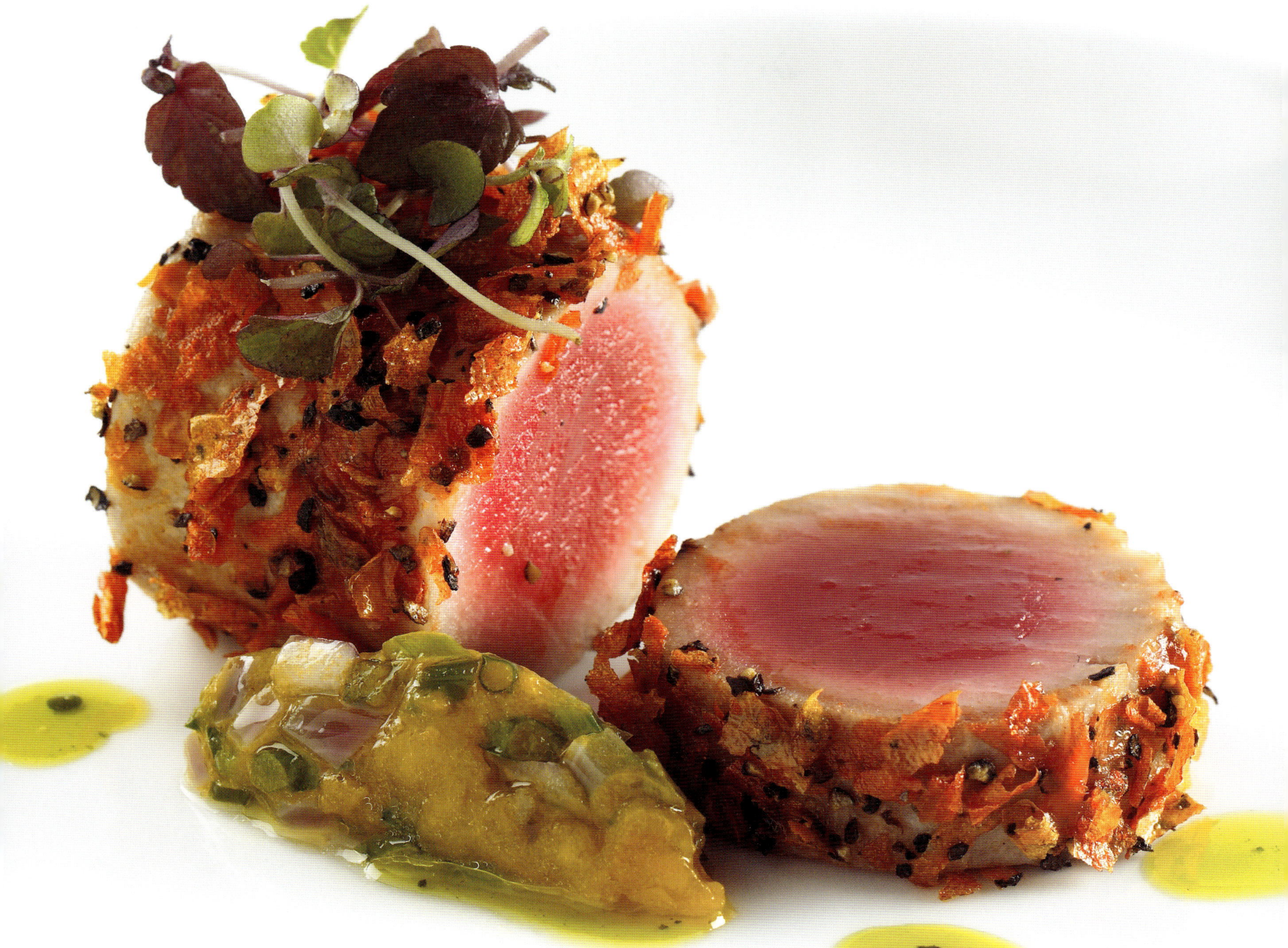

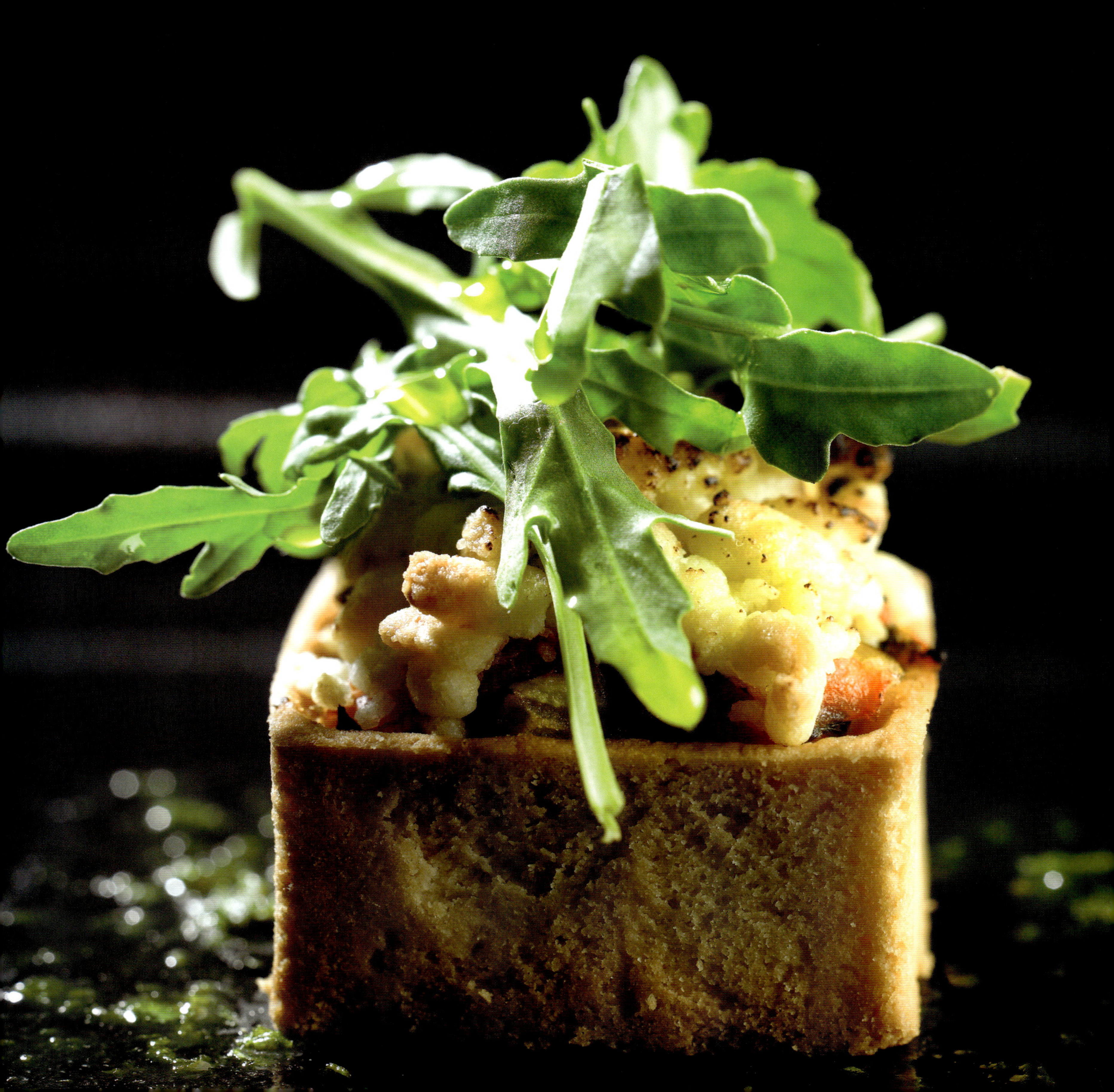

BLACK KUMATO CRUMBLE WITH ARUGULA PESTO

ARUGULA PESTO

50 gr	pine nuts
200 ml	olive oil
40 gr	garlic
250 ml	tightly packed fresh basil
250 ml	tightly packed arugula
80 gr	grated parmesan cheese

Crush pine nuts in a blender and add olive oil and garlic. Add the basil, arugula and blend for 1 minutes. Add the cheese and blend for an additional 1 minute.

CRUMBLE TOPPING

250 gr	flour
130 gr	butter
50 gr	sugar
5 gr	salt

Merge all components and grate through a large hole grater.

SAVORY DOUGH

350 gr	flour
120 gr	butter
5 gr	salt
5 gr	fresh oregano, chopped
30 ml	milk

Mix all components to a dough consistency. Cover and refrigerate for 1 hour.

BLACK KUMATO TOMATO FILLING

100 gr	black kumato tomatoes, diced
10 gr	onion, chopped
5 ml	basil, chopped
1 pc	garlic clove, chopped
30 ml	olive oil
	salt and pepper

Sauté the onions and garlic in olive oil for 1 minute. Add the diced black tomatoes and cook for 2 minutes. Add the basil, salt and pepper.

ASSEMBLY

Roll out the savory dough to 3mm thickness and line a buttered square baking mold.
Add the black tomato filling and finish with a layer of crumble.
Bake at 180° Celsius for 10 minutes.
Brush the plate with arugula pesto and serve crumble tart on top.
Garnish with a few leaves of arugula tossed in vinaigrette.

PASTEL TOMATO SALAD WITH WHITE BALSAMIC

FOR THE PASTEL TOMATO SALAD

30 gr	red tomatoes sliced
30 gr	yellow tomatoes wedges
30 gr	green zebra tomatoes wedges
30 gr	cherry tomatoes sliced
30 gr	black pear tomatoes sliced in half
20 gr	rocket lettuce
50 gr	white balsamic vinaigrette
5 ml	blue basil
	rock salt and pepper

Toss components together and season with rock salt and fresh ground pepper. Drizzle additional white balsamic vinaigrette over salad.

WHITE BALSAMIC VINAIGRETTE

200 ml	white balsamic vinegar
400 ml	olive oil
10 ml	dijon mustard
10 ml	shredded african basil
	salt and pepper to taste

Blend the mustard with the white balsamic vinegar and slowly add the olive oil. Adjust seasoning and finish with shredded African basil.

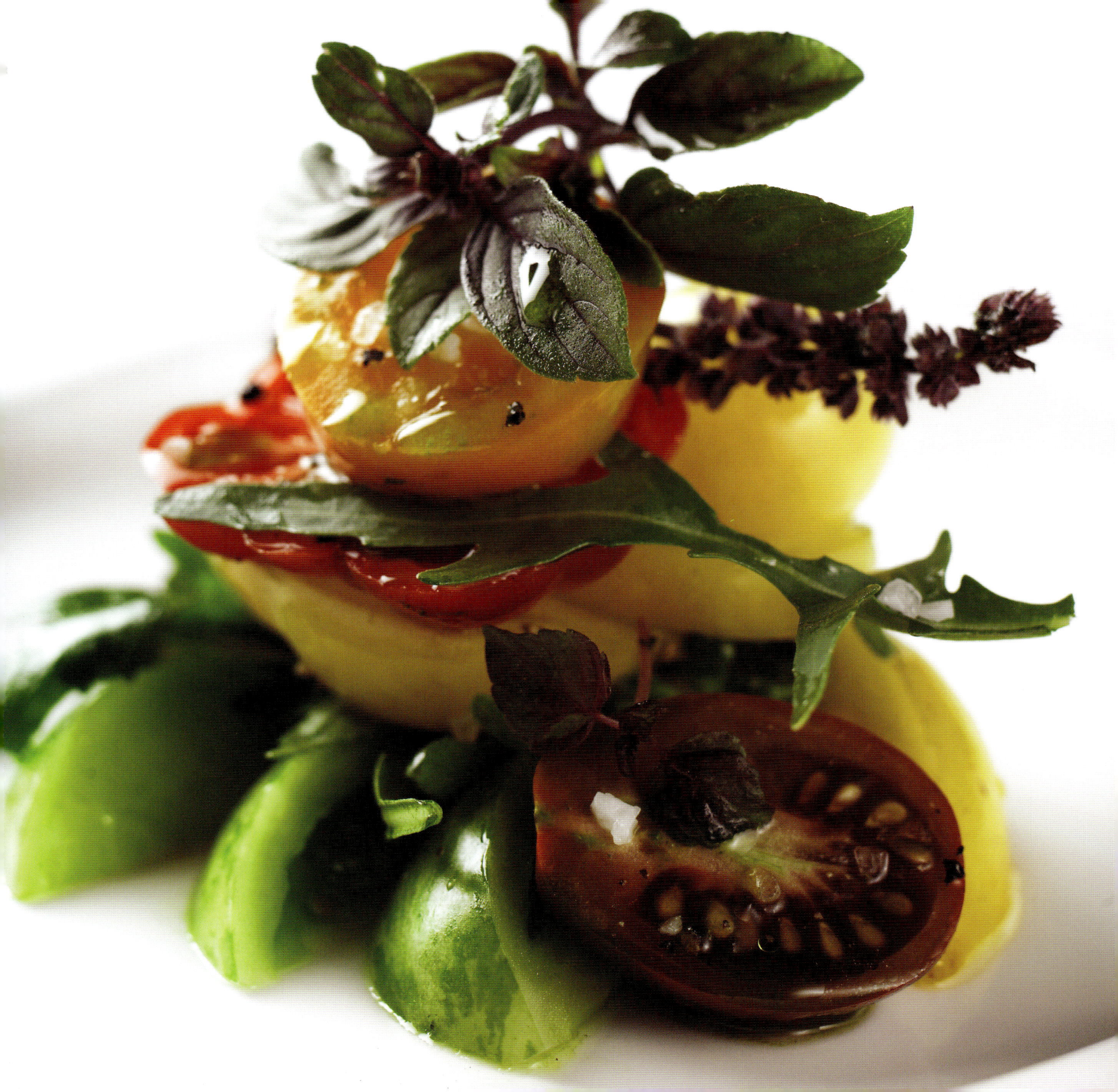

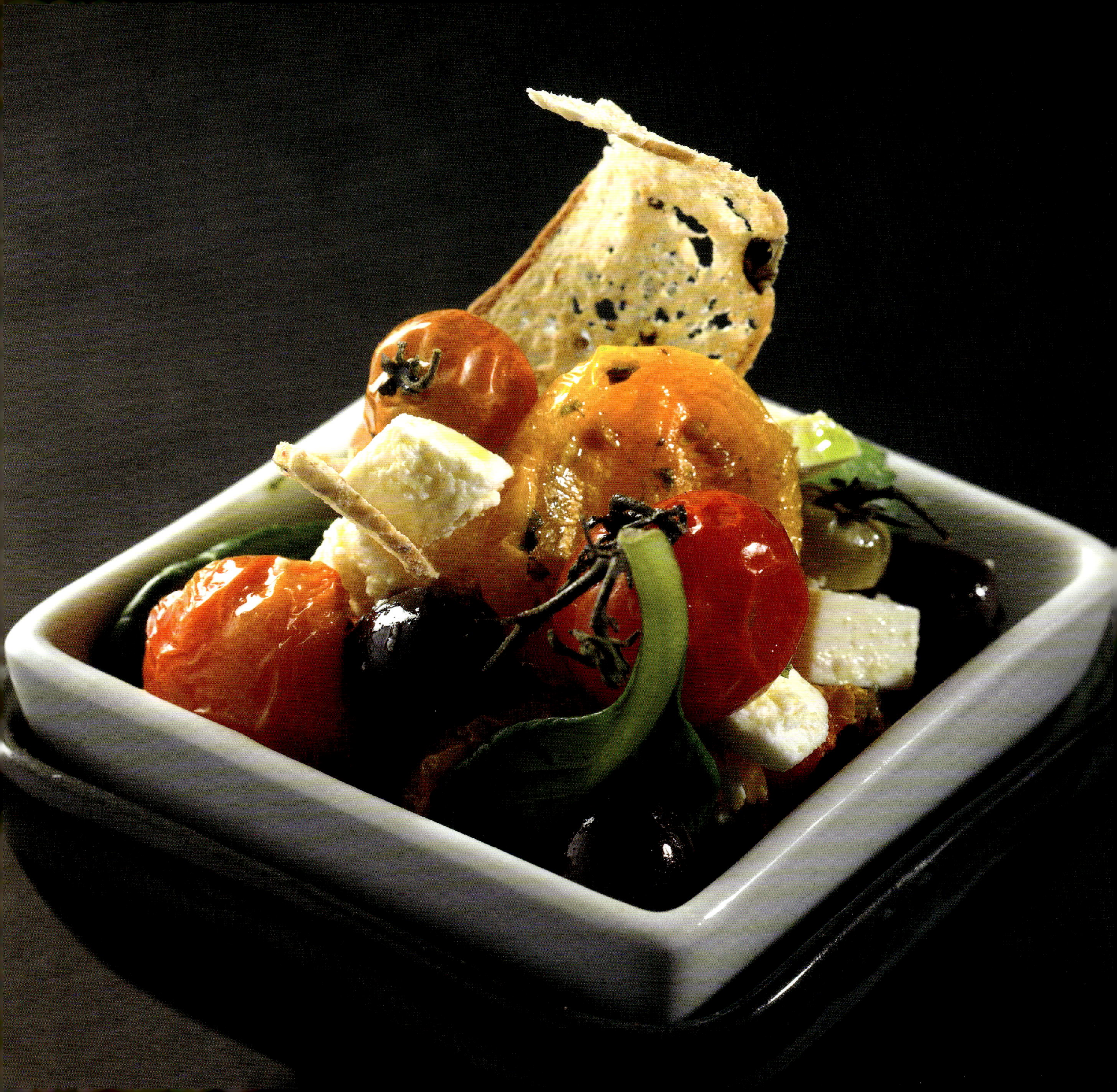

OVEN-DRIED TOMATOES WITH FETA AND OREGANO

FOR THE TOMATOES
100 gr	roma tomatoes
100 gr	yellow tomatoes
100 gr	jelly bean tomatoes
45 ml	virgin olive oil
2 pc	garlic cloves, sliced
5 ml	chopped oregano
	salt and pepper

DYNAMICS
Slice all tomatoes lengthwise and season with salt and pepper. Lay out the tomatoes on a tray and drizzle with olive oil. Sprinkle with oregano and layer with sliced garlic.
Place in a 100° Celsius oven for 2 hours.

FOR THE SALAD
50 gr	feta cheese
100 gr	oven-dried tomatoes
30 gr	kalamata olives
20 gr	baby greens
30 ml	sherry vinaigrette
	salt and pepper

Toss all components and season.

Garnish with black olive toast.

VINE TOMATO AND RED ONION SALAD WITH RED WINE VINAIGRETTE

FOR THE TOMATOES AND RED ONIONS

400 gr	vine tomatoes
100 gr	red onions, sliced
50 gr	arugula
70 ml	red wine vinaigrette
	rock salt and pepper

Blanch tomatoes in boiling water for 5 seconds and plunge into ice water. Peel tomatoes.
Slice off the top third of all tomatoes and reserve. Using a spoon remove half of the pulp from the inside of the tomatoes. Sprinkle with rock salt and pepper.
Merge the vinaigrette, red onions, arugula and fill tomato shell.
Place the reserved top back on tomato. Carefully slice the filled tomato in half vertically.

Serve with crispy tomato skin and rock salt.

FOR THE RED WINE VINAIGRETTE

500 ml	red wine
80 ml	red wine vinegar
80 gr	shallots, chopped
200 ml	olive oil
	salt and pepper

Reduce red wine to 100 ml. Cool. Merge all components.

Serve with balsamic reduction.

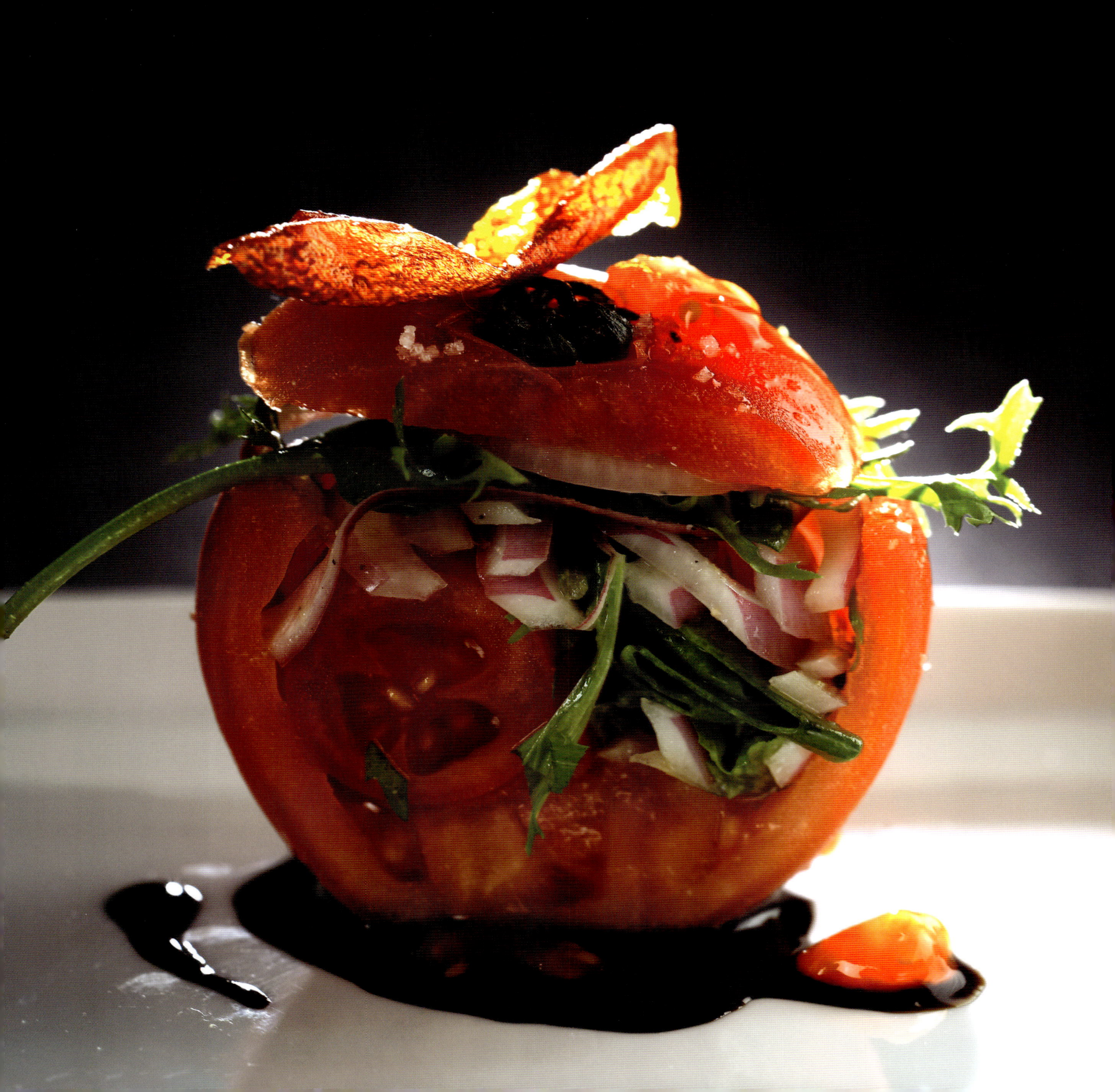

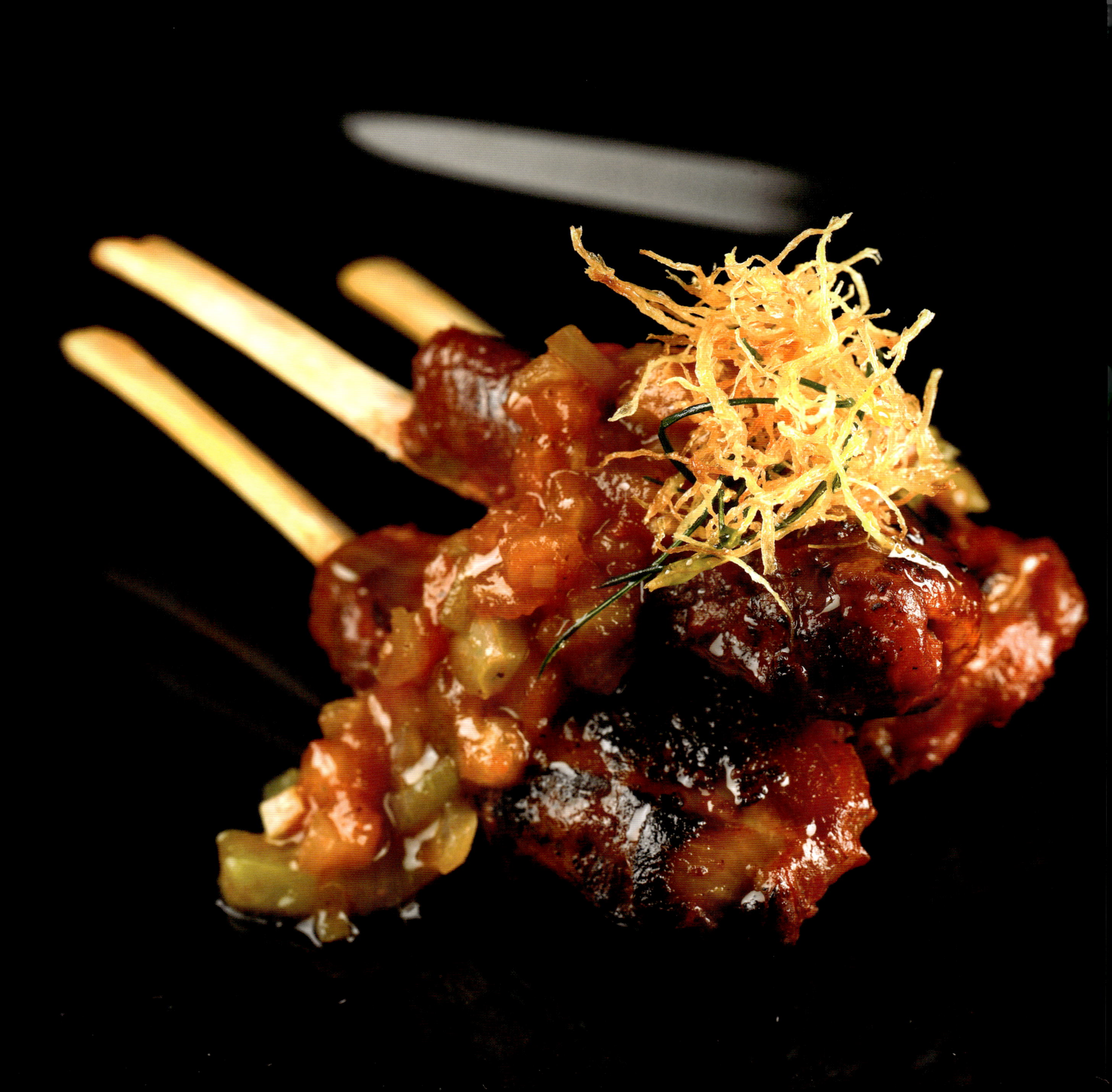

MONGOLIAN BABY PORK SHANKS WITH GINGER AND TOMATO

FOR THE SHANKS
- 1 kg   trimmed baby pork shanks
- 1 pc   red onion, sliced
- 2 pc   garlic, chopped
- 1 pc   red chili, chopped
- 10 ml   coriander seed crushed
- 2 pc   star anise
- 200 ml   red wine vinegar
- 400 ml   red wine
- 400 ml   chicken stock
- 10 ml   liquid smoke flavor
- 300 gr   fresh plum tomatoes
- 500 ml   veal jus
- hints of rosemary and thyme.

Season and sear the pork shanks in a heavy pan. Add onions, garlic, chili, coriander, star anise to the pan and cook slowly for 10 minutes.
Deglaze with the vinegar and wine, reduce to half and add the remaining components and continue to cook over low heat for 1 hour.

FOR THE GINGER-TOMATO STEW
- 100 gr   tomatoes, chopped
- 5 ml   ginger, minced
- 50 gr   onions, chopped
- 10 ml   coriander, chopped
- 30 ml   olive oil
- salt and pepper

Sweat the ginger and onions in olive oil for 2 minutes. Add remaining components and cook for an additional 10 minutes.

Garnish with deep-fried shredded ginger.

BANANA LEG TOMATOES WITH CRISPY SKIN PORK BELLY

FOR THE BANANA LEG TOMATOES

200 gr	banana leg tomatoes cut in half
5 gr	sugar
20 ml	butter
5 ml	flat leaf parsley, coarsely chopped
20 ml	honey
	salt and pepper

In a pan melt the sugar, butter and honey. Add the banana leg tomatoes and stir. Season with salt and pepper. Place the coated tomatoes on a sheet and bake at 180° Celsius for 8-10 minutes.
Remove from oven and toss with chopped parsley. Strain to remove pan juices. Blend the pan juices to a foam and spoon over the tomatoes when ready to serve.

FOR THE CRISPY PORK BELLY

2 kg	pork belly
5 pc	whole garlic cloves
5 ml	thyme, chopped
5 ml	rosemary, chopped
	salt and pepper

Heat the oven to 220° Celsius.
Make small incisions in the pork and push the whole garlic cloves into the meat. Liberally season the meat side with the salt, pepper and herbs. Season the pork skin with salt.
Heat a heavy roasting pan with the olive oil. Place the pork belly skin side up in the hot roasting pan and cook in the oven for 20 minutes. Reduce the heat to 180° Celsius and continue to cook in the oven for 45 more minutes.

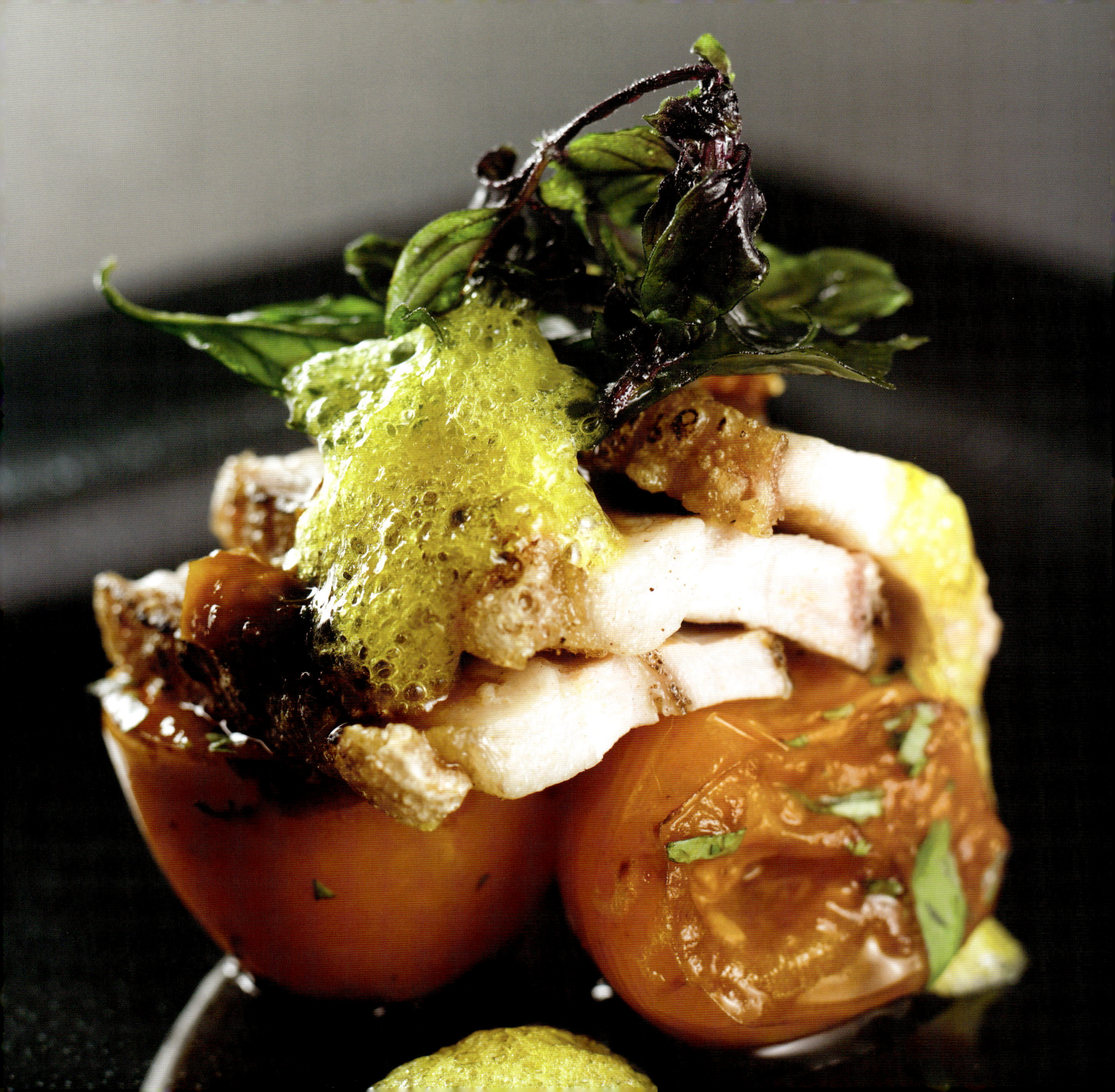

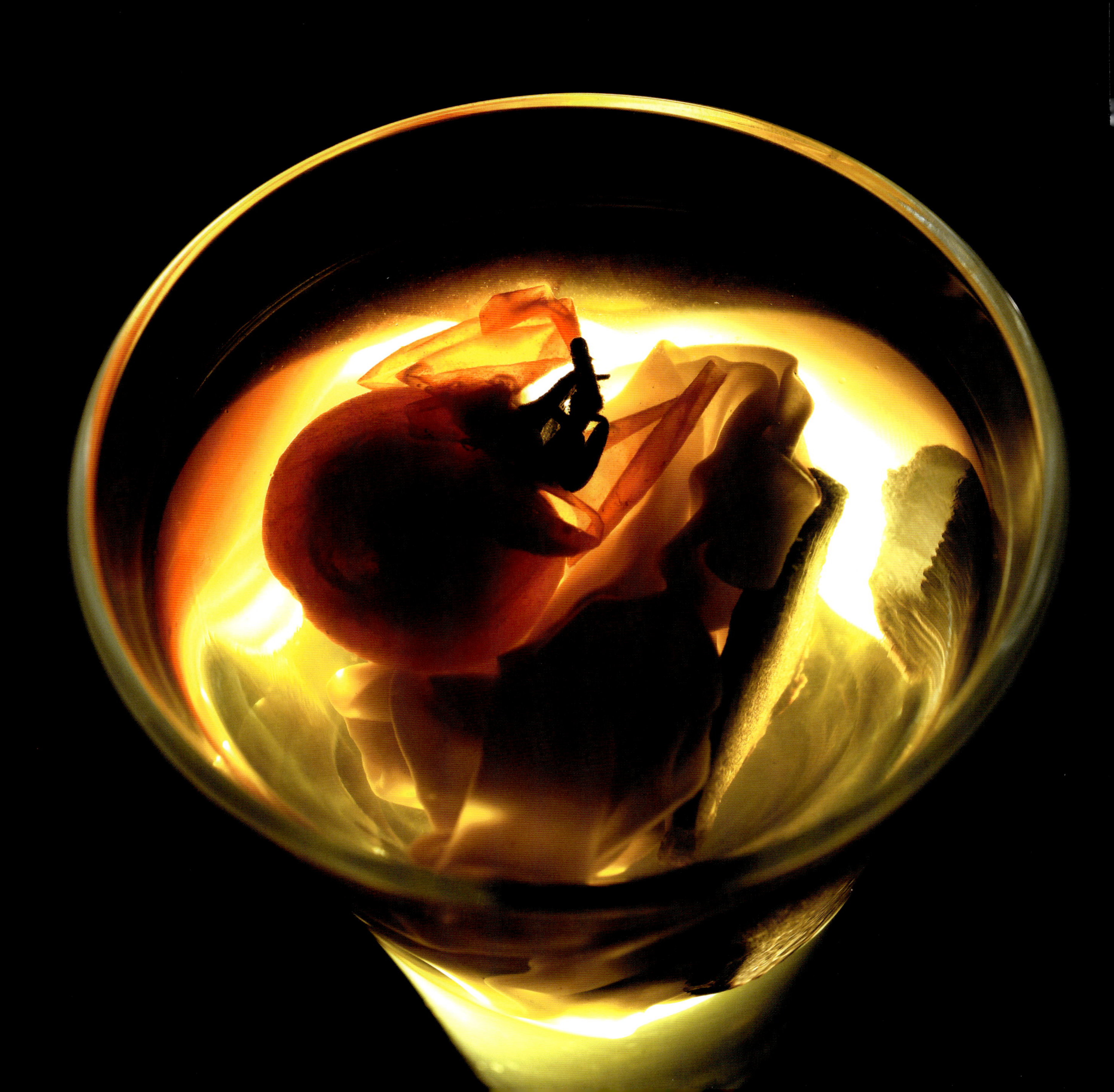

SMOKED ORANGE TOMATO CONSOMMÉ WITH SCALLOP WONTON

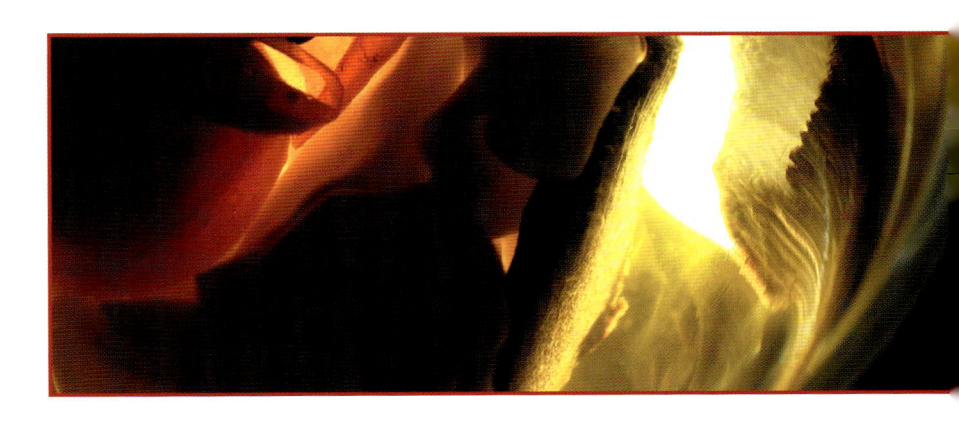

FOR THE CONSOMMÉ

300 gr	roasted smoked orange tomatoes, chopped (see recipe index)
50 gr	celery, diced
50 gr	carrots, diced
50 gr	leeks, chopped
50 gr	onions, chopped
4 pc	whole garlic cloves
3 lt	fish stock
8 pc	egg whites, whipped
100 gr	scallop meat, minced
2 pc	sprigs of rosemary
2 pc	sprigs of thyme
	salt and pepper

Merge all components and mix well to incorporate egg whites. Cook as a traditional consommé and strain.

FOR THE SCALLOPS WONTONS

120 gr	whole scallops
2 pc	egg whites
20 ml	whipping cream
50 gr	scallop meat, diced
30 ml	spring onions, chopped
15 ml	ginger water
	wonton wrappers

Blend the whole scallops with egg whites, cream and season. Add the diced scallop meat and spring onions. Place filling into center of wonton wrapper and fold inwards to form a pocket.

Blanch in salted water for 3 minutes and drain.

Garnish soup with baby tomatoes.

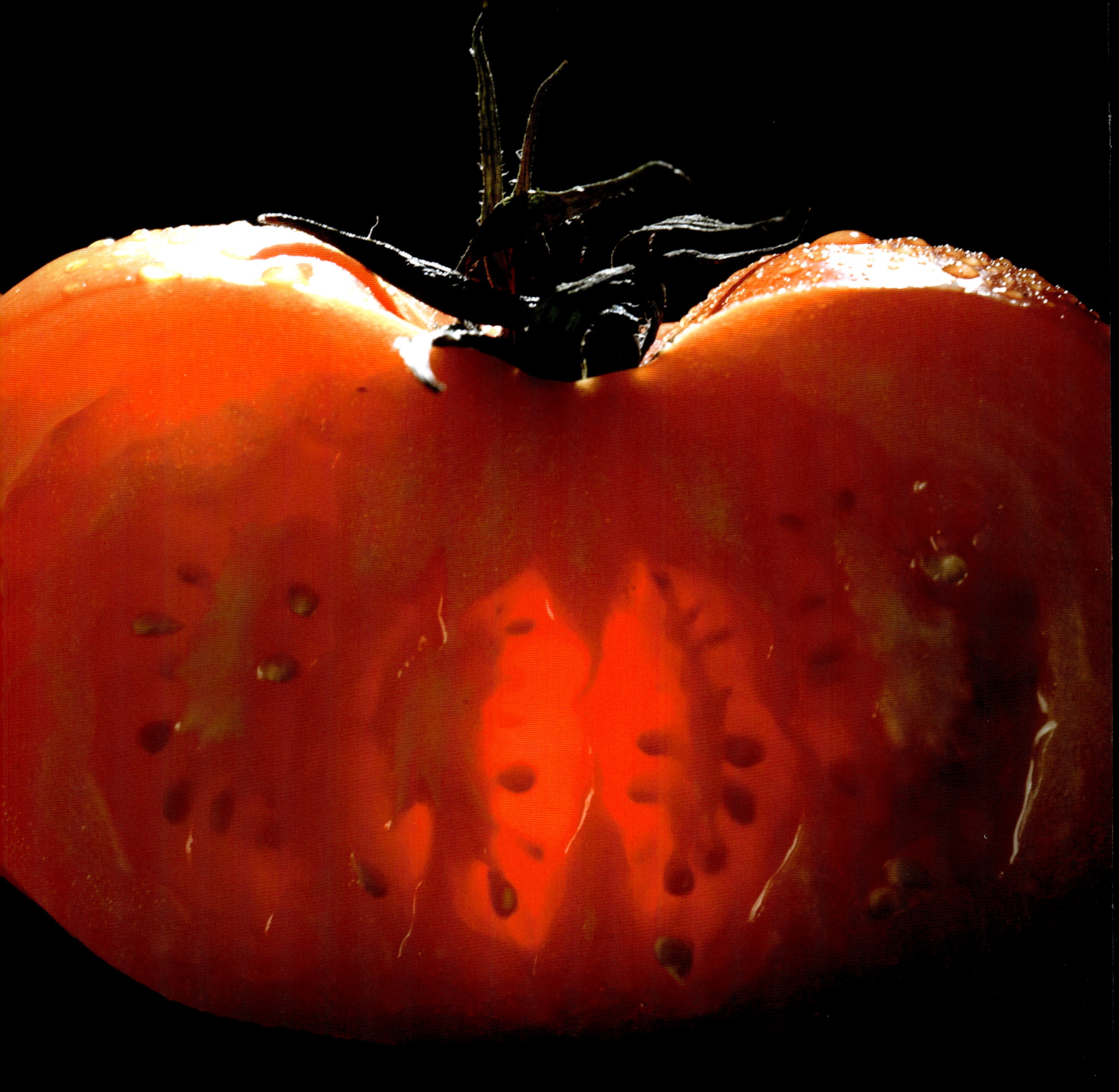

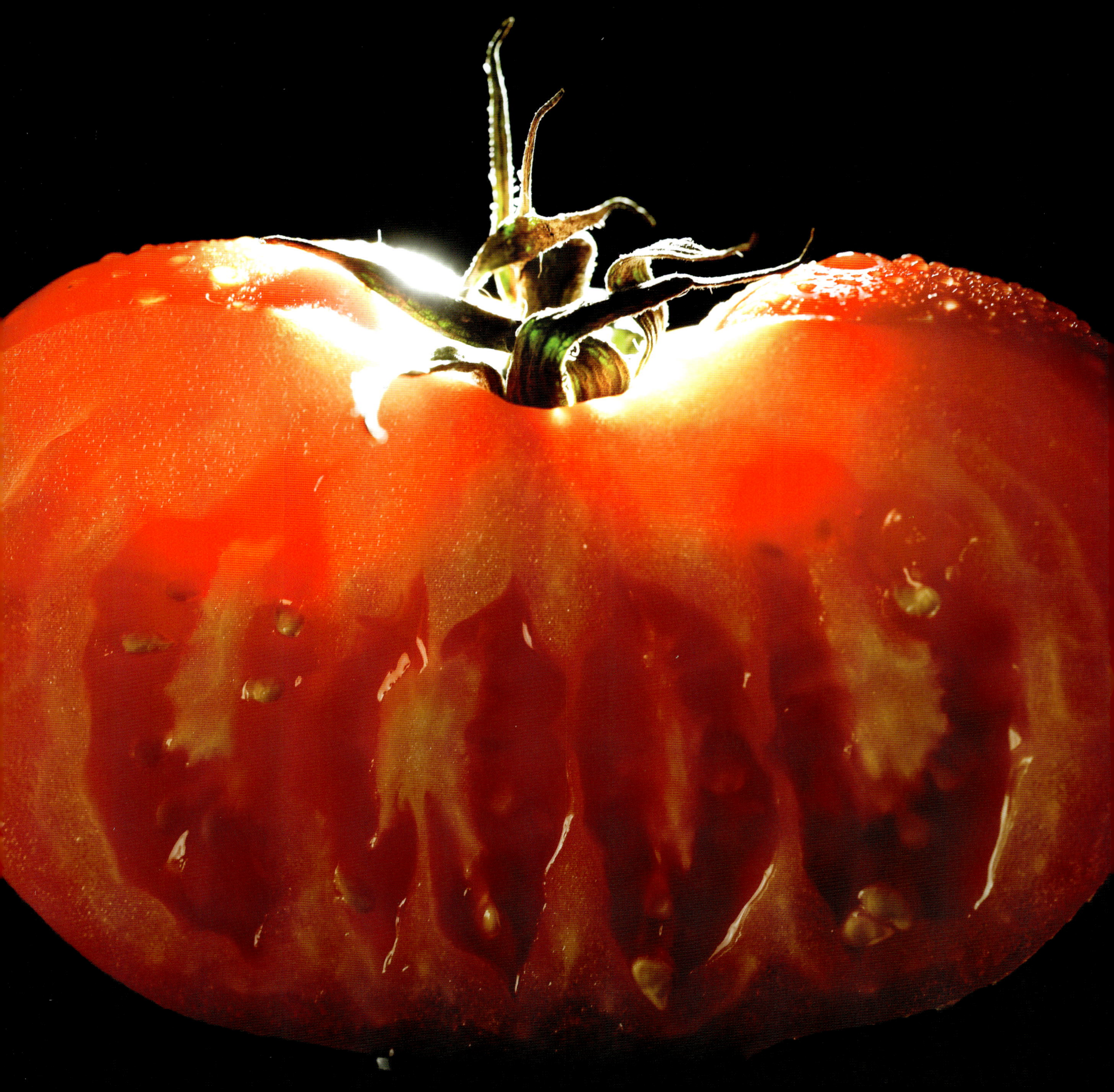

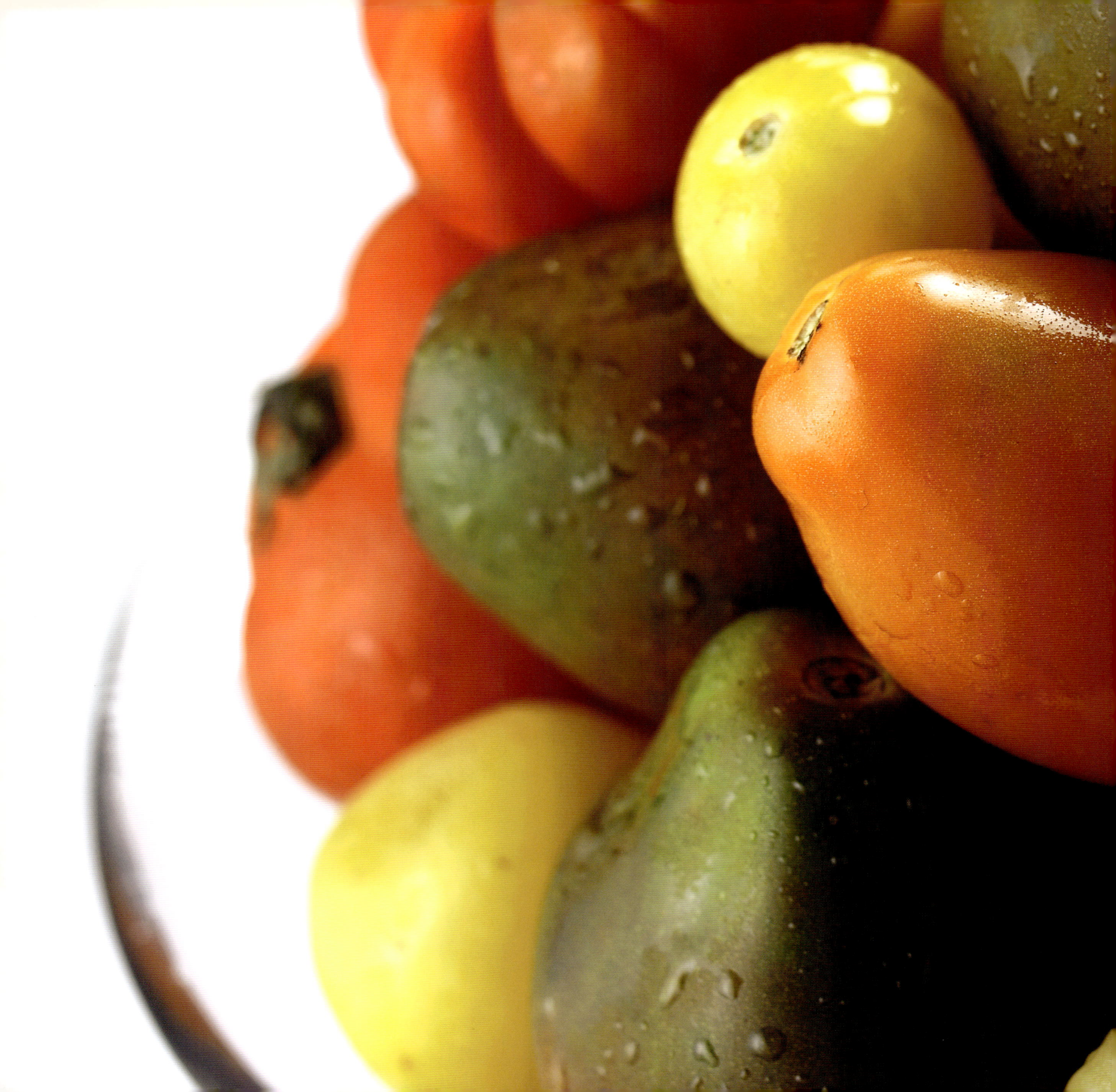

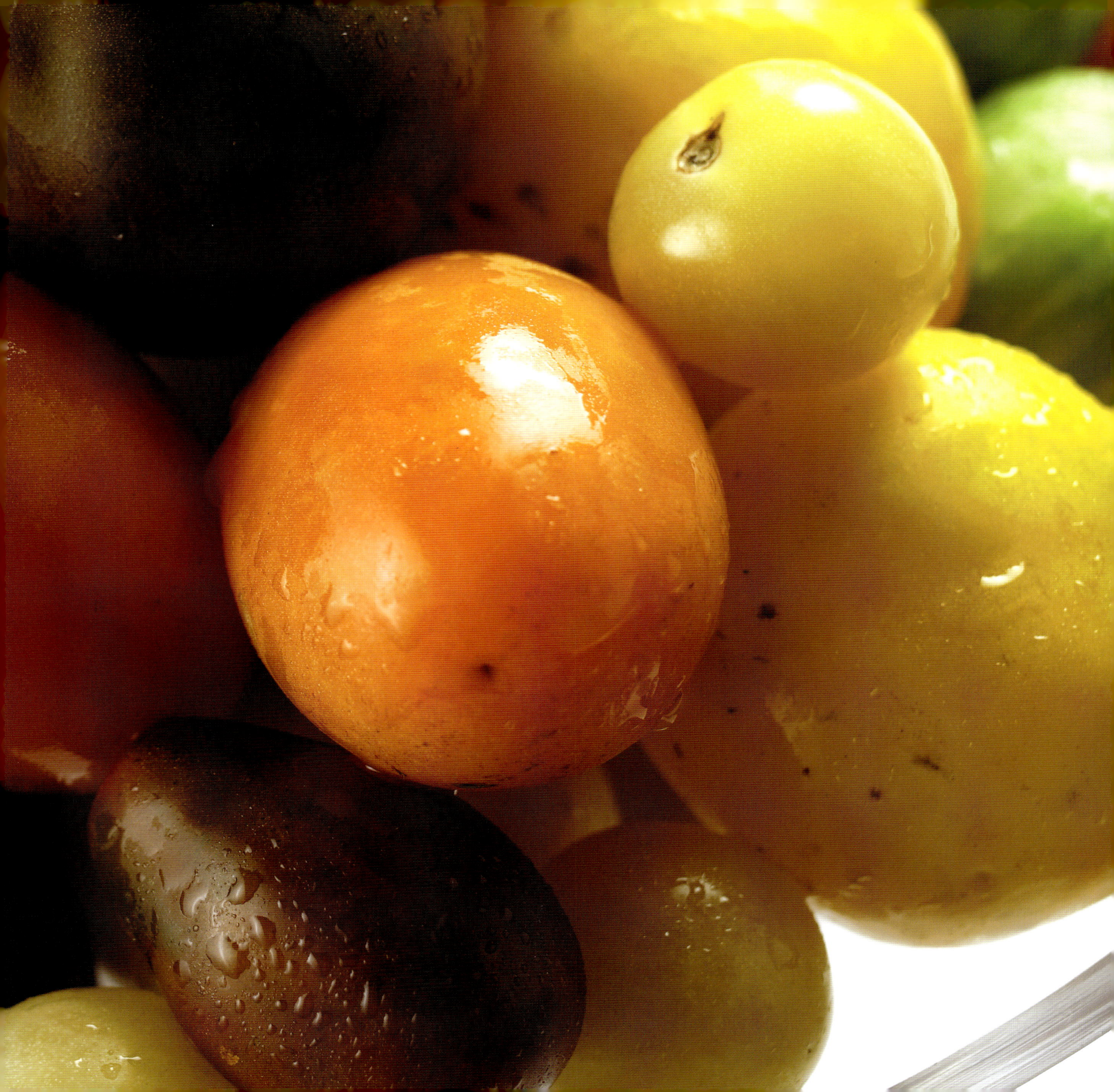

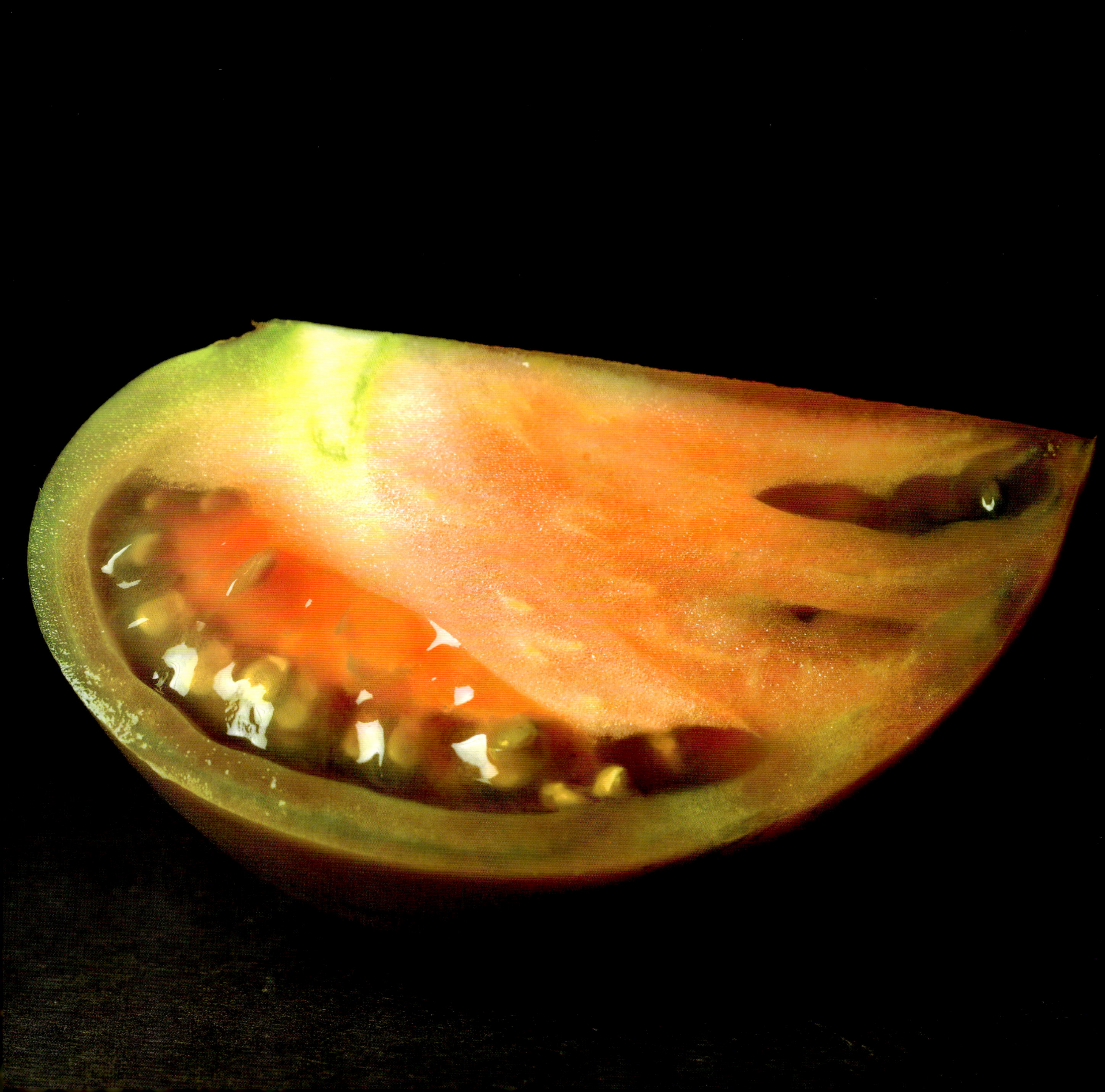

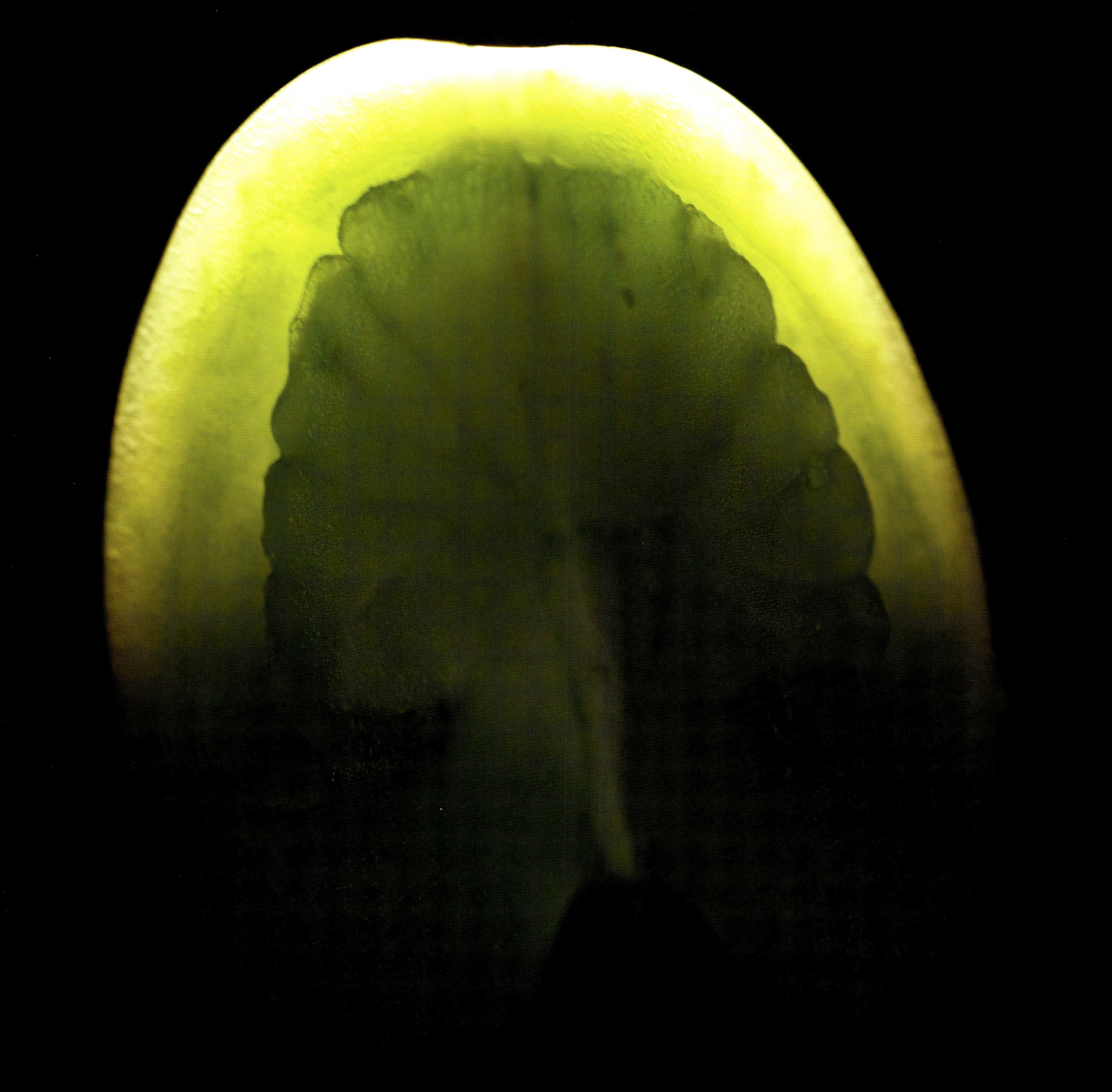

BEEF STEAK TOMATOES AND SMOKED SALMON TARTAR WITH BASIL

FOR THE TARTAR
- 50 gr   tomatoes, diced skinless and seedless
- 50 gr   smoked salmon, diced
- 5 ml   italian parsley, chopped
- 5 ml   basil, chopped
- 20 gr   onions, diced
- 20 ml   lemon juice
- 20 ml   olive oil
- salt and pepper

Merge all components in a large bowl. Season with salt and pepper.

BASIL-BALSAMIC DRESSING
- 200 ml   balsamic vinegar
- 400 ml   olive oil
- 30 ml   dijon mustard
- 5 ml   fresh basil
- salt and pepper

Blend all components and season with salt and pepper.

FOR THE TOMATO TULIP
- 220 gr   flour
- 220 gr   butter
- 200 gr   egg whites
- 30 gr   icing sugar
- 50 ml   tomato paste
- 5 gr   black sesame seeds
- salt

Merge all components and spread onto a greased baking tray to form a circle. Bake at 200° Celsius. When half baked, remove from oven and cut small circles with a ring cutter.
Return to the oven and bake until golden brown.

ASSEMBLY
On a plate, place a ring mold and spoon in the tartar and press lightly with the back of a Drizzle with basil-balsamic dressing.

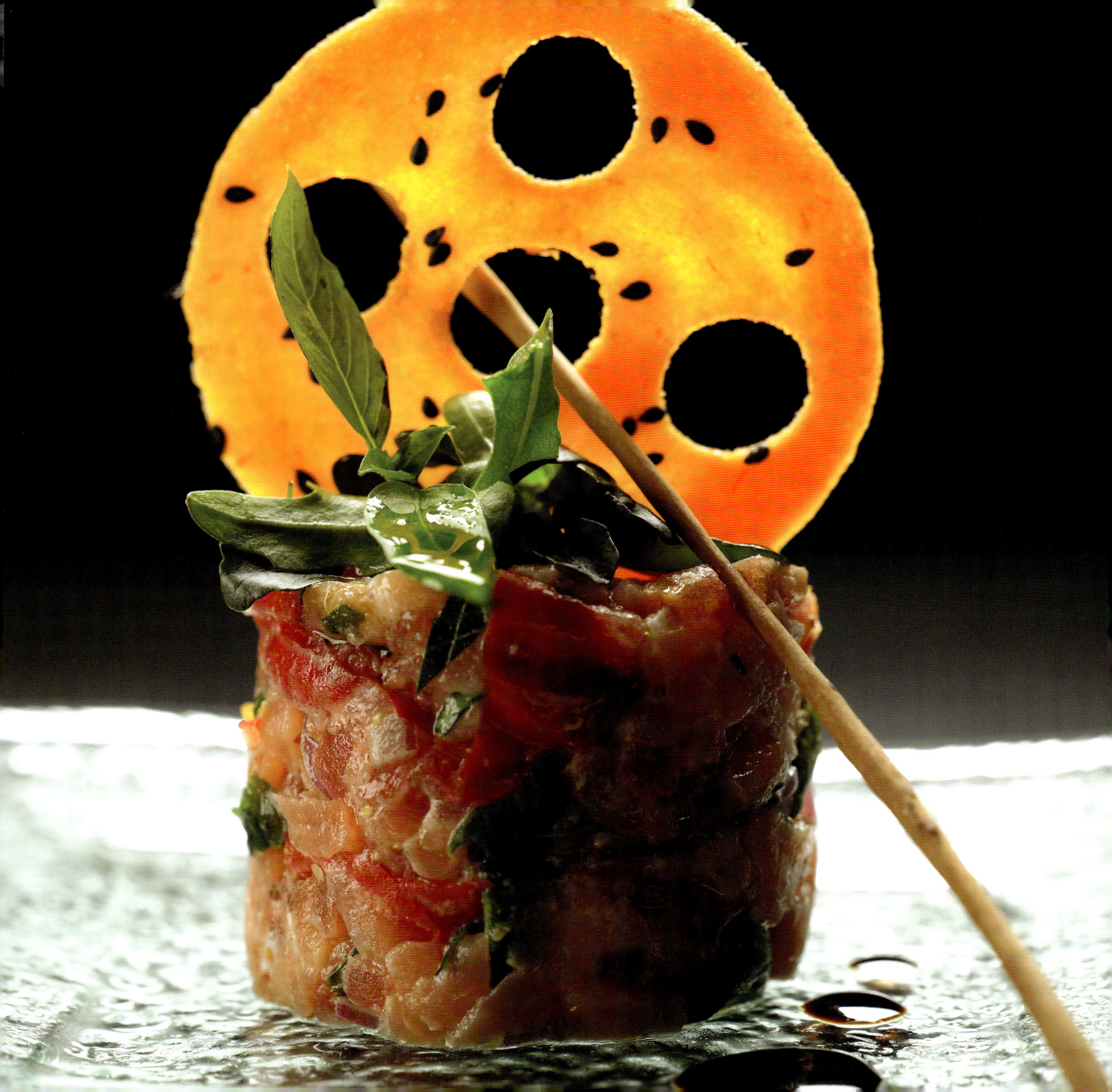

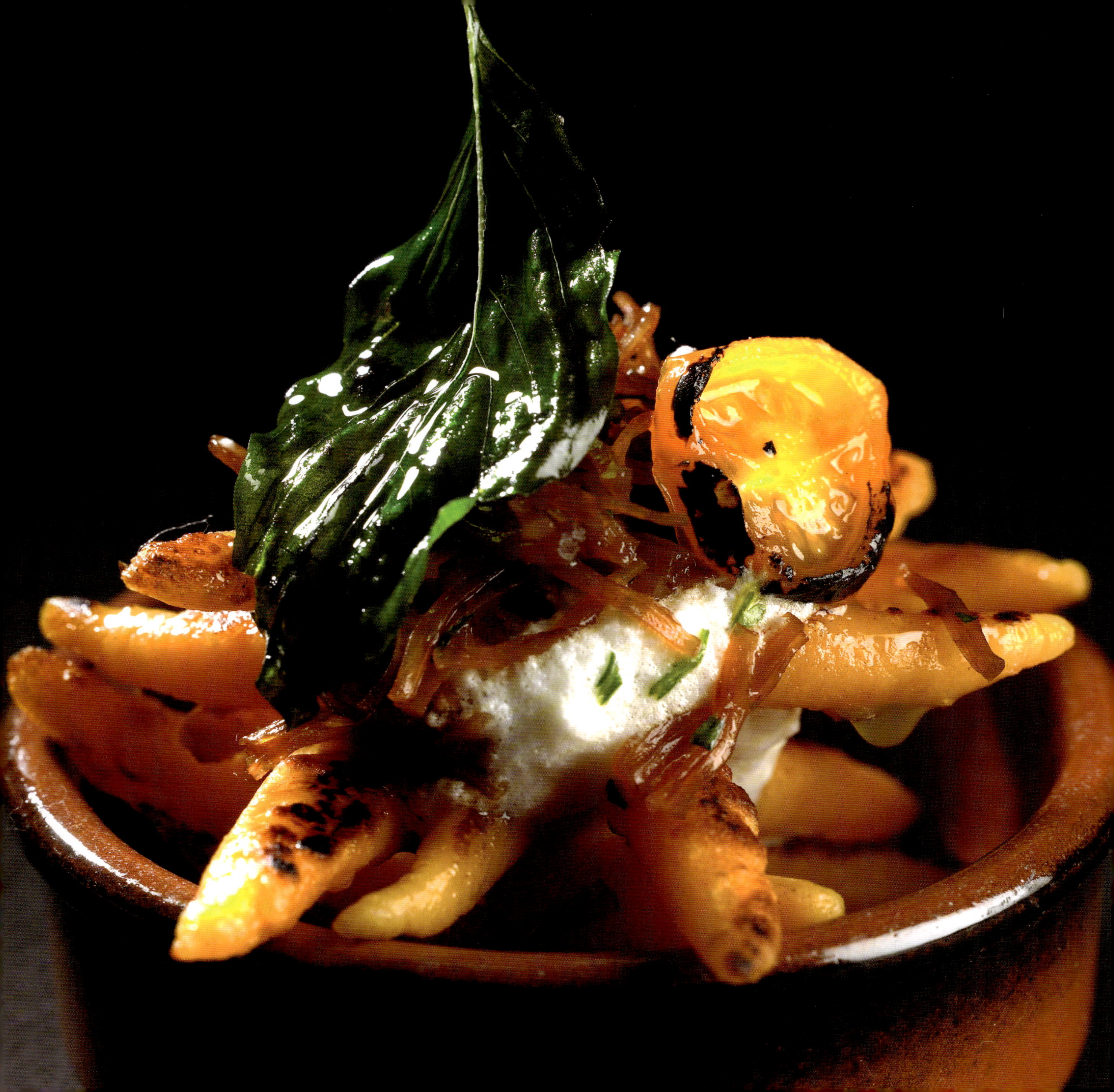

TOMATO GNOCCHI WITH MASCARPONE AND CONPOY

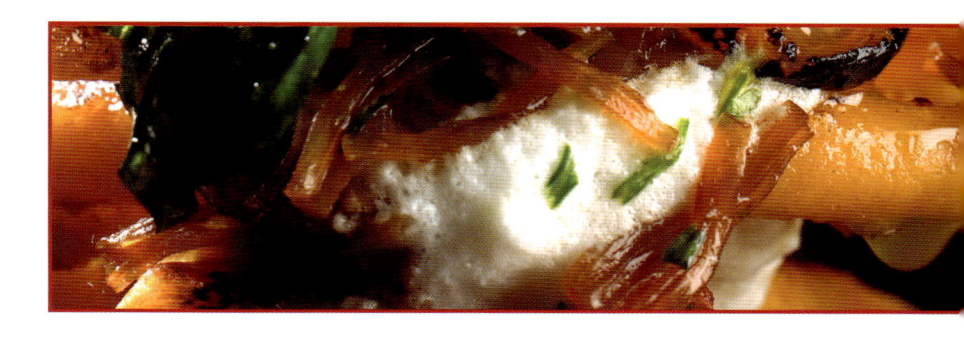

TOMATO GNOCCHI
1 kg	potatoes
300 gr	flour
2 pc	egg yolks
120 gr	tomato paste
60 gr	butter
150 gr	dry white bread crumbs
	salt and pepper

Boil peeled potatoes and drain well, process through a food mill. Merge all ingredients to a dough consistency. Roll gnocchi dough into small finger shaped dumplings and poach in salted water. Drain and pan-fry in butter.

MASCARPONE CREAM
100 ml	whipping cream
50 ml	chicken stock
100 gr	mascarpone cheese
50 ml	white wine
	salt and pepper

Bring cream, wine and stock to a boil for 5 minutes. Blend in mascarpone cheese and season.

BRAISED CONPOY
100 gr	dried scallops (conpoy)
100 ml	soy sauce
20 gr	ginger, chopped
2 pc	garlic cloves
20 ml	peanut oil
100 ml	chinese cooking wine
300 ml	chicken stock

Soak the dried scallops in soy sauce and chicken stock overnight.
Sweat the ginger and garlic in peanut oil. Add all components. Cook over low heat for 1 hour.
Adjust seasoning.

ASSEMBLY
in a serving bowl, spoon in the gnocchi and top with the mascarpone cream and conpoy, garnish with crispy basil.

VALENCIA ORANGE TOMATO RAVIOLI WITH LOBSTER, SAGE AND TOMATO STEW

FOR THE PASTA DOUGH

1 kg	semolina flour
100 gr	orange tomato pulp
8 pc	eggs
25 ml	olive oil

Merge all components to form traditional pasta dough. Cover and let rest for 1 hour before using.
Roll out the pasta dough and cut into 6 cm round disks.
Spoon the filling in the center of the pasta disk and top with another disk of pasta. Using a little egg yolk secure the sides and press edges lightly.
Poach in boiling salted water, remove and toss with a small amount of butter.

FOR THE FILLING

100 gr	lobster meat, cooked chopped
20 gr	whipping cream
20 gr	noilly prat
15 ml	italian parsley, chopped
1 pc	egg white
	salt and pepper

Merge all components and refrigerate for 1 hour.

FOR THE SEMI-DRIED ORANGE TOMATO SAUCE WITH VANILLA

50 gr	semi-dried Valencia orange tomatoes
15 ml	onion, chopped
½ pc	vanilla bean
30 ml	white wine
30 ml	whipping cream
15 ml	butter

Sweat the onion and orange tomatoes in the butter. Deglaze with white wine. Add the vanilla and cream, cook for 2 minutes and let sit in the pot to infuse flavors. Remove vanilla bean and scrape vanilla seeds into sauce. Blend.

LOBSTER SAGE-TOMATO STEW

100 gr	tomatoes, skinless and seedless
50 gr	lobster meat, diced
3 pc	fresh sage leaves, chopped
5 ml	garlic, chopped
30 gr	butter
30 ml	onions, chopped
30 ml	olive oil
	salt and pepper

Sautée the lobster in 15 grams of butter for 2 minutes and remove from the pan. Add remaining butter and all other components to the pan. Cook over low heat for 10 minutes. Return the lobster to the pan and cook for 1 minute. Spoon the stew onto plate and place ravioli on top.

Garnish with crispy parsley.

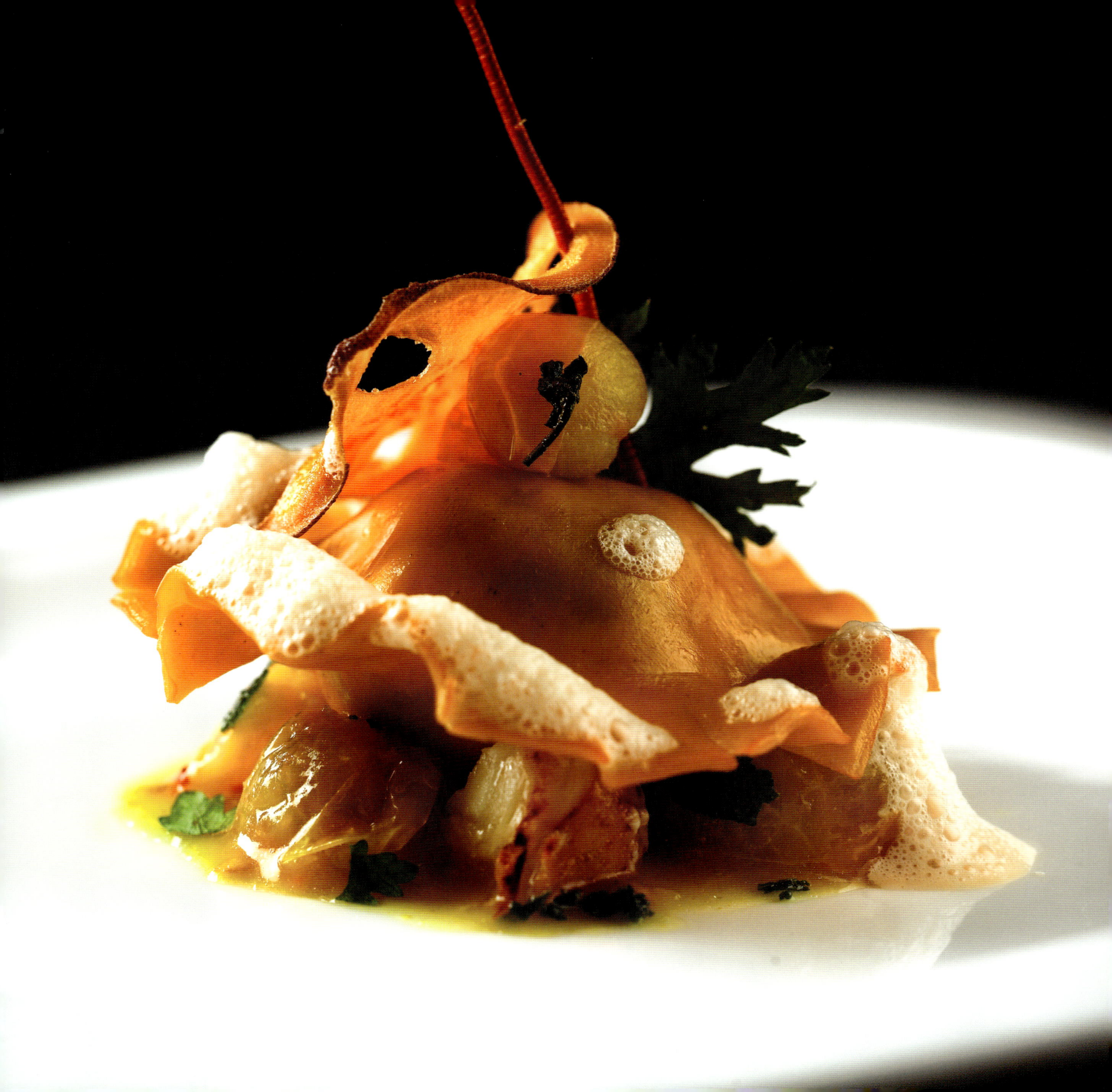

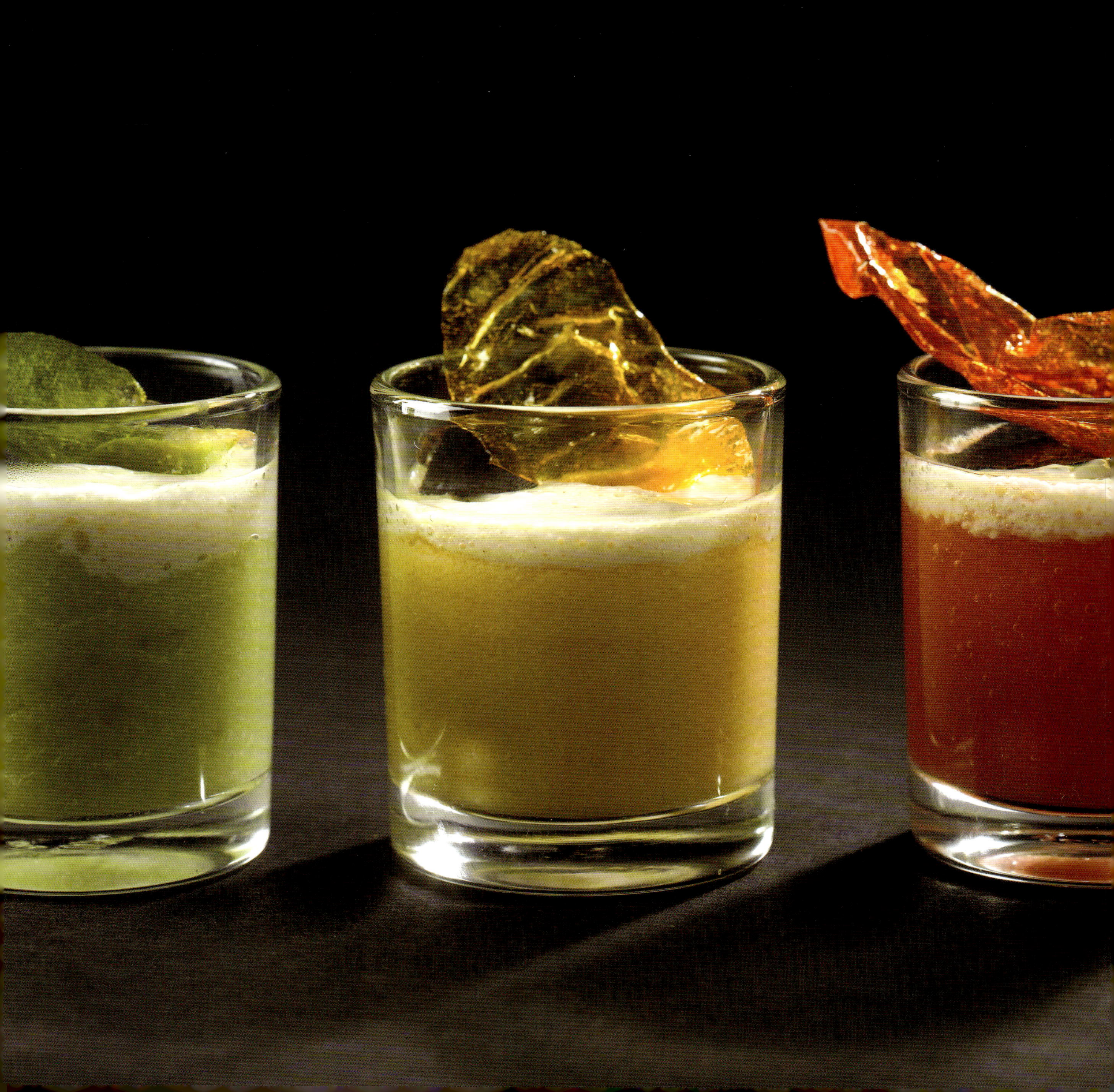

THREE TOMATO PURÉE WITH TRUFFLES

FOR THE GREEN TOMATO PURÉE

100 gr	green tomatoes, skinless and seedless
10 ml	olive oil
5 ml	truffle oil
20 gr	truffle juice
5 gr	truffles, sliced
5 gr	sugar
	salt and pepper

Sweat tomatoes in olive oil. Add remaining components and cook for 10 minutes.
Purée and strain.

RED TOMATO PURÉE

100 gr	red tomatoes, skinless and seedless
10 ml	olive oil
5 ml	truffle oil
20 gr	truffle juice
5 gr	truffles, sliced
5 gr	sugar
	salt and pepper

Sweat tomatoes in olive oil. Add remaining components and cook for 10 minutes.
Purée and strain.

YELLOW TOMATO PURÉE

100 gr	yellow tomatoes, skinless and seedless
10 ml	olive oil
5 ml	truffle oil
20 gr	truffle juice
5 gr	truffles, sliced
5 gr	sugar
	salt and pepper

Sweat tomatoes in olive oil. Add remaining components and cook for 10 minutes.
Purée and strain.

BLACK TRUFFLE CHANTILLY CREAM

60 gr	double cream
20 gr	truffle juice
50 gr	white wine
50 gr	chicken stock
5 gr	truffle, chopped
	salt and pepper

Reduce chicken stock and wine to 1/3rd. Add truffle juice and double cream and simmer until thick. Blend.

BLOODY MARY TOMATO

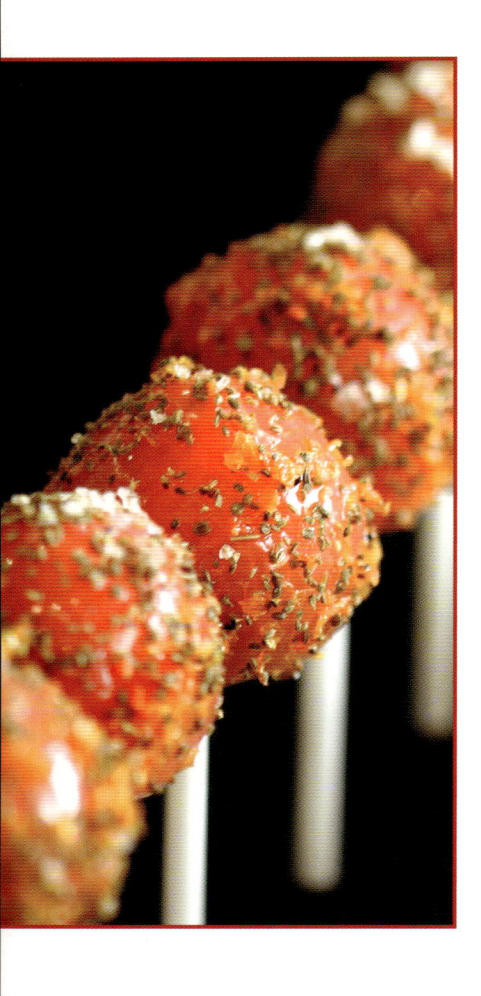

FOR THE TOMATOES
- 60 gr   vodka jelly
- 5 ml   tabasco
- 150 gr   tomato juice
- 15 ml   lemon juice
- 10 ml   worchestershire sauce
- 30 ml   celery juice

Mix tomato juice, Worcestershire, celery juice and Tabasco. Season.
Blanch the cherry tomatoes for 5 seconds in boiling salted water and plunge into ice water. Remove skins. Make a small incision to remove the juice and some of the pulp. Place on lollipop sticks. Using a syringe fill tomato juice into the skewered tomatoes.

VODKA JELLY
- 50 gr   vodka
- 7 gr   gelatin leaves
- 50 ml   celery stock

Bring 25gr of vodka to a boil and flambé. Add the remaining vodka and the celery stock. Reduce heat and add soaked gelatin leaves to dissolve.

ASSEMBLY
Dip the tomatoes in the vodka jelly and sprinkle with celery seed, rock salt and black pepper. Roll in tomato flakes.

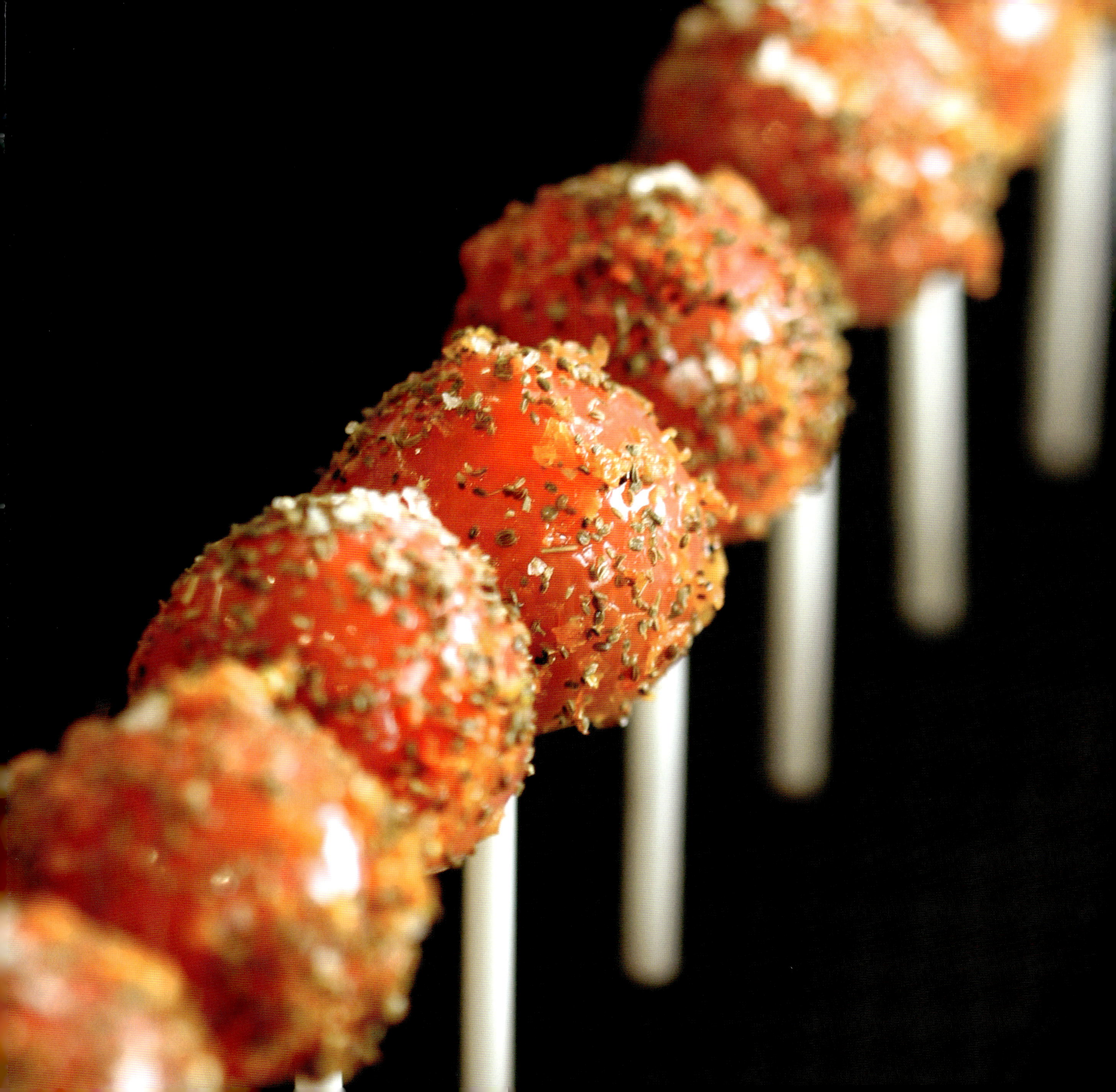

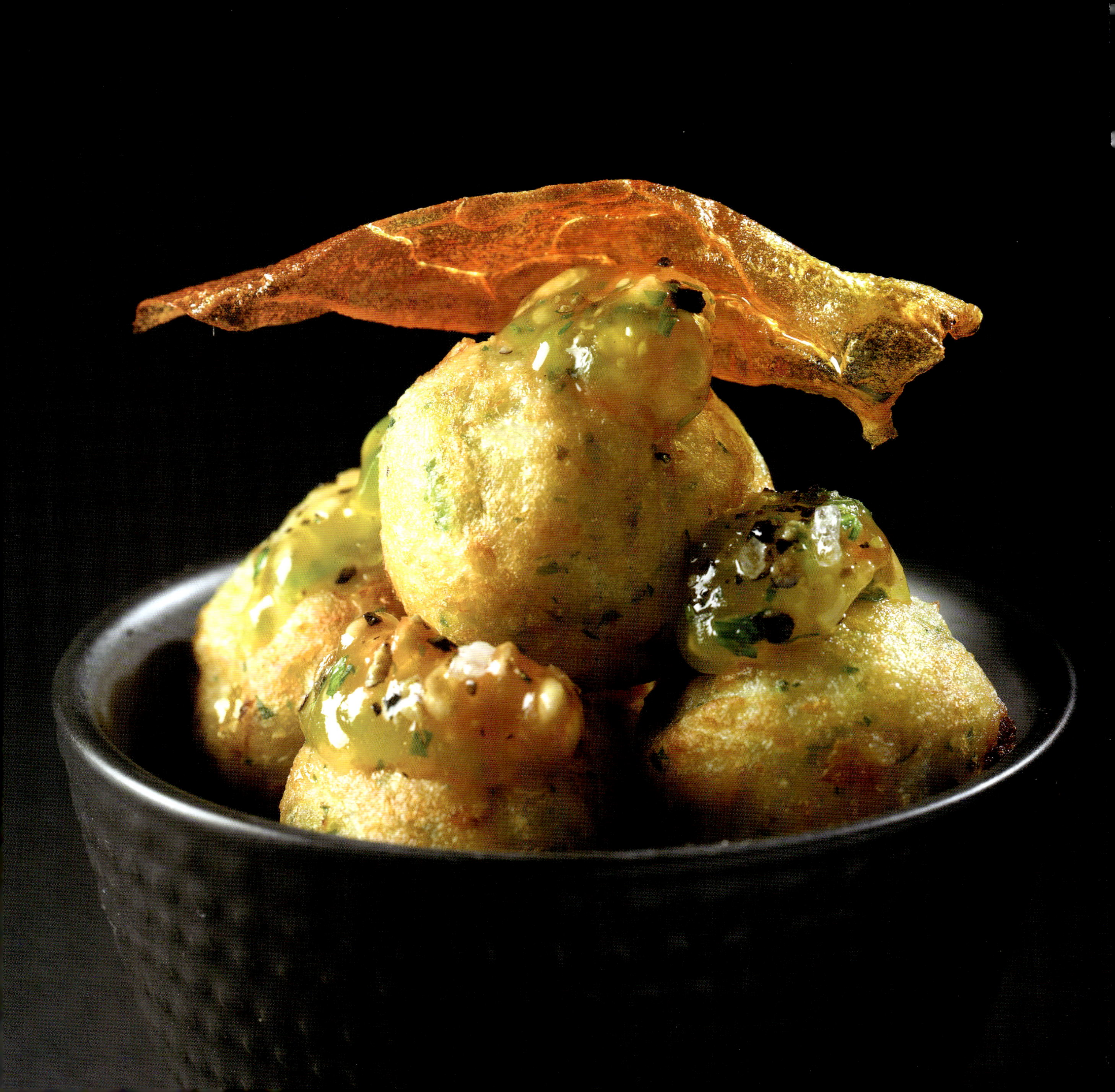

BACALAO DUMPLINGS WITH WARM TOMATO PULP

BACALAO DUMPLINGS

200 gr	steamed and flaked salted cod
150 gr	choux pastry dough
50 gr	onions, chopped
50 gr	heirloom tomatoes, diced
10 gr	parsley, chopped
	salt and pepper

Merge all components and refrigerate for 1 hour. When chilled, form small ball shapes and deep fry to a golden brown. Spoon tomato pulp over the dumplings and decorate with flat leaf parsley

CHOUX PASTRY DOUGH

250 gr	butter
500 gr	water
250 gr	flour
10 gr	sugar
5 gr	salt
8 pc	whole eggs

Bring water, sugar and salt to a boil and add the butter. Reduce the heat and stir in the flour while continuously stirring. When flour is fully incorporated, cook for 2 more minutes.
Remove from heat and allow to cool slightly before adding the eggs one at a time while
continuing to stir.

TOMATO PULP

50 gr	heirloom tomatoes, skinless and chopped
10 gr	garlic, chopped
30 ml	olive oil
	rock salt and pepper

Heat the oil and sweat the garlic for two minutes. Add the tomatoes and season. Set aside in a warm place to allow the flavors to blend.

CHILLED OX HEART TOMATO MARTINI

FOR THE ICE CUBES
200 gr   ox heart tomatoes
1 pc   rosemary
500 ml   tomato water

Cook all components for 5 minutes. Blend and strain. Pour into ice cube trays and freeze.

FOR TOMATO WATER
Place 1 kg of tomatoes in cheese cloth and crush by hand.
Hang to drain for 24 hours.

FOR THE MARTINI
30 ml   gin
30 ml   vermouth
60 ml   tomato water
10 ml   campari

Merge all components.
Add the frozen tomato cubes, olives and serve.

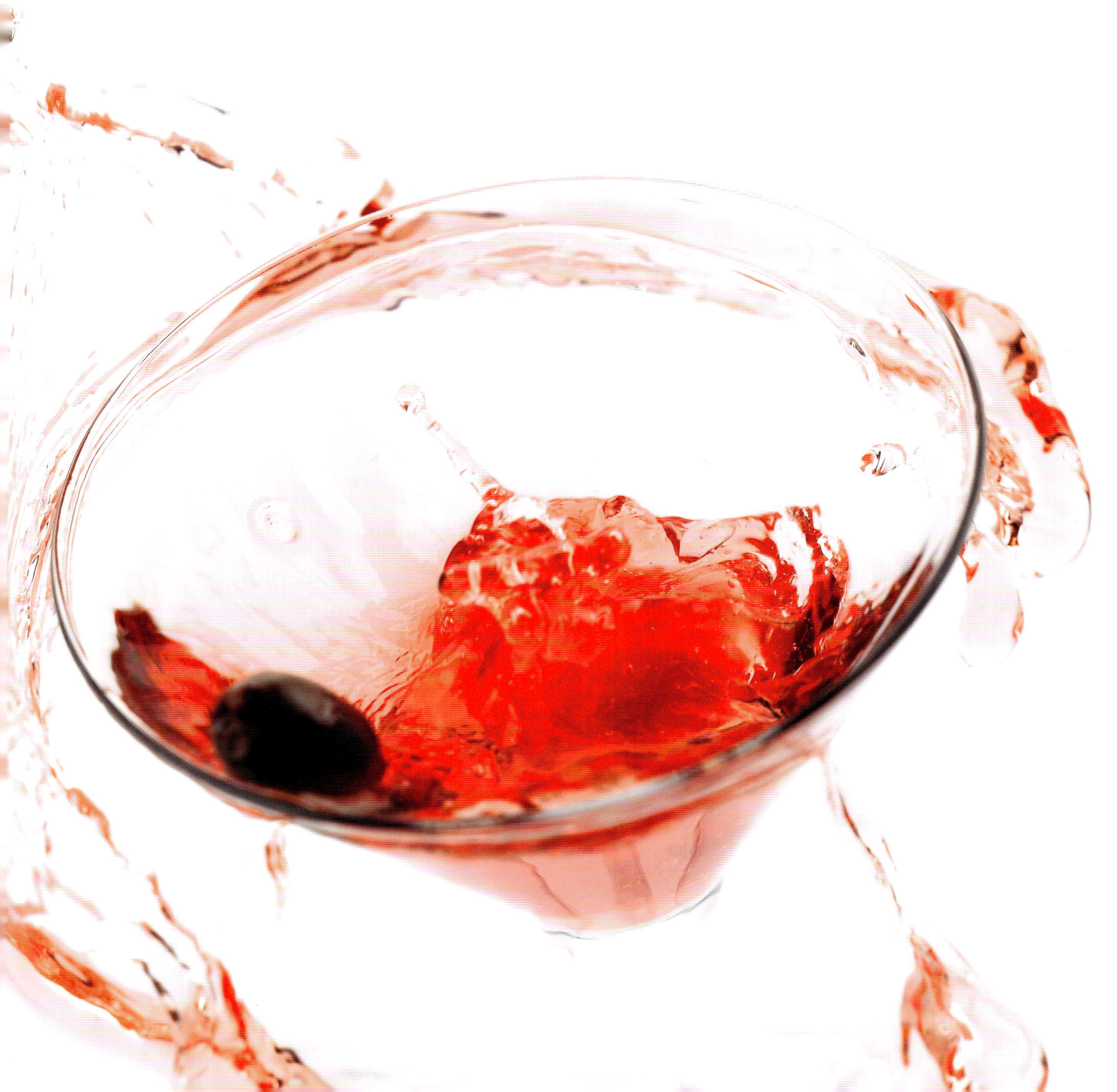

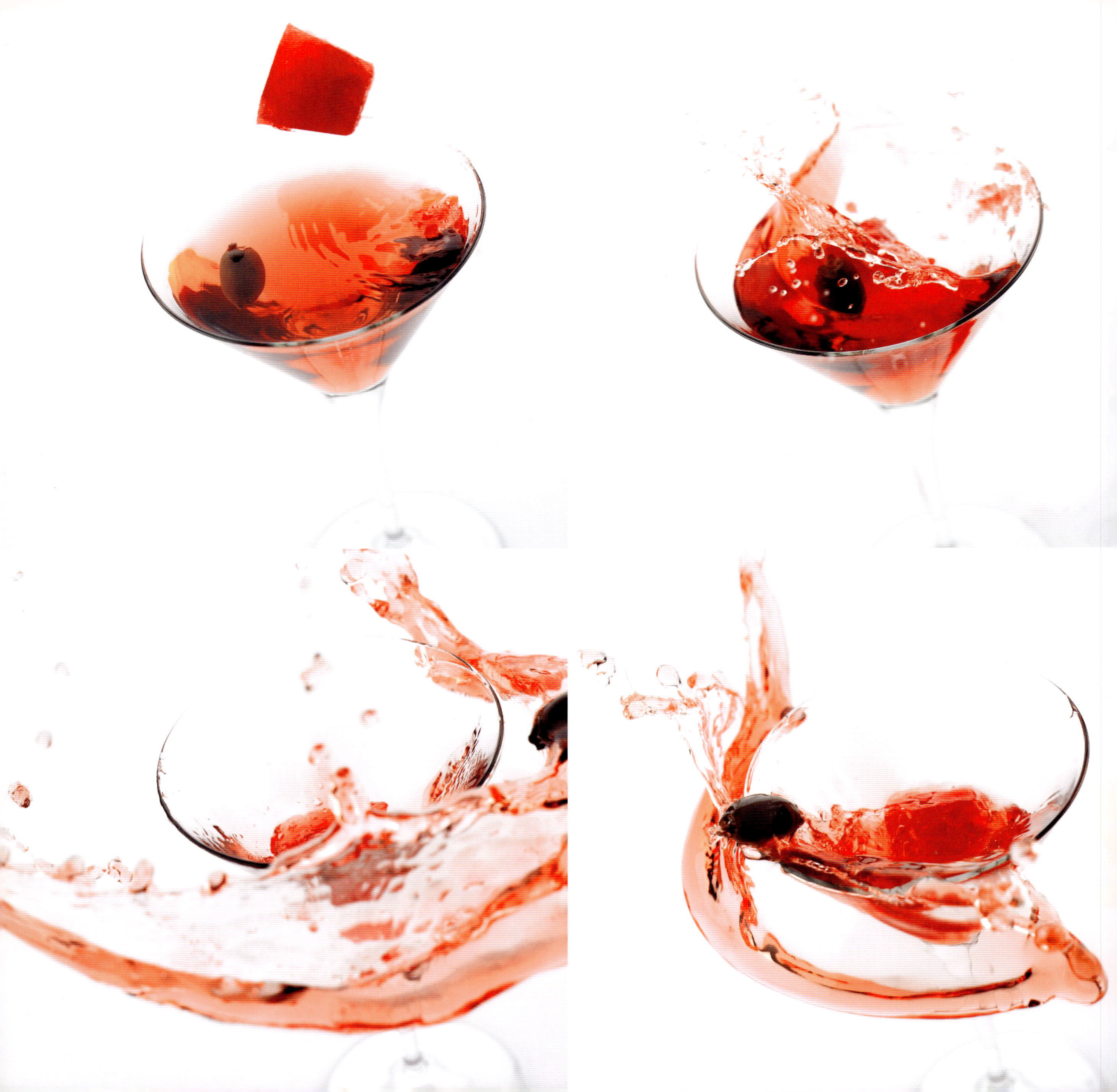

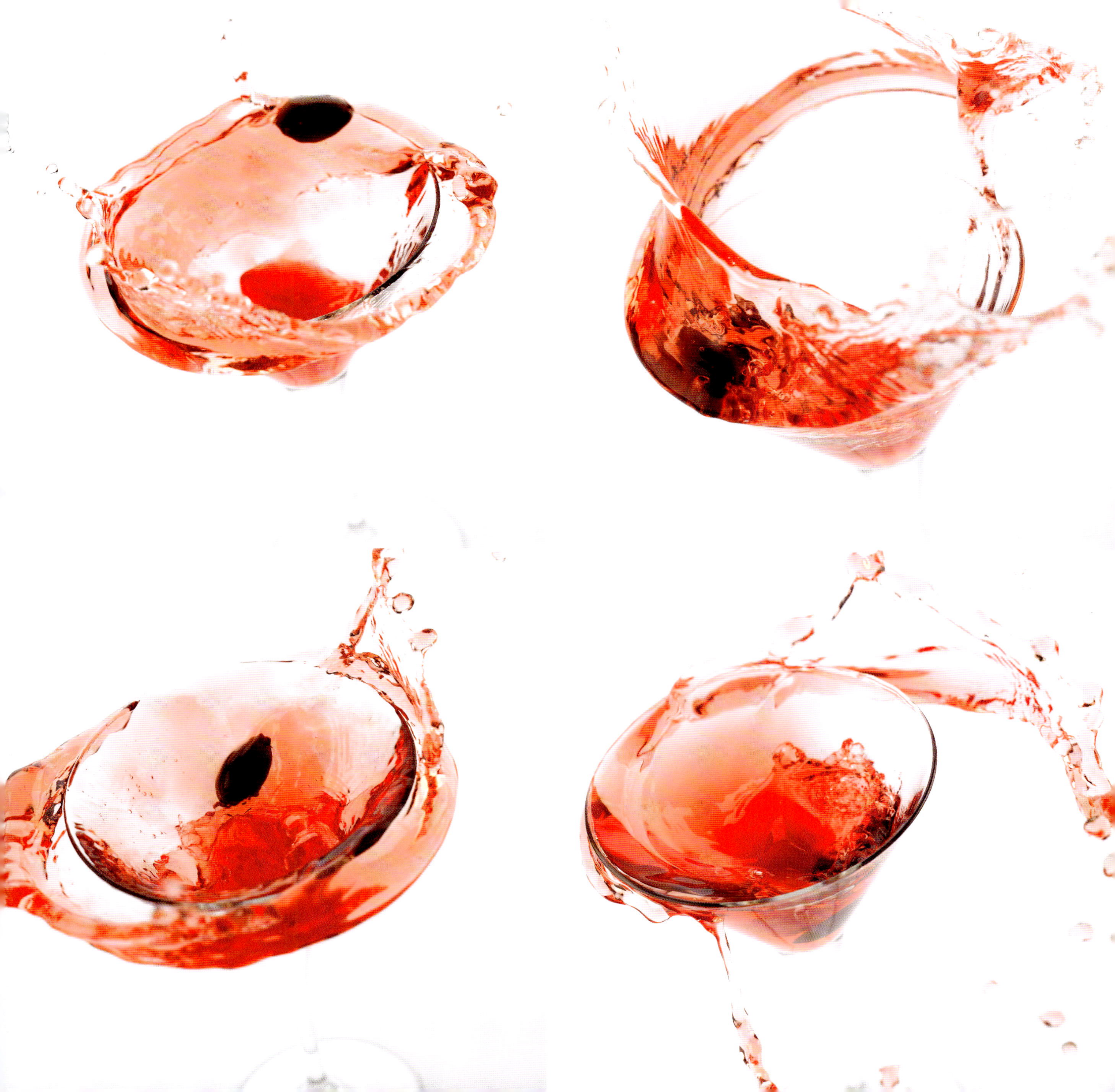

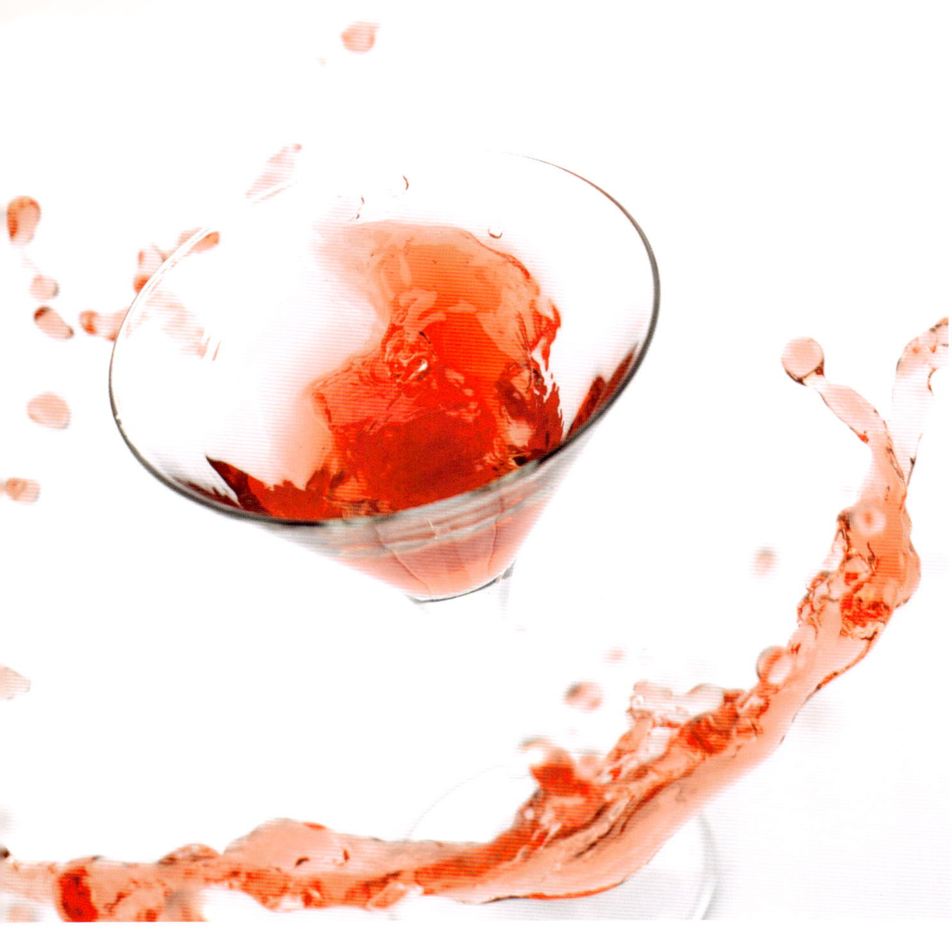
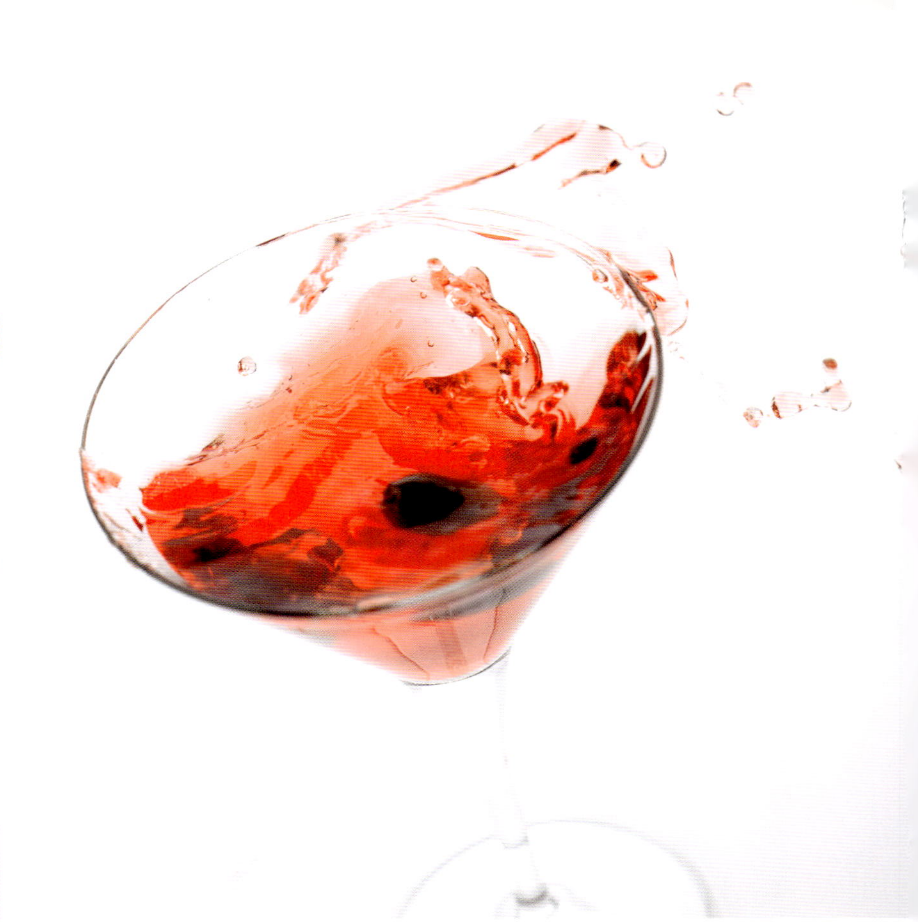
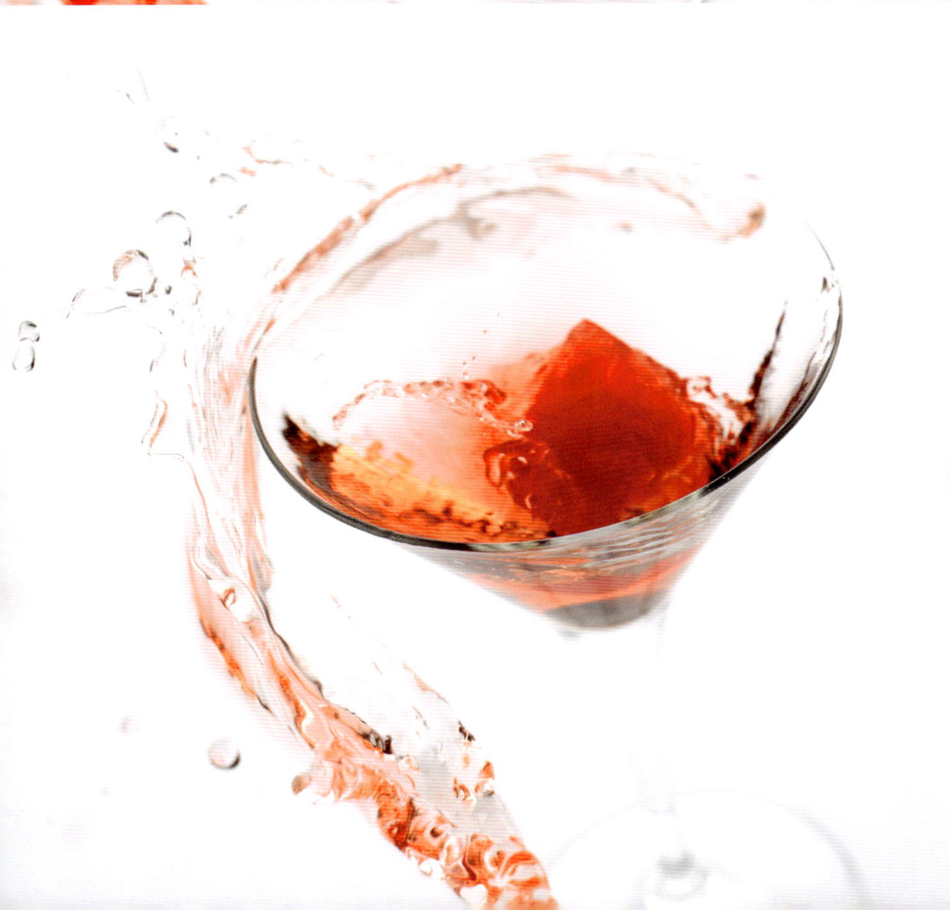
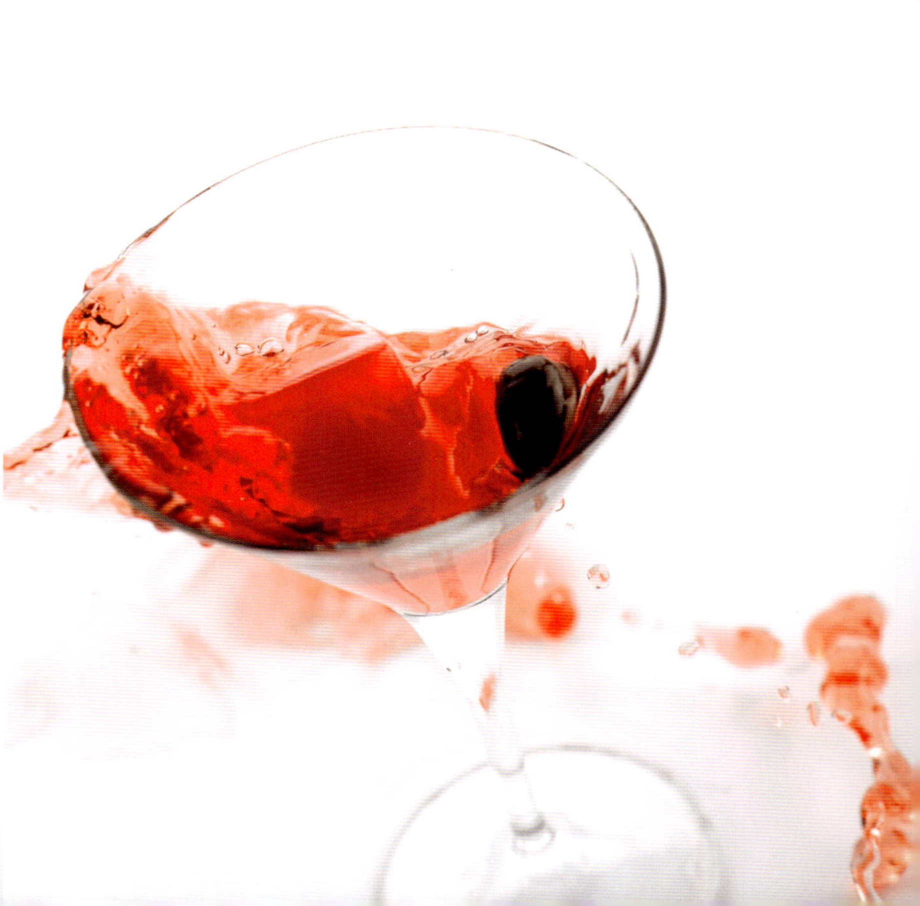

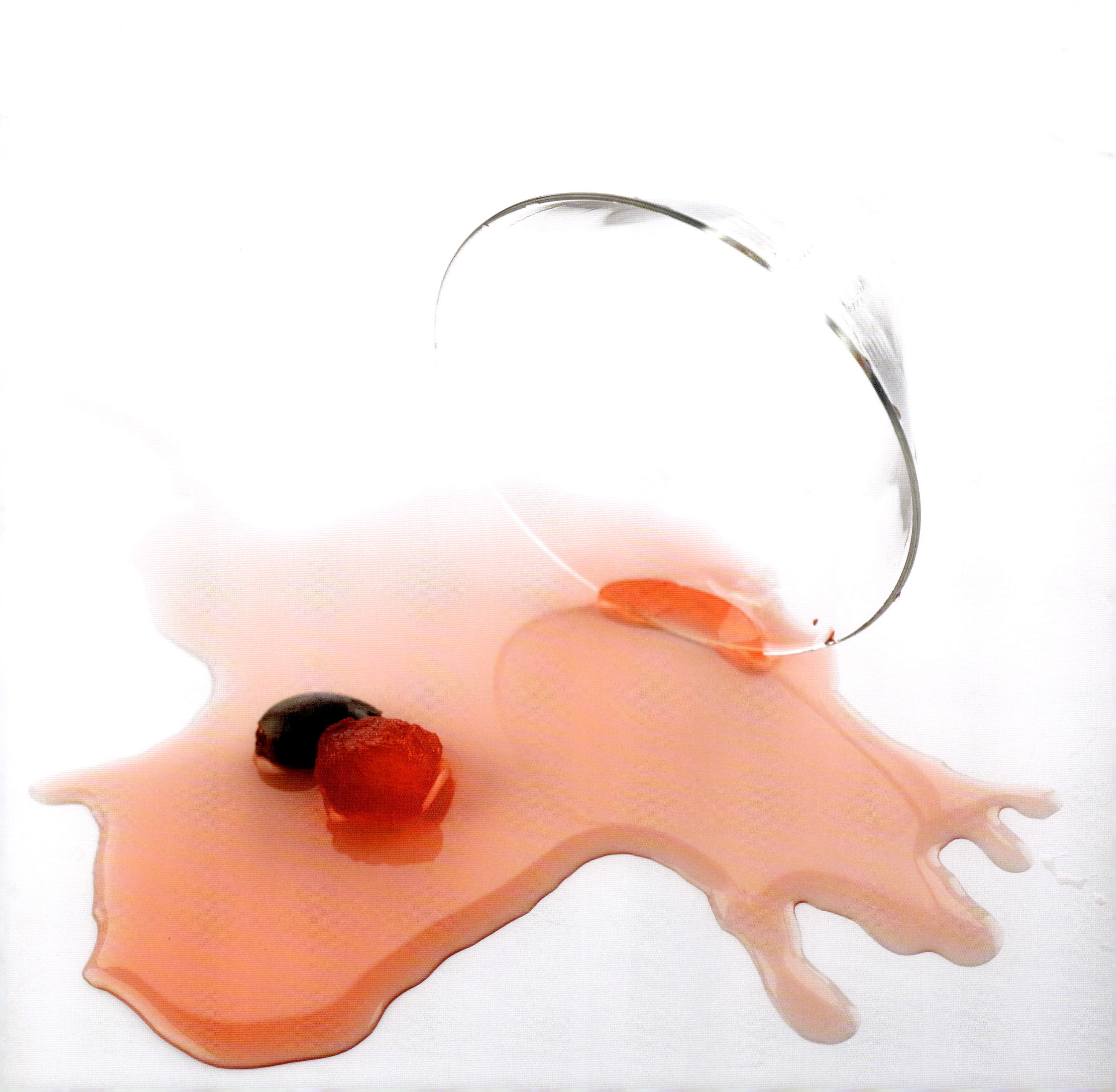

Santa Lucia Grape, bell shaped, sweet and flavorful. Gets sweeter in hotter weather

Kumato, European black tomato with sweet complex flavor

Matt's Wild Cherry, small in size but packs a big tomato flavor

Yellow Lollipop, tart-lemony flavor with a hint of sweetness

Momotaro, Japanese pink fleshed tomato, sweet, firm with great shelf life

Coustralee, European heirloom, deep red color with intense tomato flavor

Green Zebra, the original heirloom with a tangy lingering flavor. Great on its own or in salads

German Pink, very meaty heirloom with excellent flavor and very little seeds

Pineapple Heirloom, large bicolor red and yellow with sweet intense flavor

Mountain Spring, a beef steak tomato, meaty, firm and flavorful

Purple Calabash, The most truly purple tomato available, uniquely shaped with a rich flavor

Tigerella, colorful tomato with smooth skin and great flavor

Mixed Currant Tomatoes, these tiny varieties are colorful, acidic and crisp

Pink Dandy, an Asian variety of the Roma, but smaller yet meaty with great flavor

Cherokee Purple, an heirloom with soft flesh and a lot of juice

Mixed Treasure Chest Heirlooms, great mixture of heirlooms each variety with its own distinctive flavor

Emerald Green, meaty and fruity tomato

Organic Beef Steak, large solid fruit, a chef's favorite for its great flavor and long shelf life

Spring Tomatoes, meaty firm tomato with well balanced flavor

Red, Yellow and Orange 100's, intense sweet in flavors

Micro Sugar Lumps, a rainbow of colors packed with flavor

Super Snow White, very sweet, ivory colored tomatoes, about the size of a ping pong ball

Banana Legs, banana shaped with very few seeds and a bold sweet flavor

Black Pear, similar to Bartlett pear, very meaty with sweet flesh

Plum Lemon, canary yellow, grows to about 3 inches, looks like a lemon. It has a very refreshing flavor

Yellow Flammè, a well balanced tomato, sweet and salty, ideal in salads and appetizers

Garden Peach, a special heirloom, sweet yellow tomato with a fuzzy peach like skin

Red Wonder Boy, meaty flesh with a great tomato favor

Kaleidoscope Ox Heart, bicolor with strong flavors

Pink Heirloom, versatile meaty tomato with very few seeds and excellent flavor

Bicolor Heirloom, wonderful flesh exploding with flavor

Red Copia, stunning tomato with red and gold streaks, juicy with great flavor

RECIPES

ACHIOTE MARINADE

40 gr	achiote paste
60 gr	orange juice
5 gr	chopped ginger
5 gr	chopped cilantro
10 gr	sugar

Blend all ingredients in a high speed blender until smooth.

BALSAMIC REDUCTION

1 lt	balsamic vinegar
50 gr	honey
150 ml	port wine
2 pc	bay leaf
1 pc	rosemary sprig

Cook and reduce to 300 ml. Strain.

BARLEY COUS COUS

200 gr	barley flour
100 gr	semolina flour
4	whole eggs

Mix all ingredients together to form dough. Cover and refrigerate for 2 hours. Remove from refrigerator and grate with a medium hole grater.

DASHI

1 lt	cold water
40 gr	konbu-kelp with a few knife cuts to release the flavor
30 gr	large bonito flakes

Boil the water and konbu for 10 minutes. Strain. Return to the stove and bring to a boil and add bonito. Simmer for 2 minutes. Remove from heat rest for 10 minutes. Strain.
Use dashi as a stock for soups and sauces.

RED WINE VINAIGRETTE

400 ml	olive oil
200 ml	red wine vinegar
1 pc	clove of garlic chopped
5 ml	basil leaves chopped
	Salt and pepper

Merge all components.

SHERRY VINAIGRETTE

300 ml	sherry vinegar
600 ml	olive oil
20 ml	dijon mustard
1 pc	garlic clove, chopped
	salt and pepper

Merge all components.

SMOKED ORANGE TOMATOES

200 gr	peeled and seeded orange tomatoes
30 ml	fresh thyme
	rock salt

Lay the tomatoes on a baking tray and liberally season with salt and sprinkle with thyme leaves.
Place tomatoes in a 'hot smoker' with apple wood chips for 15 minutes.
Cover with plastic and refrigerate for 5 hours.

TOMATO PASTE

5 kg	tomatoes
300 ml	olive oil
	salt

Blanch the tomatoes in salted water. Plunge in ice water and remove peel and seeds. Chop the tomatoes and place in a colander for one hours to remove the liquid.
Heat olive oil and add chopped tomatoes and salt.
Cook over low heat for 3 hours. Remove and puree while still hot. Return to stove and cook for an additional 1 hour.

TOMATO SEED OIL

200 g	tomato seeds
200 ml	grape seed oil
1 pc	rosemary sprig

Heat half the oil and add the tomato seeds, cook over low heat for 20 minutes. Remove from the heat and add remaining oil and rosemary.
Leave to infuse for 24 hours.

TOMATO TULIP

450 gr	flour
450 gr	butter
400 gr	egg white
80 gr	icing sugar
30 ml	tomato paste
	salt

Merge all components and spread on a greased baking tray forming a circle. Bake at 200° C until half cooked. Remove from oven and cut small circles with a ring cutter.
Return to oven and continue to bake until golden.

WHITE BALSAMIC DRESSING

200 ml	white balsamic vinegar
400 ml	olive oil
30 ml	dijon mustard
	salt and pepper

Merge all components.

COMPONENT DESCRIPTIONS

CHICK PEA FLOUR
can be found in most Indian stores.

BALSAMIC REDUCTION
a great finish to almost any salad, only a few drops is enough.

TOMATO WATER
cut tomatoes into quarters and wrap in a clean towel. Squeeze with your hands for 2 minutes and then hang it to drain for 24 hours.

TOMATO FLAKES
crush dried tomato skins to a small flake, they're ideal for crusting fish and meat.

TOMATO PASTE
can be made from a variety of different tomatoes although certain types of tomatoes are more suitable as they contain less juice and are meatier.

TOMATO CHIPS
tomato skins deep fried until crispy. Season with salt and pepper, they have a natural sweet flavor and work wonders as a garnish.

BRUCCIO CHEESE
a soft cheese curd indigenous to Corsica; it's versatile and generally used in the same way as ricotta.

BOCCONCINI CHEESE
soft bite size mozzarella.

SWEETBREADS
the thymus gland of milk-fed veal or young calves.

KNÖDEL
a bread dumpling consisting of day old bread.

BARLEY COUSCOUS
pasta style dough made from semolina.

WON TON SKINS
thin pliable Asian dough sheets made of flour, eggs and water. They can be boiled or deep fried.

GNOCCHI
a small potato or semolina dumpling.

SALSIFY
a long parsnip-shaped root vegetable.

BACALAO
salted cod fish, used in Mediterranean cuisine. The fish must be soaked in three changes of water to extract the salt. It is usually steamed or grilled.

SOY BEAN FLOUR
used extensively in Japanese cuisine, it has a sweet nutty flavor.

CRUMPET
also known as thousand hole bread, usually served with butter and syrups.

JALOUSIE
French style pastry usually filled with fruit and jam.

BILTONG
a South African dried meat jerky which can be comprised of any number of animals. The meat is marinated, spiced and air-dried for at least seven days.

CONPOY
dried scallop used mostly in Cantonese cuisine. It has a strong flavor that works well with spiced sauces or as a condiment with vegetables.

FEUILLE DE BRICK
thin French dough pastry usually sold in large round sheets. The texture is similar to Asian spring roll wrappers but is more suited for baking or pan-frying. Can be found in specialty food stores.

BUCKWHEAT FLOUR
or kasha flour is used mostly for soba noodles and blinis.

DASHI
a Japanese stock used for soups and sauces.

SEMI DRIED TOMATOES
are well seasoned with salt and pepper, fresh herbs and garlic and slow dried at 60° Celsius up to ten hours, they can generally be purchased prepared in most delicatessens.

SUN DRIED TOMATOES
can be purchased in delicatessens or specialty stores, they posses a very intense flavor.

AFRICAN BASIL
a hybrid basil that can grow up to four feet tall, younger leaves are used much like green or purple basil, thicker leaves are mainly used for decorative purposes.

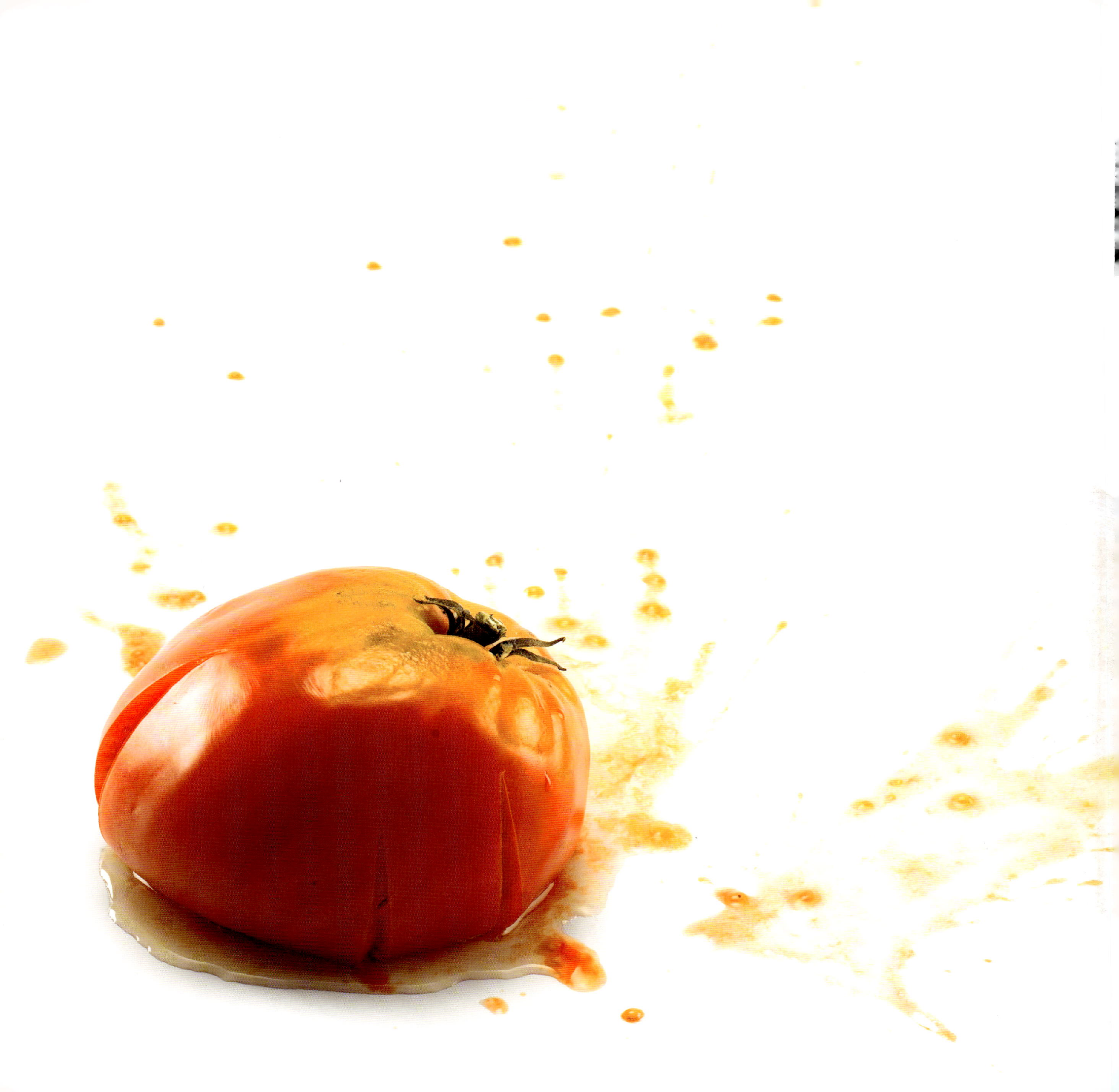

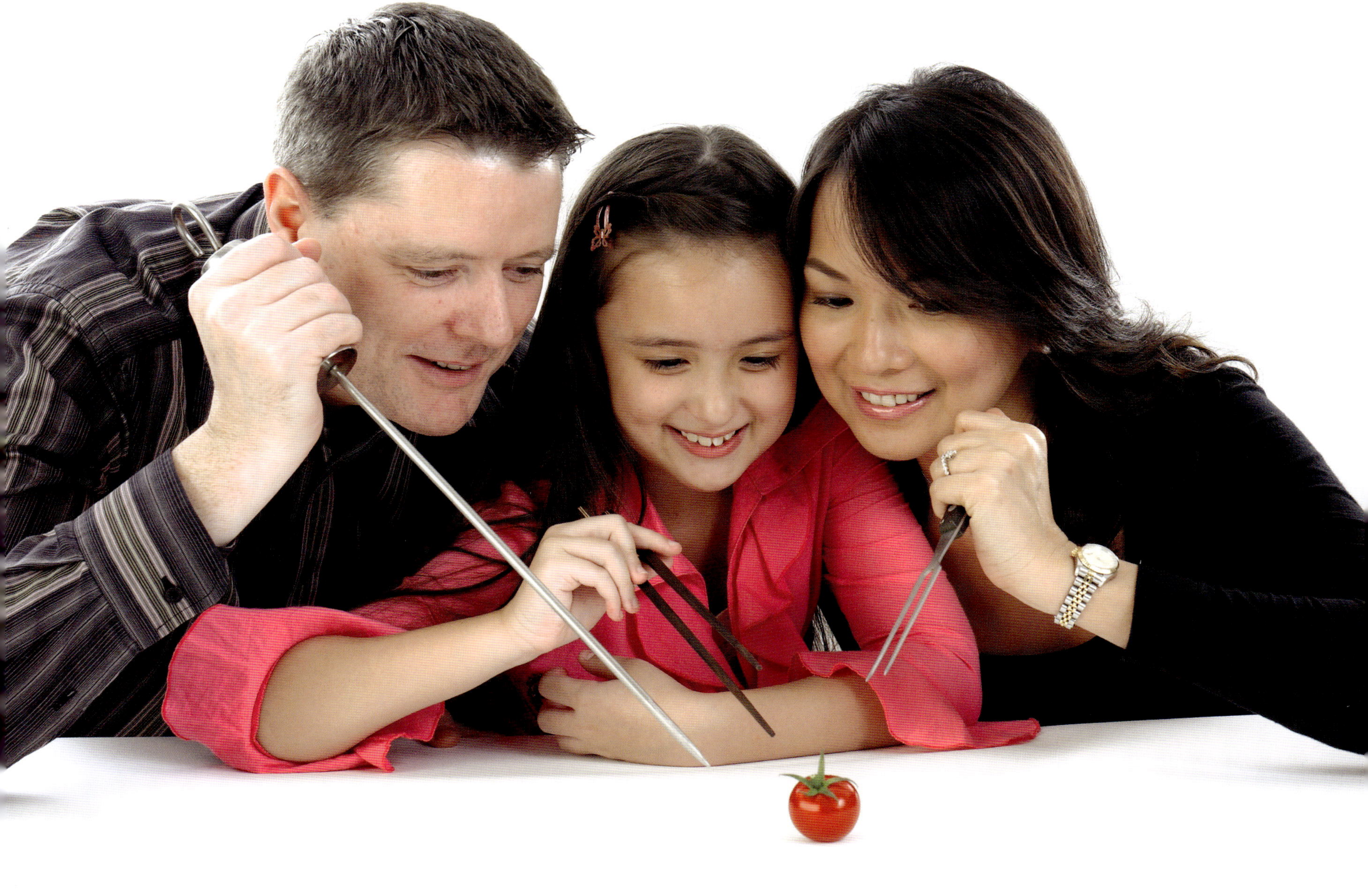